The Academy of International Business

Published in association with the UK and Ireland Chapter of the Academy of International Business

Titles already published in the series:

International Business and Europe in Transition (Volume 1)
Edited by Fred Burton, Mo Yamin and Stephen Young

Internationalisation Strategies (Volume 2)
Edited by George Chryssochoidis, Carla Miller and Jeremy Clegg

The Strategy and Organization of International Business (Volume 3)
Edited by Peter Buckley, Fred Burton and Hafiz Mirza

Internationalization: Process, Context and Markets (Volume 4)
Edited by Graham Hooley, Ray Loveridge and David Wilson

International Business Organization (Volume 5)
Edited by Fred Burton, Malcolm Chapman and Adam Cross

International Business: Emerging Issues and Emerging Markets (Volume 6)
Edited by Carla C. J. M. Millar, Robert M. Grant and Chong Ju Choi

International Business: European Dimensions (Volume 7)
Edited by Michael D. Hughes and James H. Taggart

Multinationals in a New Era: International Strategy and Management (Volume 8)
Edited by James H. Taggart, Maureen Berry and Michael McDermott

International Business (Volume 9)
Edited by Frank McDonald, Heinz Tusselman and Colin Wheeler

Internationalization: Firm Strategies and Management (Volume 10)
Edited by Colin Wheeler, Frank McDonald and Irene Greaves

The Process of Internationalization (Volume 11)
Edited by Frank MacDonald, Michael Mayer and Trevor Buck

International Business in an Enlarging Europe (Volume 12)
Edited by Trevor Morrow, Sharon Loane, Jim Bell and Colin Wheeler

Managerial Issues in International Business (Volume 13)
Edited by Felicia M. Fai and Eleanor J. Morgan

Anxieties and Management Responses in International Business (Volume 14)
Edited by Rudolf Sinkovics and Mo Yamin

Corporate Governance and International Business (Volume 15)
Edited by Roger Strange and Gregory Jackson

Contemporary Challenges to International Business (Volume 16)
Edited by Kevin Ibeh and Sheena Davies

Resources, Efficiency and Globalisation (Volume 17)
Edited by Pavlos Dimitratos and Marian V. Jones

International Business

New Challenges, New Forms, New Perspectives

Edited by

Simon Harris
University of Edinburgh Business School, UK

Olli Kuivalainen
Lappeenranta University of Technology, Finland

and

Veselina Stoyanova
University of Edinburgh Business School, UK

palgrave
macmillan

First published 2012 by
PALGRAVE MACMILLAN

Palgrave Macmillan in the UK is an imprint of Macmillan Publishers Limited, registered in England, company number 785998, of Houndmills, Basingstoke, Hampshire RG21 6XS.

Palgrave Macmillan in the US is a division of St Martin's Press LLC, 175 Fifth Avenue, New York, NY 10010.

Palgrave Macmillan is the global academic imprint of the above companies and has companies and representatives throughout the world.

Palgrave® and Macmillan® are registered trademarks in the United States, the United Kingdom, Europe and other countries.

ISBN: 978–0–230–32098–7

This book is printed on paper suitable for recycling and made from fully managed and sustained forest sources. Logging, pulping and manufacturing processes are expected to conform to the environmental regulations of the country of origin.

A catalogue record for this book is available from the British Library.

A catalog record for this book is available from the Library of Congress.

10 9 8 7 6 5 4 3 2 1
21 20 19 18 17 16 15 14 13 12

Printed and bound in Great Britain by
CPI Antony Rowe, Chippenham and Eastbourne

Contents

Tables

Figures

Acknowledgements

Many thanks to the University of Edinburgh Business School for hosting the 38th Annual Conference of the Academy of International Business, United Kingdom and Ireland (UKI) Chapter. Particular thanks to Simon Harris (Conference Chair) and the associated staff and doctoral students at the University of Edinburgh Business School.

Foreword

The 38th Annual Conference of the Academy of International Business, United Kingdom and Ireland (UKI) Chapter, was held at the University of Edinburgh Business School on 14–16 April 2011. This book reflects the contributions to the conference, and its theme – International Business: New Challenges, New Forms, New Perspectives – has offered the book a suitable title.

The 'new challenges' that we addressed are reflected in the first two parts of this book. Part I, 'The New Challenges of of Corporate Social Responsibility in Emerging Markets', reflects a concern shared in many sections of society in many parts of the world, and since the businesses concerned are often international, this has become the concern for International Business research as well. The second challenge is reflected in Part II, 'The New Challenges of ODI in China', a major international business phenomenon of our times. This is a challenge for the firms facing it, for the firms facing new competition from it, and for the countries that are hosting it. The new 'forms' that the conference addressed are reflected in Part III, 'The New Forms of International Small Businesseses', which focuses on one particular form that has received increasing attention from International Business researchers in recent years: the international growth of the smaller firms, including international new ventures.

A major focus of the conference this year, and something of an innovation for the Academy of International Business, was its engagement with practitioners of International Business, reflected in Part IV, 'The New Practices of International Business'. We are grateful for the courage shown by our pioneers in this experiment in which, in a special programme of keynote interviews attended by scholars and practitioners alike, leading scholars interviewed successful practitioners of International Business. Edited transcripts of these interviews are included in Part IV.

The 38th Annual Conference attracted 230 participants, almost half of them from outside the UK or Ireland. The Academy of International Business is the main forum for International Business and International Management research in the United Kingdom and Ireland, and its federated position within the wider Academy of International Business community links it to work advancing world-wide. Our website (www. aib-uki.org) provides details and links.

Heinz Tüselmann
Chair, Academy of International Business
UK and Ireland Chapter

Contributors

Frederick Ahen is a researcher at the University of Turku, Finland. Frederick holds a BSc in Economics and International Business from the Università Politecnica delle Marche, Italy and an MSc in International Business from the London South Bank University. Frederick's main research interests include corporate responsibility, sustainability, institutional analysis and the pharmaceutical industry.

Kenneth Amaeshi is Senior Lecturer in Strategy and International Business at the University of Edinburgh Business School and Visiting Professor at the Lagos Business School, Pan-African University, Nigeria. He is Associate of the Doughty Centre for Corporate Responsibility and Visiting Fellow of the Cranfield School of Management; Associate of the Centre for the Study of Globalisation and Regionalisation at the University of Warwick; and was Visiting Scholar at Said Business School, University of Oxford. His research focuses mainly on: sustainable finance and innovation, comparative corporate social responsibility, commercialization of intellectual property assets, governance of innovation networks and multinational corporations in developing economies. Previously he worked as a management consultant to multinational corporations in oil and gas, financial services, telecommunication and aviation industries in Africa and Europe.

Tamer Cavusgil is Fuller E. Callaway Professorial Chair and Director, Institute of International Business, Robinson College of Business, Georgia State University. Tamer specializes in the internationalization of the firm, global strategy, emerging markets and buyer–seller relationships in cross-border business. Tamer has authored more than a dozen books and over 180 refereed journal articles.

Diana A. Filipescu completed her PhD in Business Economics at the Autonomous University of Barcelona. Her main research interests are firms' internationalization, R&D strategies and family businesses. Her research was presented in several conferences such as ACEDE, McGill IE, EIBA, AOM and AIB. Some of her main teaching courses are International Business and International Marketing Strategies at the Autonomous University of Barcelona's Foundation.

Lan Gao is Research Associate in the School of Business and Economics, Loughborough University. She holds an MSc in Finance and

Management and a PhD in International Business and Strategy from Loughborough University. Her research interests concern human mobility, knowledge transfer and the internationalization of Chinese firms.

Pervez N. Ghauri is a full-time professor at Kings College, University of London. He has written more than ten books and numerous articles on international marketing and international business topics. Pervez's main research areas are internalization process, entry strategies and negotiations. His publications include *The Internationalization of the Firm; The Global Challenge for Multinational Enterprises* and *International Business Negotiations*.

Birgit Hagen has a PhD from the Vienna University of Economics and Business Administration with a specialization in International Marketing/International Finance. She has held various marketing positions in Austria, worked in international and strategic marketing in France, and was Business Unit Manager in Italy for a multinational enterprise. She completed her doctoral studies at the University of Pavia in 2009 where she now holds a research position and collaborates in various national and international research projects on Small and Medium-Sized Enterprise (SME) internationalization. Her areas of research are: SME internationalization, strategic orientation, international marketing and international entrepreneurship.

Simon Harris researches how the managers of growth businesses develop their strategies, the people and considerations involved, particularly for their development in new areas and territories. He is particularly interested in the relationships that help this process. He has worked with the managers of young growth companies as well as of large multinational firms in Scotland, the Netherlands, France, Germany, Sweden, China, Italy and Finland on their strategic development and on their international growth.

Olli Kuivalainen is Professor of International Marketing at the School of Business, Lappeenranta University of Technology, Finland. His research interests are in the areas of international entrepreneurship, and strategic management, marketing and internationalization of knowledge-intensive firms, the focus especially being on firms operating in the domains of media and information and communication technologies. He has published articles in the *Journal of World Business, Journal of International Marketing, Technovation, International Journal of Production Economics* and *Journal of International Entrepreneurship*, among others.

Yong Kyu Lew is a PhD candidate in the Comparative and International Business Group at Manchester Business School (MBS), UK, and a doctoral researcher at MBS-CIBER (Comparative and International Business Research Centre). He holds a master's degree from Cranfield School of Management, UK and his research focuses on international strategic alliances, interfirm governance and innovation.

Jia Li is a PhD researcher at University of Edinburgh Business School. He also holds an MSc in International Business and Emerging Markets from University of Edinburgh Business School. His research focuses on transaction costs economics, institutional theories, emerging markets and transitional economies and trading companies.

Ling Liu is Lecturer at University of Edinburgh Business School. Her research in International Business focuses on the internationalization of firms from emerging economies and foreign direct investment.

Xiaohui Liu is Professor of International Business at the School of Business and Economics, Loughborough University. She received her PhD in International Economics from the University of Birmingham. She has published widely, with publications in *Journal of International Business Studies, Research Policy, Entrepreneurship Theory and Practice, Management International Review, Journal of World Business, International Business Review, International Journal of Human Resource Management* and *Management and Organisation Review*. She has received the Best Paper award from the Academy of International Business (UK) and the International Association for Chinese Management Research. She is the Editor of the *International Journal of Emerging Markets* and the Secretary-General of the Chinese Economic Association (UK).

Volker Mahnke is a Professor of International Business and Director of Research at the University of Edinburgh Business School. His research interests are in strategic management of technology, knowledge management and IT-enabled innovation. His work has been published internationally on conferences and in journals including *Journal of Governance and Management* as well as *Management International Review*. He has edited and co-authored books on knowledge management, strategic management and entrepreneurship.

Frank McDonald is Professor of International Business at Bradford University School of Management and Director of the Bradford Centre in International Business. He is the former Chair of the Academy of International Business, UK and Ireland Chapter. His research focuses on strategic issues connected to the subsidiaries of MNCs and internationalization strategies. He has authored or edited 13 books and 40 journal articles.

Jorge Mongay is Lecturer in International Business at the Autonomous University of Barcelona (FUAB), ESIC Business School and Arcadia University, holding professional experience as an Export Area Manager. He completed his Doctor of Business Administration degree at SBS Swiss Business School (Zurich). He is author of several academic articles and textbooks and reviewer of the International Academy of Business and Economics (IABE).

Niina Nummela is a Professor of International Business at the Turku School of Economics at the University of Turku. Her areas of expertise include international entrepreneurship, cross-border acquisitions, interfirm cooperation and research methods. She has published widely in academic journals, including the *Journal of World Business*, the *Management International Review*, the *European Journal of Marketing*, the *International Small Business Journal* and the *Journal of Engineering and Technology Management*, among others. She has also contributed to several internationally published books, and edited a book for Routledge (Taylor & Francis Group) entitled *International Growth of Small and Medium Enterprises*.

Taekyung Park is a full-time lecturer of strategic management at Yeungnam University. He received his PhD from the University of Hull in the UK. His research interests include international entrepreneurship, technological capability and absorptive capacity in technology-based small firms. His research has been published in *Technovation, International Journal of Human Resource Management, The Korean Small Business Review,* among others.

Sami Saarenketo is a Professor of International Marketing at the School of Business, at Lappeenranta University of Technology, Finland. His primary areas of expertise are international entrepreneurship, international marketing and interfirm cooperation in technology-based small firms. He has published widely on these issues in *Journal of World Business, International Business Review, European Business Review, European Journal of Marketing* and *Journal of International Entrepreneurship*, among others.

Thor Sigfusson is pursuing a PhD degree in International Business at the University of Iceland with emphasis on networks and international entrepreneurship. Thor has written extensively on business and economics and he has published five books. He has a master's degree in Economics from the UNCC in the United States. Thor was a guest scholar at Stanford University, 2010, and the University of Edinburgh, 2010–2011. Thor is the founder and director of the Iceland Ocean Cluster.

Thor has 15 years experience in leadership and management. He has been a managing director of Sjova (The Ocean Insurance Company), managing director of the Iceland Chamber of Commerce and the National Committee of the International Chamber of Commerce and Vice President at the Nordic Investment Bank in Helsinki. He was the chairman of the Iceland Confederation of Employers in 2008–2009. Thor is currently a board member or co-founder of several new star-tups in Iceland in diverse areas such as IT, education and recycling. He served as a senior adviser to the Minister of Finance in Iceland and as a board member of several government bodies such as the Iceland University Hospitals, 1994–1996. Thor was a board member of Reykjavik University, 2004–2006, and chairman of the board of Arvakur newspaper and internet publishing house, 2008–2009.

Rudolf R. Sinkovics is Professor of International Business and Co-director of the Comparative and International Business Research Centre at Manchester Business School, UK. He has published on inter-organizational governance, the role of ICT in firm internationalization and research methods in international business. Recent work focuses on rising powers, emerging market firms and drivers of economic change. He received his PhD from Vienna University of Economics and Business (WU), Austria, in 1998. His work has appeared in International Business and International Marketing journals such as *Journal of International Business Studies, Management International Review, Journal of World Business, International Business Review* and *International Marketing Review*.

Veselina Stoyanova is a PhD candidate and researcher in Strategy and International Business at the University of Edinburgh Business School. Her main research interests are in the field of companies' sustainability strategies in emerging market countries, stakeholder engagement strategy, CSR and trust building and repairing strategies. Some of her work has been presented at AIB and EGOS conferences.

Yue Xu is a lecturer on International Business at the Hull University Business School, UK. She is also the Programme Leader of the MSc in International Business at the Centre for Regional and International Business (CRIB). She completed her PhD study at Cranfield School of Management on the entry strategy of multinational banks in China in 2008. Since then she has been working intensively in the area of Chinese outward direct investment (ODI).

Antonella Zucchella is Full Professor of Marketing and International Entrepreneurship at the University of Pavia, Italy. She is also President of the Centre for Research in International Business, CIBIE, of the University of Pavia and Director of the Business and Management Department. She is author of many national and international publications in the fields of international entrepreneurship, international strategic management and marketing.

Introduction

Simon Harris, Olli Kuivalainen and Veselina Stoyanova

New industries, new types of firms and organizations, new types of people, and new nations are increasingly practicing international business, and are doing it in new ways and within new structures. The rapid change we witness in the types of international businesses, and in how they practice international business, continues unabated. This presents managerial challenges and new international competition for those doing it. For example, new global multinationals may not long have been SMEs (Small or Medium Enterprises), and many are emerging from countries that are only recently industrializing. Established MNEs (Multinational Enterprises) are doing business in entirely new ways, and are encountering new opportunities and difficulties. Those of us making sense of these trends may need new techniques and new theoretical frameworks.

This collection of 13 chapters addresses two of these new challenges: new forms of international small businesses and new practices in managing them. They are drawn from contributions given at the 38th Academy of International Business (United Kingdom and Ireland chapter) conference that was held at the University of Edinburgh Business School in April 2011, and chaired by Simon Harris. The chapters are laid out in four parts. The first addresses a new challenge that represented a special theme at the conference: corporate and social responsibility in international businesses.

The second reflects another challenge that was also a special theme at the conference: the growing phenomenon of Chinese outward direct investment. The third part reflects an area where there was considerable interest and many contributions: that of the new forms of international small businesses, particularly of international new ventures.

The fourth reflects a new innovation at the conference, which was intended to integrate the worlds of research in international business with the world of practice, in order to enable us to observe, reflect and learn from new practices in international business. Two of the chapters in this last part reflect conference sessions which gave us the opportunity to learn from the voices of experience since we had invited experienced researchers to interview experienced and successful international business leaders on stage. One session addressed the management of large complex collaborative projects, the other addressed the management of the process of internationalization.

Part I: The New challenges for corporate and social responsibility in international businesses

Part I contains three chapters on the new challenges for corporate and social responsibility (CSR) in international businesses, introduced by Kenneth Amaeshi and Veselina Stoyanova.

In Chapter 1, Jorge Mongay and Diana A. Filipescu report on a study that finds a high level of interdependence between the ease of doing business and the perceived level of corruption. Corruption and the ease of doing business have been widely analysed independently, but research has insufficiently focused on the correlation between the two, and their interdependence. This chapter describes a research study that empirically explores the level of correlation between corruption and ease of doing business in 172 nations, employing data from the Corruption Perception Index and Doing Business rankings. The study finds a high interdependence between the two variables. This high level of interdependence represents an interesting contribution to research on the issue of corruption within an international business perspective.

In Chapter 2, Veselina Stoyanova suggests that different institutional logics can coexist, which, in this case, explains heterogeneous CSR practices within the Bulgarian wine industry. She bases this on a study of CEOs of Bulgarian small- and medium-sized wineries, which explores ways business leaders in SMEs perceive and practice their firms' social responsibilities towards society, and what institutional factors influence these business practices. Applying neo-institutional theory, the study finds that CSR activities in SMEs are mostly encouraged either by inter-organizational level factors such as pressures from customers and suppliers, or by individual level factors, such as the managers' individual characteristics. It therefore contradicts previous research studies by indicating that there is a convergence of socially responsible practices within the same sectoral and geographical contexts.

In Chapter 3, Frederick Ahen argues that the weak institutions common to developing economies mean that the political power of Multinational corporations (MNCs) alter the rules of the game, which has implications for sustainable development in those territories. This study is driven by the increased social and political attention given to the issue of corporate responsibility, so it addresses the need for a new theoretical framework that will assist the study of institutions and their role in developing economies. Based on a meta-theoretical analysis using institutional theory, the study argues that supranational organizations deserve credit for their roles in developing economies. It suggests that, in the absence of strong institutional structures or NGOs in developing economies, actualizing responsible actions to meet sustainability goals will be ineffective or impossible, because of corporate political power, bargaining power and political action. The chapter contributes a systematic institutional theory analysis contextualized within developing economies, using a 'second best' theoretical lens, which results in a novel framework that offers valuable insights.

Part II: The New challenges of outward direct investment in China

Part II contains three chapters on new challenges from Chinese outward direct investment (ODI), introduced by Ling Liu. In Chapter 4, Lan Gao and Xiaohui Liu report a study that finds Chinese state-owned enterprises have difficulties in effectively and efficiently configuring their resources, sourcing externally and coordination their activities. They also face institutional intervention at home and political risks abroad. This is an important contribution because extensive research into the rapid internationalization of Chinese firms has not yet explored the challenges faced by firms themselves. To explore this issue, and to capture the challenges caused by both internal and external factors, the study combines the dynamic capability perspective with the institution-based view and qualitatively explores four case studies of Chinese state-owned enterprises. The researchers undertook semi-structured interviews with senior managers in the organizations to generate an in-depth understanding of the issues.

In Chapter 5, Yue Xu compares existing studies of Chinese ODI. The review finds four key determining factors that have been co-evolving to form the Chinese ODI strategy in Africa. These are: political alliances; bi-liberal trade; aid; and contractual projects. The study described in this chapter aims to understand the evolution of Sino-African political and economic policies that shape the development of Chinese ODI in Africa. The chapter thereby makes three contributions. First, it provides a review of Chinese ODI in a specific region with a large number of the least developed countries. Secondly, it examines the motive for seeking natural resources, which is relevant to both the home and host markets. Thirdly, it provides an historical perspective for understanding the pattern of Chinese ODI and economic relations over the past six decades.

In Chapter 6, Jia Li and Ling Liu shows the interconnected roles played by particular organizations, in this case export trading companies, and the institutional context of a transitional economy, in this case China. The chapter examines the interaction between institutions and organizations by investigating export trading companies in China, which it takes as an example and a focus for this interaction in the context of a transition economy, adopting both transaction cost and institutional perspectives. The exploratory study suggests that institutions in a transitional economy may generate additional transaction costs when direct exporting. Here, export trading companies play a crucial role in reducing institution-related costs by linking domestic producers and foreign buyers. Export trading companies may thereby be making a significant contribution to the exporting performance of China.

Part III: The New forms of international small businesses

Part III contains four chapters, introduced by Olli Kuivalainen and Simon Harris. In Chapter 7, Niina Nummela and Sami Saarenketo challenge the view that it is mainly external factors that drive the foreign operation modes chosen by firms, and they highlight the importance of the firms own internal strategic factors. Their chapter adopts foreign operation modes and strategic decision-making viewpoints longitudinally to describe the internationalization process in a small software international new venture (INV). The study confirms that foreign operation modes are used in different mode combinations. But it also contributes by challenging earlier studies in suggesting that instead of being the result of market-level evaluation, INV mode change may be based on company-level strategy decisions, even if the timing of those decisions is determined by market-level factors. The drivers of mode change may be motivated by increasing control and their partners' commitment, but also by the company's desire to manage its international growth and geographically spreading value network. Internal factors appear to be at play here, and not only the external ones on which previous research has concentrated. Within these, financial and ownership factors may significantly influence decisions that lead to change of foreign operation mode.

In Chapter 8, Antonella Zucchella and Birgit Hagen investigate the potential of the internet in sustaining SME internationalization processes, drawing on two case studies of internet-based firms. It investigates, first, how e-commerce start ups embrace new technology to implement an international strategy from the outset and, secondly, whether, and how, the internet plays a role as the venture develops. The study finds that the key to international growth is not the outside factor of the internet in itself. Rather, it is the firm's ability to develop a coherent set of organizational capabilities that will enable it to exploit the global opportunities that e-business presents. Here, in particular, the firm's internal capabilities for managing portfolios of customers seem to be most critical for these internet-based firms' success.

In Chapter 9, Frank McDonald and Taekyung Park examine whether the number of key resources employed by SMEs affects their performance (as measured by satisfaction with foreign market growth and share of sales from international activities) or their competence to work in foreign markets. Unlike most previous studies of the drivers of international performance by SMEs, their study seeks evidence on the effect not only of the type of resources that affect performance, but also on their number or intensity of use. Analysis of a survey of early internationalizing South Korean SMEs reveals that the number of networks accessed by the firms, and the number of employees devoted to international business activity, positively affects performance. This novel approach offers some evidence of value both for public policy and to managers about how to plan more effectively and manage the internationalization processes of early internationalizing SMEs.

In Chapter 10, Thor Sigfusson and Simon Harris argue that that cyberspace may lead to a paradigm shift in the relationship formation of international entrepreneurs and offer three propositions about how it might do this, drawn from previous research and evidence. First, in presenting new tools for relationship building, maintaining networks on Facebook, LinkedIn and Twitter, for example, cyberspace opens up opportunities to forge ties with a large number of people. International entrepreneurs can hold and manage large portfolios of weak, sometimes 'sleeping' relationships that can be activated to expand into a new territory. Secondly, cyberspace tools present an effective virtual system that rapidly enables a semi-strong form of trust to develop within a system of virtual embeddedness that reduces the risks of loss of trust and is entirely sufficient for the cooperative behaviour that the entrepreneurs seek. Thirdly, it is a facility that may or may not be adopted by international entrepreneurs rather than a necessary force for change. International entrepreneurs will adopt it in different ways according to their own orientations. Some will hold relatively small internet relationship networks; others will hold large networks of weaker ties, resulting in greater diversity in international entrepreneurs' development strategies for relationship networks.

Part IV: The New practices of international business

Part IV comprises three chapters, introduced by Simon Harris. The first two comprise lightly edited transcripts of conversations held as a public session at the conference. In Chapter 11, Tamer Cavusgil interviews three managers experienced in managing complex cross-border collaborative (CCBC) projects. In a session chaired by Volker Mahnke, he discusses these issues with Hillary Sillitto of the Thales group, Hermine Schnetler of the UK Astronomy Technology Centre, and Paul Holbourn, from the Selex Galileo group. Discussion topics raised some of the most salient problems managers face and pinpointed rewarding research avenues in tackling the challenges in organizing multinational projects such as CCBCs. They include: the risks involved in complex cross-border collaborative projects; the motivation for undertaking them; the meaning of success and failure; how to manage for success in them; the role of the contract; dealing with conflicts; competing while collaborating within them; the management of complexity and loss of control; moral hazard; timescales; the political dimension; and doing business in the BRIC (Brazil, Russia, India and China) countries.

In Chapter 12, Pervez Ghauri interviews four managers experienced in managing the process of internationalization. In a session chaired by Simon Harris, he discusses this issue with Carla Mahieu of Aegon, formerly of Philips, Ian Stevens, of Mpathy and formerly of Optos, Paul D'Arcy, from Raytheon, and Arten Moussavi, whose new INV BioFood Nutrition follows his previous international entrepreneurial experience. Discussion topics included: the process of deciding where and how to internationalize; the partnerships involved in international business; dealing with uncertainty and change in overseas territories; the opportunities and challenges for emerging markets of internationalizing; the risks of counterfeit goods and the problems of intellectual property protection; learning in the internationalization process; and the issue of ethical behaviour in international business.

In Chapter 13, Yong Kyu Lew and Rudolf Sinkovics usefully show how focal firms in alliances generate innovation from within those alliances by gaining access to complementary overseas resources, by internalizing these, by developing new products, and by commercializing them. They draw on the findings of previous international business research which indicates that global technology alliances can be useful ways for firms to acquire complementary resources, to develop new business models and to help them penetrate new markets. To investigate the interrelationships between complementary resources, global technology alliances, and innovation capabilities in a 'high-tech' market context, they then study a global technology alliance between a South Korean personal computer software firm and its global hardware and software technology partners, which involves them undertaking interviews with senior managers and drawing on secondary sources of information. This study contributes not by showing that the alliance is useful, but by showing *how* it is.

Conclusion

This book provides a number of useful contributions to knowledge on the theme, International Business: New Challenges, New Forms, New Practices, with contributions not only from colleagues from universities around the world, but also, for the first time, from experienced practitioners as well. The goal is to stimulate new areas of relevant and useful research that will help our understanding of, and practitioners' performance within, the new and unfolding world of international business.

Part I

The New Challenges of CSR in Emerging Markets

Kenneth Amaeshi and Veselina Stoyanova

Are CSR practices suitable and relevant in all institutional contexts? To what extent and under what conditions can CSR practices be enacted in weak institutional contexts? These are some of the pressing questions confronting international businesses as they transverse transnational borders. Answers to these questions are not made simpler by the fact that the suitability of CSR across institutional contexts is often taken for granted and most CSR theoretical frameworks and discourses often assume strong institutional contexts in their accounts. Aguilera and Jackson (2003, p.247), for instance, developed '... a theoretical model to identify and explain the diversity of corporate governance across advanced capitalist economies', while Matten and Moon (2008, p.406) in their theorization of the explicit and implicit model of CSR assumed '... some basic institutional prerequisites for CSR', founded on the essential characteristics of the advanced capitalist economies:

> First, we assume a functioning market in which corporations have discretion over their responses to market, social, or political drivers. Second, we assume functioning governmental and legal institutions that guarantee, define, and administer the market and act on behalf of society to address instances of market failure. Third, we assume that these institutions neither capture nor are captured by market actors. And fourth, we assume a civil society that institutionalizes and articulates social values and preferences, to which government and market actors respond.

Continuing, Matten and Moon recognized and emphasized that:

> This idealized system masks great variety in the structure of markets and the nature of the firm, in the accountability of the government and the

operation of the judiciary, and in the freedom of civil society. Opportunities for irresponsibility increase in the absence of these conditions, as is evident in much of sub-Saharan Africa and the former Union of Soviet Socialist Republics (USSR), with, for example, monopolistic companies exploiting capitalist economies or governments substituting regulation and administration of markets with rent seeking. (Matten and Moon, 2008, pp.406–7)

It cannot be denied that the advanced capitalist economies have become the global yardstick for assessing responsible and irresponsible business behaviours. Based on this line of thinking, economic systems could be classified as either weak or strong (Aguilera and Jackson, 2003) or a success or failure (Wood and Frynas, 2006), depending on how much they reflect the essential characteristics of the advanced capitalist political economies – i.e. functioning, independent and free markets, governments, civil societies and legislative institutions.

However, if one accepts the view that '... CSR is located in wider responsibility systems in which business, governmental, legal, and social actors operate according to some measure of mutual responsiveness, interdependency, choice, and capacity' (Matten and Moon, 2008, p.407), one must doubt the efficiency and effectiveness of CSR in weak institutional contexts. Even if one accepts the point that there can also be responsibility where there are no '... markets and business autonomy, as demonstrated by myriad cases of individual, family, tribal, religious, charitable, and feudal responsibility ...' (Matten and Moon, 2008, p.407) it raises questions about the function and relevance of CSR in different institutional contexts. This is particularly the case since there is a growing tendency to globalize CSR practices articulated within advanced capitalist economies as the panacea for most global challenges – including poverty, inequality, human rights abuses, climate change, bribery and corruption, *et cetera* – especially in developing economies.

This further strengthens the perspective that firms are products of their cultural and social milieu and, as such, calls into question, the current trend towards the globalization of CSR through multinational corporations and multinational institutions. These multinational bodies tend to work from the assumption that the global economic system is converging. While the theory of global economic system convergence seems plausible, it has been confirmed that business practices are socially and contextually bounded. In other words, CSR practices are functions of their institutional contexts, and this view is mainly informed by the understanding that institutions shape '... how stakeholders' interests are defined ... aggregated, and represented with respect to the firm' (Aguilera and Jackson, 2003, p.450). This approach to understanding CSR practices has, in the main, drawn significantly from literature on comparative institutionalism (e.g. Matten and Moon, 2008; Campbell, 2007; Aguilera et al., 2006).

However, most of these institutionalist accounts tend to adopt a macro (national level) characteristic, which appears to suggest some kind of organizational field homogeneity within national institutional contexts. Whilst the introduction of a comparative institutionalism perspective to the CSR literature is innovative and worthwhile, at least in wresting CSR from the domineering grip of managerialist theorizations (Owen et al., 2000; Gray, 2002; O'Dwyer, 2002, 2003), it appears to underemphasize possible heterogeneities that could exist within national institutional boundaries. These heterogeneities have been picked up by a related stream of literature that emphasizes sectoral differences as the main sources of variations of CSR practices (Griffin and Weber, 2006). The significance of sectors in accounting for corporate actions is also gradually permeating and unsettling the core tenets and foundations of national business systems and comparative capitalism, which are in orientation macro-centric. Scholars promoting the sector-based perspective argue that national business systems are not necessarily homogenous but are most of the time concatenations of heterogeneities or, at best, 'models within models' (Deeg and Jackson, 2007, p.154).

An anchor for the sector-based argument is that some sectors are constitutively and uniquely transnational social spaces.[1] As such, their practices cannot be fully accounted for by national institutional boundaries. In some instances, these transnational social spaces could be more influential on corporate practices than national institutional contexts and vice versa. The oil and gas sector in Nigeria, for instance, is heavily driven more by global than local practices (Ite, 2004, 2005; Frynas et al., 2006; Frynas, 1999; Amaeshi and Amao, 2009), since the major actors in the sector are MNCs which tend to retain their home country influences, albeit with slight modifications (Whitley, 1999a,b). The two streams of literature on the influence of national institutional boundaries and transnational social spaces, respectively, on corporate actions, therefore, appear to be in constant contestation in accounting for variations of CSR practices across institutional contexts, albeit with inconclusive outcomes.

The chapters in this part focus on the need to recognize the importance of contexts – and more especially the interplay of contexts – in the study of CSR amongst international businesses and emerging markets. In Chapter 1 of this part Mongay and Filipescu explore the issue of corruption and its interdependence with the ease of doing business in 172 countries. Chapter 2 unveils the case of CSR in small- and medium-sized companies in an emerging market country in transition. Part I of the book concludes with a study of the issue of 'second best' institutions and global sustainability in developing countries.

Note

1. Borrowing from Morgan (2001): I take 'transnational space' to refer to an arena of social action distinct from that of the 'national' context. It is an arena of social inter-action where the main modes of connection between groups cross national bound-aries.... Transnational social space implies a more open-ended set of cross-border connections between multiple nodes in which the forms of interaction become more than simply the sum of interactions between different 'national' units; it constitutes an arena in which new social actors may emerge, which may be labelled 'transna-tional communities' (p.115).

References

Aguilera, R. and Jackson, G. (2003) 'The Cross-National Diversity of Corporate Governance: Dimensions and Determinants', *Academy of Management Review*, **28(3)**, 447–65.

Amaeshi, K. and Amao, O. (2009) 'Corporate Social Responsibility in Transnational Spaces: Exploring the Influences of Varieties of Capitalism on Expressions of Corporate Codes of Conduct in Nigeria', *Journal of Business Ethics*, 86 (2), 225–39.

Campbell, J. L. (2007) 'Why would Corporations Behave in Socially Responsible Ways? An Institutional Theory of Corporate Social Responsibility', *Academy of Management Review*, 32(3), 946–67.

Deeg, R. and Jackson, G. (2007) 'The State of the Art: Towards a More Dynamic Theory of Capitalist Variety', *Socio-Economic Review*, 5, 149–179.

Frynas, J. G. (1999) *Oil in Nigeria: Conflict and Litigation between Oil Companies and Village Communities* (Munster, Hamburg and London: Lit Verlag).

Frynas, J. G., Mellahi, K. and Pigman, G. A. (2006) 'First Mover Advantages in International Business and Firm-specific Political Resources', *Strategic Management Journal*, 27(4), 321–45.

Griffin, J. J. and Weber, J. (2006) 'Industry Social Analysis: Examining the Beer Industry', *Business & Society*, 45, 413–40.

Ite, U. E. (2004) 'Multinationals and Corporate Social Responsibility in Developing Countries: A Case Study of Nigeria', *Corporate Social Responsibility and Environmental Management*, 11(1), 1–11.

Ite, U. E. (2005) 'Poverty Reduction in Resource-rich Developing Countries: What have Multinational Corporations Got to Do with it?', *Journal of International Development*, 17(7), 913–29.

Matten, D. and Moon, J. (2008) '"Implicit" and "Explicit" CSR: A Conceptual Framework for a Comparative Understanding of Corporate Social Responsibility', *Academy of Management Review*, 33(2), 404–24.

Morgan, G. (2001) 'Transnational Communities and Business Systems', *Global Networks* 1(2), 113–130.

O'Dwyer, B. (2002) 'Managerial Perceptions of Corporate Social Disclosure: An Irish Story', *Accounting, Auditing & Accountability Journal*, 15(3), 406–36.

O'Dwyer, B. (2003) 'Conceptions of Corporate Social Responsibility: The Nature of Managerial Capture', *Accounting, Auditing & Accountability Journal*, 16(4), 523–57.

Owen, D. L., Swift, T. A., Humphrey, C. and Bowerman, M. C. (2000) 'The New Social Audits: Accountability, Managerial Capture or the Agenda of Social Champions?', *European Accounting Review*, 9(1), 81–98.

Whitley, R. (1999a) *Divergent Capitalisms. The Social Structuring and Change of Business Systems* (Oxford: Oxford University Press).

Whitley, R. (1999b) 'Firms, Institutions and Management Control: The Comparative Analysis of Coordination and Control Systems', *Accounting, Organizations and Society*, 24, 507–24.

Wood, G. and Frynas, J. G. (2006) 'The Institutional Basis of Economic Failure: Anatomy of the Segmented Business System', *Socio-Economic Review*, 4(2), 239–77.

1
Are Corruption and Ease of Doing Business Correlated? An Analysis of 172 Nations

Jorge Mongay and Diana A. Filipescu

Introduction

Corruption and its implications in international business trading and investments represent an increasing interest for academicians. It is extremely important to understand how corruption affects economic growth directly, by shifting the allocation of public funds, and, indirectly, by changing the incentives, prices, and opportunities faced by entrepreneurs (Jain, 2002). Corruption refers to behaviour that violates the trust placed in public officials and serves to destabilize the basis on which generalized interpersonal trust relies and increases the risks faced by the entrepreneur (Anokhin and Schulze, 2009).

Although the economic development and international business literature is aware of the negative effect that corruption has on firm behaviour (Uhlenbruck et al., 2006), foreign direct investment (Hannafey, 2003; Lenway and Murtha, 1994), and mode of entry decisions (Rodriguez et al., 2005), evidence about the relationship between corruption and ease of doing business is scarce. This is precisely the niche that we aim to fill in this chapter. Although corruption and ease of doing business have been widely analysed independently, there is a lack of research focused on the correlation between the two magnitudes, and their interdependence.

This chapter aims to answer the question empirically: 'Are corruption and ease of doing business correlated?' In order to do so, we follow the arguments of academicians and employ data from the Corruption Perception Index and Doing Business rankings, analysing a total of 172 countries. We begin with a brief review of the literature on corruption and ease of doing business, and then turn to the task of developing and testing the data. We conclude with a brief discussion of the results of this study and their implications for theory and practice, highlighting at the end the main future lines of research.

Literature review

Defining corruption can be a difficult task since its definition is determined by how it is measured and modelled. However, a general definition of corruption would highlight the idea that it refers to acts in which the power of public office is used for personal gain in a manner that disregards the rules of the game (Jain, 2002). Certain illegal acts such as fraud, money laundering, drug trades and black market operations do not constitute corruption, in and of themselves, because they do not engage the use of public power. However, people who carry out these activities must often involve public officials and politicians if these operations are to succeed and hence these activities rarely proceed without extensive corruption.

Corruption has been studied in relation to a variety of indicators of economic welfare, including: per capita growth in GDP (Kaufmann and Kraay, 2003); the United Nations Human Welfare Index (Rose-Ackerman, 2004); bond spreads (Ciocchini et al., 2003); income inequality (Carmignani, 2005; Li et al., 2000); capital investment and foreign direct investment (Lambsdorff, 2003; Mauro, 1995); and total factor productivity (Lambsdorff, 2003; Rivera-Batiz, 2002).

Jain (2002) emphasizes the existence of three elements which determine corruption. First, there is the type of power which would include authority to design regulations as well as to administer them. This is known as discretionary power. Secondly, there must be economic rents associated with this power. Thirdly, the judicial system must offer a sufficiently low probability of exposure or penalty for illegal behaviour. Corruption occurs when higher rents are associated with abuse of discretionary powers, net of any illegal payments and penalties associated with such a misuse.

One of the main concepts taken into consideration with regards to corruption is the role of historical and geographical factors, as well as of governments. Results highlighted that government indeed matters in important ways in its impact on corruption, both issues – size and scope of the government – positively affecting it. In a recent meta-analysis, Doucouliagos and Ulubasoglu (2008) confirm that the quality of a nation's governance (corruption being one of its central elements) moderates a variety of important economic indicators and thus plays a key role in shaping economic performance across nations. At the same time, the historical inertia of institutions that induce corruption persists, although sometimes geographical factors can mitigate it, as described by Goel and Nelson (2010). The role that corporations have to play in anti-corruption efforts has been researched using several indexes and ranking, such as The Bribe Payers Index, Corruption Perception Index (CPI) and Doing Business rankings (Calderón et al., 2009).

In developing countries with high levels of corruption, people are often forced into small business entrepreneurship because larger, more efficient firms do not exist, while in developed countries low corruption means that people choose entrepreneurship as a better mean of innovation, as described by Mitchell and Campbell (2009).

Research about measuring corruption in infrastructure suggests that a focus on bribe payments as the indicator of the costs of corruption in infrastructure may be misplaced (Kenny, 2009). The analysis of the effect of corruption on investment growth carried out by Asiedu and Freeman (2009) shows it varies significantly across regions: corruption has a negative and significant effect on investment growth for firms in transition countries but has no significant impact for firms in Latin America and sub-Saharan Africa. The role of trust in the corruption-efficiency relationship has been analysed as well by Li and Wu (2010) who argue that, in countries with a relatively low level of trust, corruption tends to be more predatory.

Failure to control the forms of corruption causes a country to resort to other measures of trade, such as the black market. Furthermore, when the existing laws and policies make it extremely difficult to execute international business, citizens turn to the black market as a way of bypassing the legal system and executing their business transactions. For example, when certain licences and certificates are difficult to obtain legally without bribing the distributing officials, people in need of these licences and certificates must resort to purchasing them on the black market (Mocan, 2008).

Therefore, it is obvious that corruption is an important factor to be analysed. However, despite the vast evidence which has been highlighted here, academicians stress the lack of studies focusing on corruption within an international business perspective (Jain, 2002; Anokhin and Schulze, 2009).

Excessive amounts of the various forms of corruption, as well as political instability, often prevent a country from participating in international business transactions. Countries where bribery and extortion occur quite frequently are less likely to enforce international trading and investing laws. Without a guarantee of the enforcement of these laws, people are hesitant to invest in these countries due to the fear that their investments will not be protected (Husted, 1999). Mauro (1995) aims at identifying the channels through which corruption and other institutional factors affect economic growth, quantifying the magnitude of these effects. His results show that when corruption in a country reduces foreign investments there, economic growth in the country also declines. Furthermore, Wei (2000) analyses the effect of corruption on foreign direct investment, showing that an increase in the estimated level of corruption within a country results in a fall in incoming foreign direct investment. This study also shows that the United States and other OECD countries dislike investing in corrupt countries because political corruption inherently violates democratic principles. In line with these results are the ones of Habib and Zurawicki (2002), who highlight that foreign direct investment avoids corruption mainly because it is wrong and it creates operational inefficiencies.

With economic growth stagnating due to a lack of foreign investment, caused by corruption, a country must resort to other methods of gaining revenue such as exporting valuable natural resources or illegally selling products on the black market. Relying upon natural resources as a country's biggest source of revenue can cause devastating problems for the majority of a country's population and perpetuate corruption within that country. If a country only has one resource for export, the country's wealth lies in the hand of those who work to export this resource, which is often only a small percentage of the overall population. Because the government is dependent upon the export revenue to function, it is also forced to cater to the interests of the resource exporters. This leaves the wants and needs of a vast majority of the population entirely unaddressed. For example, in Kenya, 87 per cent of the population were forced to pay bribes to get access to the cities' water networks, as described in the paper 'The Anti-Corruption Solution: Keeping the Millennium Development Promise' (Transparency International 2010). With the actions of the government determined by the resource exporters, corruption in the country continues and the government fails to build the necessary infrastructure. Also, the majority of the citizenry remains poor because government officials and the exporters themselves pocket the revenue from the exports. For example, Nigeria exported a large portion of the world's oil supply, earning over $300 billion in revenue. However, this money was pocketed by oil distributors and by the government officials that these distributors had paid off. This left the rest of the population extremely poor, with only $300 per capita in 2000, and lacking high living standards, with just 60 per cent of the population literate (Hill, 2005).

Because corruption within a country only fosters more corruption, a vicious circle of corruption results, breaking free of which is almost impossible. However, many countries, particularly the United States and Western European nations, strive to combat the forces of corruption. In the 1970's, the United States passed the Foreign Corrupt Practices Act to prevent bribery of foreign government officials. Prior to this act there had been many instances of American businessmen bribing foreign government officials who had jurisdiction over the businesses of these Americans. The bribes were conducted to facilitate the starting and maintaining of their businesses. The Act also stipulated that offshore businesses keep open records, which can be reviewed to determine any violations of the law (Hill, 2005). Enforcement of this Act had proved difficult in the past but, more recently, more highly developed organizations, such as the Organization of Economic Cooperation and Development and Transparency International, have fought to prevent corruption in international business transactions around the world. In 1997, members of the OECD agreed to frame and pass laws within their respective nations to prevent any occurrence of bribery (Hotchkiss, 1998). Transparency International has created various goals for fighting corruption, which they hope to meet by

2050 ('The Anti-Corruption Solution: Keeping the Millennium Development Promise'). Members of the OECD did most to fight corruption in international business in the past but now emerging markets are striving to fight corruption as well, in order to make themselves more attractive to foreign investors.

It has been emphasized that corruption not only deters foreign direct investment (Hannafey, 2003; Mauro, 1995; Wilhelm, 2002) but also influences the source of investment, such that corrupt nations tend to attract foreign direct investment from other corrupt nations, and less corrupt nations tend to attract foreign investments from less corrupt nations (Hellman and Kaufmann, 2004). Firms with better technologies, human capital or training programmes are unwilling to enter markets where gains may be more than offset by the potential costs of corruption. Corrupt nations are thus less likely to benefit from investment by high quality companies that employ sophisticated technologies (Anokhin and Schulze, 2009). Equally important, corruption affects the type of entry strategies that multinational enterprises employ when considering expansion into other nations (Rodriguez et al., 2005; Uhlenbruck et al., 2006). Wei and Smarzynska (2000) find that firms from less corrupt home nations are more likely to enter using direct investment and to export more sophisticated technology to the host country.

Research about country innovativeness and the difficulty of doing business has been also done by Di Pietro (2009) using cross country regression analysis for the year 2007 on a cross section of over a hundred countries to look at the relationship between country innovativeness and the difficulty of doing business, and to test the hypothesis that there is negative relationship between country innovativeness and the difficulty of doing business (positive relationship between innovativeness and the ease of doing business).

The idea 'ease of doing business' is explored by Stading and Altay (2007). This research provides insight into the 'ease of doing business' construct. Factor analysis of survey respondents – supply managers in the electronics industry – was used to test the 'ease of doing business' construct, which includes three dimensions – information and material services, financial contract services and personal relations services. The impact of legal requirements on the regulations of starting up a business in 47 sub-Saharan African economies (SSA) is investigated by Kabongo and Okpara (2009). The research examines data from the World Bank Annual Report on the Ease of Doing Business and World Bank Development Indicators. Findings indicate that the historical origins of SSA countries do not play a determinant role in the number of procedures required to start a new business.

After reviewing the literature which concentrates on corruption we proceed with the formulation of the main research question of this study, precisely: 'Are corruption and ease of doing business correlated?' Corruption seems to affect the level of investment, entrepreneurial incentive, and the design or implementation of rules or regulations regarding access to resources and assets within a country (Jain, 2002). In addition to economic growth rates, corruption can influence the income distribution within a country (Brunetti et al., 1998). The need to understand exactly how corruption affects these variables becomes greater every day and the growing body of academic work on the subject presents an opportunity for scholars in various fields to contribute to our understanding of this phenomenon from different perspectives.

Methods

Corruption remains a major obstacle to international business. Despite new laws – like the Foreign Corrupt Practices Act (US Department of Justice, 1997), which fights against foreign bribery – there have been few prosecutions outside the US and honest companies are losing out to dishonest competitors on a large scale. Countries with high levels of corruption discourage companies from investing. This issue is particularly important in a decade when the ideas of Corporate Social Responsibility are gaining adepts in the fields of consumers and investors. After initial research, the most cited research project aiming to measure corruption is the CPI index – Corruption Perception Index – developed by Transparency International (2010). CPI measures the perceived level of public sector corruption in a total of 180 countries and territories around the world. It is a 'survey of surveys', based on 13 different expert and business surveys. In the construction of CPI, the valuation of the extent of corruption in countries is carried out by two groups: country experts, both residents and non residents, and business leaders. In the 2009 CPI, the following six sources provided data based on expert analysis: the African Development Bank; the Bertelsmann Foundation; the Economist Intelligence Unit; Freedom House Global Insight; and the World Bank. Three sources for the 2009 CPI reflect evaluations by resident business leaders of their own country: IMD; Political and Economic Risk Consultancy; and the World Economic Forum.

To determine the mean value for a country, standardization is carried out through a matching percentiles technique. This uses the rank of countries by each individual source. This method is useful for combining sources that have a different distribution. While there is some information loss in this technique, it allows all reported scores to remain within the bounds of the CPI, i.e. to remain between 0 and 10 points (Transparency International, 2010).

The final ranking shows a list of 180 countries ordered from least corrupt to more corrupt. Scores of less than 5 points over 10 are considered corrupt and scores in the range of 2–3 points are perceived as very corrupt nations. On the other hand, nations which show a grade of 7–8 points remain relatively clean and nations in the group of 9 points out of 10 show the best possible scores. It is important to state that Scandinavian nations appear regularly in the ranking

Table 1.1　The least corrupt nations

Ranking	Country	CPI score
1	New Zealand	9.4
2	Denmark	9.3
3	Singapore	9.2
4	Sweden	9.2
5	Switzerland	9.0
6	Finland	8.9
7	Netherlands	8.9
8	Australia	8.7
9	Canada	8.7
10	Iceland	8.7

Source: Transparency International, 2010.

Table 1.2　The most corrupt nations

Ranking	Country	CPI score
180	Somalia	1.1
179	Afghanistan	1.3
178	Myanmar	1.4
177	Sudan	1.5
176	Iraq	1.5
175	Chad	1.6
174	Uzbekistan	1.7
173	Turkmenistan	1.8
172	Iran	1.8
171	Haiti	1.8

Source: Transparency International, 2010.

as the least corrupt nations. See Tables 1.1 and 1.2, which refer to the top 10 best countries and the top 10 worst nations according to the CPI Index 2009.

'Ease of doing business' rankings

To evaluate ease of doing business is crucial for managers, in order to reduce risks and optimize set up costs. The chosen evaluation criterion for this factor is the Ease of Doing Business (Doing Business Ranking, 2010). This index ranks economies from 1 to 183. For each economy, the index is calculated as the ranking of the simple average of its percentile rankings on each of the 10 indicators covered in the research project.

According to the Doing Business Ranking (2010), the 10 indicators which make up the ranking are the following:

1. Starting a business: procedures; time; cost; and paid-in minimum capital to open a new business.

2. Dealing with construction permits: procedures; time and cost of obtaining construction permits; inspections and utility connections.
3. Employing workers: difficult of hiring index; rigidity of hours index; difficulty of redundancy index; redundancy cost.
4. Registering property: procedures; time and cost of transferring commercial real estate.
5. Getting credit: strength of legal rights index; depth of credit information index.
6. Protecting investors: strength of investor protection index; extent of disclosure index; extent of director liability index; and ease of shareholder suits index.
7. Paying taxes: number of payments; time to prepare; total taxes; and share of profit before all taxes.
8. Trading across borders: documents; time and cost to export and import.
9. Enforcing contracts: procedures; time and cost of resolving a commercial dispute.
10. Closing a business: recovery rate in bankruptcy.

Doing Business Project and the Number of Contributors (Table 1.3) shows the total number of managers and experts who contributed to the creation of the index. This table shows the number of experts that the Doing Business Project consults (Doing Business Ranking, 2010):

The purpose of this research, as mentioned in the introductory section, is not to show the total number of countries analysed in both classifications but to show some of the best and worst countries with regard to the ease of doing business. These are highlighted below, in Table 1.4 and Table 1.5.

Table 1.3   Number of contributors

Indicator set	Number of contributors
Starting a business	1403
Dealing with construction permits	639
Employing workers	997
Registering property	1010
Getting credit	1713
Protecting investors	877
Paying taxes	926
Trading across borders	1455
Enforcing contracts	1029
Closing a business	863

Source: Doing Business Ranking, 2010.

Table 1.4   The most competitive countries in 'Doing Business'

Ease of Doing Business rank	Country
1	Singapore
2	New Zealand
3	Hong Kong, China
4	United States
5	United Kingdom
6	Denmark
7	Ireland
8	Canada
9	Australia
10	Norway

Source: Doing Business Ranking, 2010.

Table 1.5   The least competitive countries in 'Doing Business'

Ease of Doing Business rank	Country
183	Central African Republic
182	Congo Democratic Republic
181	Guinea-Bissau
180	Sao Tomé and Principe
179	Congo Republic
178	Chad
177	Venezuela
176	Burundi
175	Eritrea
174	Niger

Source: Doing Business Project, 2010.

Results

The question that this chapter tries to answer is the extent to which the variables 'corruption' and 'ease of doing business' show interdependence. For this purpose both variables have been analysed statistically using a bivariate correlation analysis. A total of 172 countries have been analysed, comparing their position in the CPI Ranking and their position in the Ease of Doing Business ranking. Both rankings show the results related to year 2009. Next, 10 nations which show higher dispersions in both rankings – outliers – have been eliminated from the list in order to simulate a new correlation analysis without the most disperse sample units.

First, some descriptive statistics of the data are provided, including the mean and standard deviation of the variables 'corruption' and 'ease of doing business', for both analyses (Tables 1.5 and 1.6). Our data supports Jain (2002),

Table 1.6 Descriptive statistics

Variable	Number of observations	Mean	Std Dev.	Min	Max
Sample of 172 nations					
cpi	172	88.21512	50.67111	1	179
db	172	92.4593	54.11341	1	183
Sample of 162 nations					
cpi	162	88.85185	51.25278	1	179
db	162	93.34568	54.68559	1	183

showing that corruption levels seem to be the highest in Asia, where between 25 and 40 per cent of politicians and between 15 and 33 per cent of public servants are corrupt, and the lowest in Oceania, where all the numbers are below 10 per cent.

The analysis uses the Pearson's correlation coefficient between two variables which is defined as the covariance of the two variables divided by the product of their standard deviations:

$$\rho_{X,Y} = \frac{cov(X,Y)}{\sigma_X \sigma_Y} = \frac{E\left[(X - \mu_X)(Y - \mu_Y)\right]}{\sigma_X \sigma_Y},$$

where E is the expected value operator.

The first analysis includes the complete list of the 172 nations. The results derived from this analysis show a correlation of 0.785, a high correlation which can be interpreted as high interdependence between the two variables (Table 1.7).

Discussion

This research aimed to fill an observed niche in the literature, focusing on the relation between corruption and ease of doing business, precisely to see whether these variables – which, to our knowledge, have never been analysed together – were correlated or not. In order to do so, a total of 172 countries have been taken into consideration, comparing their position in the Corruption Perception Index and the Ease of Doing Business ranking for the year 2009. The results showed a high degree of interdependency between the two variables, being thus in line with existing literature focused on corruption and international business development. Of course, it would be reasonable to expect these results. As highlighted in the literature review, corrupt nations tend to make business more difficult and complex and, by contrast, transparent countries

Table 1.7   Correlations for 172 nations

		Corruption Perception Index	Doing Business
Corruption Perception Index	Pearson correlation	1	0.785(**)
	Sig. (2-tailed)	.	0.0
	N	172	172

Note: ** $p < 0.01$ (2-tailed). The second conducted analysis included a list of 162 nations, since we eliminated 10 nations which showed higher dispersions in both rankings (sample units number 37, 43, 50, 83, 99, 115, 119, 137, 145, 161 which refer to these countries respectively: Botswana; Costa Rica; Czech Republic; Serbia; Bosnia; Kiribati; Togo; Nigeria; Nepal; Kyrgyzstan). In this case, the final results of the analysis increases significantly up to a correlation of 0.840, emphasizing a very high interdependence between the two variables (Table 1.8). Therefore, the results support our hypothesis according to which the less corrupt a nation is the easier it is to do business in it.

Table 1.8   Correlations for 162 nations

		Corruption Perception Index	Doing Business
Corruption Perception Index	Pearson correlation	1	0.840(**)
	Sig. (2-tailed)	.	,000
	N	162	162

Note: ** $p < 0.01$ (2-tailed).

tend to make things easier for foreign or local investors. As Habib and Zurawicki (2002) mention, there are several theoretical arguments, which are derived from both ethics and economics, according to which it is much more difficult to start a venture in a corrupt nation, either because managers believe it is morally wrong or because it is risky and costly, and, therefore, to be avoided.

Our data supports the statement of Mitchell and Campbell (2009), according to which in developed countries low corruption is similar to entrepreneurship as a better means of innovation. It is quite difficult for a country to be involved in international business transactions if there are excessive amounts of corruption, as well as political instability. Countries where bribery and extortion occur quite frequently are less likely to enforce international trading and investing laws. Without a guarantee of the enforcement of these laws, people are hesitant to invest in these countries, due to the fear that their investments will not be protected (Husted, 1999). This in line with the results that our study presents.

As mentioned at the beginning of this study, corruption usually involves the behaviour that violates the trust placed in public officials and serves to destabilize the foundation on which generalized interpersonal trust relies

(Anokhin and Schulze, 2009). Yet the ability to rely on others with whom the entrepreneur has only indirect contact is indispensable to the success of new ventures and the creation of high value-added product and services. Baker et al. (2005) consider that the problem here is that the decision to pursue an entrepreneurial opportunity depends on 'the portion of the value that the venture creates that the entrepreneur is able to capture for their own purposes'.

However, when looking at some specific cases, an inverse correlation is observed. In particular, let's take the case of Thailand. Thailand appears to be in a very good position for doing business with a good #12 ranking in the world as highly competitive. However, it appears at the bottom of the list related to corruption, #84 with a score of 3.4 only. The explanation for this could be found in the fact that Thailand is a developing country with great future prospects, attracting foreign businesses and making their environment favourable. Corruption does not have too much effect. This case, as well as other similar ones (i.e. Mexico, India), are quite common: multinationals decide to localize their labour force by employing local people at a lower salary, engaging in competitive international business. Another example is given by Habib and Zurawicki (2002): the case of McDonald's in Moscow and how the relative corrupt environment did not prevent the installation of a successful outlet there.

Conclusion

Putting our results into practice, the recommendation we give to managers is that they should take responsibility, before proceeding with foreign direct investments or business in overseas countries, to evaluate corruption and the ease of doing business at the same time. It is not always possible to obtain access to both factors but it is possible to say that, in general terms, both variables support each other. For this, the Doing Business Ranking (2010) stands out because it offers crucial information for managers to evaluate in order to reduce risks and optimize set up costs in a foreign country.

This study is not free from limitations. The present research only addresses questions of whether corruption and ease of doing business are correlated. There are future opportunities for research to analyse exhaustively the relation between these two factors. First of all, the presence of explanatory variables can be acknowledged, such as wealth, trade or the population of the host country. Moreover, new results can be tied in either to strategic or to ethics discussions about corruption. A further step would be to explore how perceived corruption and ease of doing business explain different aspects of the business behaviour of firms, such as exports, investments to countries and innovation capabilities. For example, Anokhin and Schulze (2009) stress that in corrupt economies foreign direct investment tends to be in the form of joint ventures – an organizational form that is associated with the use of less sophisticated managerial and production technology. Corruption thus reduces the types and amount of technical knowledge that the foreign direct investment might bring to the host nation. If results of future analyses, which employ similar data to ours, are in line with our work, an important contribution could be made to the literature. Moreover, a longitudinal analysis of changes in the indices and the relation between them over time could be an interesting empirical issue to investigate.

References

Aguilera, R.V., Williams, A. C., Conley, M. J. and Rupp, E. D. (May 2006) 'Corporate Governance and Social Responsibility: A Comparative Analysis of the UK and the US', 14(3). Available at http://www.business.illinois.edu/aguilera/pdf/CGIR%202006.pdf.

Anokhin, S. and Schulze, W. S. (2009) 'Entrepreneurship, Innovation and Corruption', *Journal of Business Venturing*, 24(5), 465–76.

Asiedu, E. and Freeman, J. (2009) 'The Effect of Corruption on Investment Growth: Evidence from Firms in Latin America, sub-Saharan Africa, and Transition Countries', *Review of Development Economics*, 13(2), 200–14.

Baker, T., Gedajlovic, E. and Lubatkin, M. (2005) 'A Framework for Comparing Entrepreneurship Processes Across Nations', *Journal of International Business Studies*, 36, 492–504.

Brunetti, A., Kisunko, G. and Weder, B. (1998) 'Credibility of Rules and Economic Growth: Evidence from a Worldwide Survey of the Private Sector', *The World Bank Economic Review*, 12(3), 353–84.

Calderón, R., Álvarez-Arce, J. and Mayoral, S. (2009) 'Corporation as a Crucial Ally against Corruption', *Journal of Business Ethics*, 87 (July), 319–32.

Carmignani, F. (2005) 'Efficiency of Institutions, Political Stability and Income Dynamics', *United Nations Economic Commission for Europe (UNECE)*.

Ciocchini, F., Durbin, E. and Ng, D. (2003), 'Does Corruption Increase Emerging Market Bond Spreads?', *Journal of Economics and Business*, 55, 503–28.

Di Pietro, W. R. (2009) 'Country Innovativeness and the Difficulty of Doing Business', *Journal of Global Business Issues*, 3(2), 69–75.

Doing Business Rankings (2010), *http://www.doingbusiness.org/rankings*.

Doucouliagos, H. and Ulubasoglu, M. A. (2008) 'Democracy and Economic Growth: A Meta-analysis', *American Journal of Political Science*, 52(1), 61–83.

Goel, R. K. and Nelson, M. A. (2010) 'Causes of Corruption: History, Geography and Government', *Journal of Policy Modeling*, 32(4), 433–47.

Gray (2002) 'Of Messiness, Systems and Sustainability: Towards a More Social and Environmental Finance and Accounting', *The British Accounting Review*, 34(4), 357–86.

Habib, M. and Zurawicki, L. (2002) 'Corruption and Foreign Direct Investment', *Journal of International Business Studies*, 33(2), 291–307.

Hannafey, F. T. (2003) 'Entrepreneurship and Ethics: A Literature Review', *Journal of Business Ethics*, 46(2), 99–110.

Hellman, J. and Kaufmann, D. (2004) 'The Inequality of Influence' in Kornai, J. and Rose-Ackerman, S. (eds), *Trust in Transition* (New York: Palgrave Macmillan).

Hill, C. W. L. (2005) *International Business: Competing in the Global Marketplace* (5th international edn, New York: McGraw-Hill/Irwin).

Hotchkiss, C. (1998) 'The Sleeping Dog Stirs: New Signs of Life in Efforts to End Corruption in International Business', *Journal of Public Policy & Marketing*, 17(1), 108–15.

Husted, B. W. (1999) 'Wealth, Culture, and Corruption', *Journal of International Business Studies*, 30(2), 339–59.

Jain, A. K. (2002) 'Corruption: A Review', *Journal of Economic Surveys*, 15(1), 71–121.

Kabongo, J. D. and Okpara, J. O. (2009) 'Does Legal Origin Explain Differences in Regulations of Business Entry? A Study of sub-Saharan African Countries', *African Journal of Business & Economics Research*, 4(2/3), 8–24.

Kaufmann, D. and Kraay, A. (2003) 'Governance and Growth: Which Causes Which?', *The World Bank Working Papers* (Washington DC: World Bank).

Kenny, C. (2009) 'Measuring Corruption in Infrastructure: Evidence from Transition and Developing Countries', *Journal of Development Studies*, 45(3), 314–32.

Lambsdorff, G. J. (2003) 'How Corruption Affects Productivity', *Kyklos*, 56, 457–474.

Lenway, S. A. and Murtha, T. P. (1994) 'The State as Strategist in International Business Research', *Journal of International Business Studies*, 25(3), 513–35.

Li, H., Xu, L. C. and Zou, H. (2000) 'Corruption, Income Distribution, and Growth', *Economics and Politics*, 12, 155–182.

Li, S. and Wu, J. (2010) 'Why Some Countries Thrive Despite Corruption: The Role of Trust in the Corruption-Efficiency Relationship', *Review of International Political Economy*, 17(1), 129–154.

Mauro, P. (1995) 'Corruption and Growth', *The Quarterly Journal of Economics*, 110 (3), 681–712.

Mitchell, D. T. and Campbell, N. D. (2009) 'Corruption's Effect on Business Venturing within the United States', *American Journal of Economics & Sociology*, 68(5), 1135–52.

Mocan, N. (2008) 'What Determines Corruption? International Evidence from Microdata', *Economic Inquiry*, 46(4), 493–510.

Rivera-Batiz, F. L. (2002) 'Democracy, Governance, and Economic Growth: Theory and Evidence', *Review of Development Economics*, 6(2), 225–47.

Rodriguez, P., Uhlenbruck, K. and Eden, L. (2005) 'Government Corruption and the Entry Strategies of Multinationals', *Academy of Management Review*, 30(2), 383–96.

Rose-Ackerman, S. (2004) 'The Challenge of Poor Governance and Corruption', *Copenhagen Consensus Challenge Paper, Copenhagenconcensus.com*.

Stading, G. and Altay, N. (2007) 'Delineating the "Ease of Doing Business" construct within Supplier-Customer Interface', *Journal of Supply Chain Management*, 43(2), 29–38.

Transparency International (2010) *http://www.transparency.org/policy_research/surveys_indices/cpi/2010*

Uhlenbruck, K., Rodriguez, P., Doh, J. and Eden, L. (2006) 'The Impact of Corruption on Entry Strategy: Evidence from Telecommunication Projects in Emerging Economies', *Organization Science*, 17(3), 402–14.

Wei, S. J. (2000) 'How Taxing is Corruption on International Investors?' *The Review of Economics and Statistics*, 82(1), 1–11. (MIT Press Journals).

Wei, S. J. and Smarzynska, B. K. (2000) 'Corruption and the Composition of Foreign Direct Investment: Firm-Level Evidence', *Policy Research Working Paper*, Series 2360 (The World Bank).

Wilhelm, P. G. (2002) 'International Validation of the Corruption Perception Index: Implications for Business Ethics and Entrepreneurship Education', *Journal of Business Ethics*, 35, 177–189.

2
'Old Wine in New Bottles'? The Meaning and Drivers of CSR in SMEs in a Transition Economy

Veselina Stoyanova

Introduction

Over the last five decades, few topics have attracted the attention of both academics and business practitioners as much as the issue of CSR, which has been widely seen as the interplay between global and local legitimacies, shaping corporate structures and influencing decision processes (Gjølberg, 2009). A quick review of the top journals in international business and international management science reveal that CSR scholarship has taken different shapes and forms through the years, applying a wide range of theoretical frameworks. Academics and practitioners have approached the issue by applying different theoretical perspectives, placing small, medium or multinational companies at the centre of their studies.

If a timeline is drawn, the development of CSR scholarship can be divided into two stages. During the first stage (1950s–1970s), researchers have been interested in defining the phenomenon and exploring what a company's responsibility should be (Carroll, 1979, 1999). The second stage of the development of CSR scholarship has been an exploratory one. Scholars have commenced not simply to discuss companies' responsibilities but to examine the processes of implementing CSR in companies' day-to-day business practices and the factors affecting these processes. During this period, scholars have proposed a wide range of new concepts (e.g. corporate social responsiveness, corporate citizenship, corporate social performance, corporate sustainability), intended to illustrate the phenomenon better and its impact on a company's business performance (e.g. Wood, 1991; Wood and Jones, 1993; Frederick, 1994; Salzmann et al. 2005). Furthermore, the second exploratory stage of CSR has undertaken four contextual forms of research query.

The first explores the CSR behaviour of multinational companies (MNCs) in Western societies, mainly comparing the socially responsible practices of companies in the United States and Western Europe (Husted and Allen, 2006; Matten and Moon, 2008; Lindgreen et al., 2008). The second group of research studies addresses CSR in the MNC subsidiaries of Western countries in developing countries (e.g. Yang and Rivers, 2009). The researchers have been interested in studying how CSR practices are transmitted from a company's headquarters to its subsidiaries abroad and what the degree of homogeneity of CSR practice is between the home country and host country contexts. Increasing competitiveness and outward foreign direct investments from BRICS countries (Brazil, Russia, India, China and South Africa) have provoked international business researchers to investigate the CSR behaviour of these emerging market countries' MNCs (e.g. Jamali and Mirshak, 2007; Gao, 2009). The fourth direction of CSR scholarship has shifted its focus from MNCs' CSR behaviour to examine CSR in small and medium sized enterprises (SMEs). However, when compared to other research topics on CSR, the issue of CSR in SMEs has been explored the least. Arguing that SMEs are not 'little big companies' and should be studied separately from MNCs (Tilley, 2000), experts in the field have focused on examining mainly the perception and main drivers of CSR in SMEs in Western countries and less systematically the business case of CSR in SMEs (e.g. Spence and Schmidpeter, 2003; Jenkins, 2006; Perrini, 2006; Jamali et al., 2009).

The narrative in these studies has been about the CSR adaptation process either in countries with a weak institutional environment, characteristic of many developing countries, or countries with strong and transparent government systems, such as those in Western states. What has emerged as an apparent gap in the CSR literature is the study of CSR in SMEs in 'transition' economies in Eastern Europe. With some exceptions, examining the behaviour of mainly international companies (e.g. Fulop et al., 2000; Korka, 2005; Koleva et al., 2010), research on the CSR behaviour of local, indigenous firms in post-socialist, Eastern European transition economies has been lacking researchers' attention.

The aim of this study is to try to bridge the gap in the literature and to explore CSR from the outlook not only of an emerging market but also from the perspective of a post-socialist European country in transition, with small and medium sized enterprises. This is particularly relevant given that two key transitional 'waves' or 'periods' can be distinguished in the history of Eastern European states. The first was marked by the change from a socialist to a market economy, and the second by the creation of the European Union (EU) and accession to the other European Union states. In countries experiencing one transition period or the other, individuals and businesses absorb new values, and challenge and restructure traditionally embedded forms of governance and business practices (Padelford and White, 2010) All are significant for understanding CSR in different contexts. To reduce the scarcity of research on

CSR in transition economies, this study focuses on the case of Bulgaria – an example of a country experienced these two periods of transitions.

Since Bulgaria's EU membership in 2007, a number of socio-economic changes have taken place in both the macro and micro-economic business environment. This has influenced not only the way business is conducted but also the way decisions are made and issues solved in regard to CSR. The current changes in Bulgaria, as a post-socialist country and the most recent member of the EU, therefore, offer an interesting empirical site for CSR scholarship. SMEs represent the driving force of the economy in the Eastern European region, and particularly in Bulgaria (Barlett and Rangelova, 1997). The changes in the institutional environment are likely to challenge old SMEs' practices and the institutional logic behind them.

This chapter aims to explore how SMEs' managers perceive social responsibility and what institutional factors drive small and medium sized firms' CSR orientation, through the lens of neo-institutional theory. This study explores the CSR issue in two tiers of analysis, looking at the firm level and trying to grasp an overview of dominant industry trends. In the next section, a short overview of the existing CSR literature in SMEs is discussed together with the theoretical perspective that this chapter adopts.

Literature review

In order to answer the research questions of this study, it is necessary to explore what the literature has suggested so far about the meaning and drivers of CSR in SMEs. To date, a number of definitions have been used as a basis for research studies looking at the CSR practices of SMEs. For example, in a review of the literature, Garriga and Mele (2004) and later Dahlsrud (2008) managed to detect 37 different definitions and concepts of CSR. When studying CSR from a pan-European context, one of the most frequently applied definitions has been the one proposed by the European Commission, stating that CSR is a 'concept whereby companies decide (voluntarily) to contribute to a better society and a cleaner environment' (2001, p.4). This definition has been used interchangeably in research exploring CSR in small or large international companies.

This study adapts the definition of CSR used by Crane, Matten and Spence (2008), which describes CSR as a company's responsibilities towards the community (customers), workplace (employees), marketplace (suppliers, business partners, government) and environment. These responsibilities can be any activities which try to build or enhance a company's relationship with these external or internal stakeholder groups which Crane and his colleagues have identified.

From the few research studies exploring the meaning and drivers of CSR in SMEs, a heterogeneity of assumptions is observed. A partial explanation for the heterogeneity of findings is the different contexts in which previous research studies have been conducted; mainly between these based in Western countries and those coming from emerging market contexts. As well as the scarcity of research on SMEs in emerging market countries, Luetkenhorst's (2004) argument is relevant. It describes the CSR engagement of smaller companies in emerging market countries as 'salient CSR'. According to the author, this phenomenon is observed when emerging markets' companies' executives engage in socially and environmentally responsible business practices and may even recognize the strategic benefits from CSR activities but at the same time they are unaware of the existence of CSR in their companies. Another supposition regarding the practice and meaning of CSR in SMEs has been proposed by Murrillo and Lozano (2006). Based on their findings, the researchers argue that in SMEs, a degree of 'specialization' is often observed. This means that smaller companies' chief executive officers (CEOs) understand CSR as a company's responsibility towards the most important group of stakeholders for the company's business. The main driver of this 'specialization' is usually the financial limitations that smaller companies tend to face (Murrillo and Lozano, 2006).

When considering the drivers of CSR in SMEs, in comparison with large companies, a number of differences become apparent. One of the most distinctive characteristics of SMEs is the informal and personal relationships that managers may have within the company's supply chain with suppliers, employees and competitors. In contrast to large companies, where CSR practices are often influenced by companies' investors, in SMEs the CSR practices are heavily driven by the beliefs and the values of the people running them (Davies and Crane, 2010, p.128). This allows for a trustful relationship and open and honest dialogue (Spence, 1999; Davies and Crane, 2010). Williamson, Wood and Ramsey's study (2006) on 31 manufacturing SMEs in the UK shows that compliance-driven factors, such as a compliance with institutional regulation, are major drivers of SMEs' environmentally responsible activities. Based on their research study's findings, the authors argue that CSR in SMEs stems from the desire of the companies to satisfy purely functional short-term needs. Jenkins (2006) and Morsing and Perrini (2009) argue that pressures from stakeholders other than government tend to impact smaller companies' CSR orientation. The company managers of four Catalan SMEs, interviewed by Murrillo and Lozano (2006), support the arguments of Jenkins (2006) and Morsing and Perrini (2009). All of the interviewed company managers stated that they measure the effect of their CSR activities in terms of the improvements of their relationships with employees and external stakeholders (Murrillo and Lozano, 2006).

SMEs operate usually in one of three business contexts in which they are likely to face pressures from multiple stakeholder groups. First, SMEs may operate as subcontractors or suppliers to MNCs. In this case, they are more likely to face pressures from a global value chain, which requires compliance with both external and internal regulations and standards, as well as adaptation of practices, reflecting the client MNC's CSR (Luetkenhorst, 2004). Secondly, SMEs may act as an independent supplier. In this scenario, managers will face both consumer pressures and institutional pressures (Luetkenhorst, 2004). A third possibility is for SMEs to operate only in the national value chain. These enterprises are more likely to adopt CSR in response to domestic regulation, pressure from domestic consumers and community issues that are problematic for a firm's success (Luetkenhorst, 2004). Other studies have described voluntary-driven factors as the most influential drivers of CSR behaviour.

Findings from a number of studies show that the motivation of SMEs to engage in CSR stems from the owner-manager or founder of the firm (Spence and Schmidpeter, 2003; Murrillo and Lozano, 2006; Ciliberti et al., 2008; Jamali et al., 2009; Morsing and Perrini, 2009; Del Baldo, 2010). Spence and Schmidpeter's (2003) research on 30 SMEs located in Germany and the UK discloses that factors such as a manager's own type of personality and connections assist SMEs in building social capital, which on the other hand benefits the development of CSR practices. Murrillo and Lozano's study (2006) links the development of CSR in SMEs to the leadership style of their managers. However, it is noticeable, when scanning the literature on CSR in SMEs, that there is a lack of research studies focusing on cases from emerging market countries. It would be interesting to find out what CSR means in these countries' contexts and what factors tend to drive socially responsible activities in a country in transition.

Theoretical framework: neo-institutional theory approach

Within the body of theoretical underpinnings of research studies on CSR, institutional theory appears to be a preferable theoretical framework when exploring socially responsible practices in cross-cultural (e.g. Aguilera and Jackson, 2003; Aguilera et al., 2006; Matten and Moon, 2008) and cross-sectorial contexts (e.g. Griffin and Weber, 2006). An explanation for this ascendancy is the general view of the firm as an institutionalized entity, dependent on external and internal institutionalized factors for a company (Scott, 1987). In this vein, research studies on CSR have focused largely on studying the role of national business systems and the varieties of capitalism across nations to account for differences and similarities in CSR practices among industrial and geographical milieus. The principal argument in these studies, mainly examining the practices of MNCs, tends to emphasize homogeneity of practice across sectors resulting from the influence of a host country's specific institutional environment or a company's own institutionally embedded characteristics from the home country government and business systems (Whitley, 1992; Doh et al., 2010).

When comparing CSR practices across nations and across sectors, there is a dearth of analysis on the CSR behaviour of companies sharing the same sectorial and geographical contexts. To narrow the identified gap in the literature, this study adopts an institutional perspective to examine the meaning and practices of social responsibility within an indigenous sector, namely the wine industry in Bulgaria, some 4000 years old, and within a single geographical context. As the focus of this study is to understand the CSR orientation of Bulgarian SMEs from the wine industry and the factors driving this orientation and CSR meaning, Oliver's (1997) interpretation of institutional theory seems to be one of the most appropriate theoretical frameworks for this study's objectives.

Drawing on Scott (1995), DiMaggio and Powell (1983) and Kostova's (1997) institutional views, Oliver (1997) extends the neo-institutional view by examining it from a firm-level context. Oliver's interpretation of institutional theory frames this study. As companies' CSR behaviour is a newly institutionalized activity in the majority of SMEs in Bulgaria, it is relevant to examine the phenomenon as interrelated processes taking place at individual (cognitive), organizational (normative) and inter-organizational (regulative) levels of analysis (Oliver, 1997, p.700). In Oliver's framework, individual level factors often refer to the manager's personal background, values and experience which directly or indirectly often influence the way decisions are made and processed. Organizational (normative) factors are internal to a firm, such as company employees, and work unions who stimulate a change in old practices or the establishment of new ones. Inter-organizational (regulative) factors are initiated usually by governmental legislation or stakeholders external to the company, such as its competitors, suppliers and customers (please see Figure 2.1).

Using Oliver's (1997) adaptation of neo-institutional theory, this chapter seeks to examine the factors that have stimulated SMEs' CEOs to adopt CSR in their companies' strategies. The chapter seeks to check the extent to which inter-organizational factors (regulatory) push CSR in the sampled companies, in comparison with other organizational (normative) and individual (cognitive) level factors.

Methodology

The aim of this research study is to examine a previously, unexplored phenomenon. Therefore it is necessary to search for any factors and details that provide a deeper understanding of the phenomenon within the context. Therefore, qualitative research rather than quantitative research methodology was more suitable for the objectives of this study.

This article adopts an exploratory qualitative research method based on face-to-face, in-depth, interviews with senior executive managers of 8 small

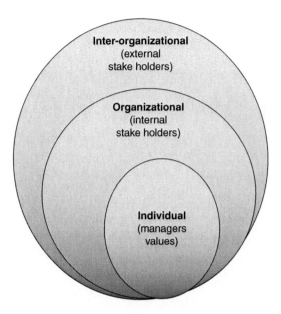

Figure 2.1   Analytical model

and medium sized wineries, located in the Southern, Northern, Western, South-eastern part of Bulgaria. Initially, 35 small and medium sized wineries randomly selected and identified from the website of the Ministry of Justice's Registry Agency of Bulgaria, where all firms registered in Bulgaria are listed. All of the firms were approached and contacted prior to the research. From all these, eight firms agreed to participate in the study. All of the interviewed respondents were CEOs who were contacted and interview meetings were scheduled. Two reasons made the choice of companies' chief executives the better choice than the selection of any other actors in the company. Generally, people working in Eastern European countries' organizations are suspicious and insecure towards people coming to interview them (Michailova, 2004). Often these people feel afraid that if they provide a 'wrong' answer, it may cost them their job (Michailova, 2004). Michailova (2004, p.371) proposes that one way to eliminate insecurity and suspicion in the interview process is to interview companies' CEOs. The second reason is linked to the fact that managers' background, experience with the company as well as their industry knowledge can be a significant source of information when assessing how individual factors influence CSR motivation (please see Table 2.1).

To ensure the validity and reliability of the findings, exactly the same semi-structured interview questions were asked in all of the eight companies with

Table 2.1 SMEs details

CEO	Labour no.	Education	Background	Market focus	Sector of operations
CEO 1	110	Home country	Family-run business, bought the company in 1996	International mainly; and a domestic niche	Specializes in the production of boutique wine; wine tourism
CEO 2	60	Home country; International	In 2002, came back from abroad after being an immigrant since 1991 and bought the company and a number of vineyards; family-business	Domestic	Specializes in the production of boutique wine; wine tourism
CEO 3	165	Home country	Worked 10 years in R&D lab in large winery, before joining in 2000 the company	Domestic mainly but also international	Wine production
CEO 4	50	Home country	Family-run business	Domestic	Wine production; wine tourism
CEO 5	40	Home country	Bought the winery in the 90s together with friends, later became the only owner	International	Wine production
CEO 6	80	International	His family has a hundred years long tradition in wine production. He inherited the family business.	International	Specializes in the production of boutique wine
CEO 7	35	Home country	Family business, started from inheriting a small vineyard from his grandfather	Domestic	Specializes in the production of organic wine
CEO 8	25	International	Family business, works with his father	Domestic	Wine production

the same number of individuals and for the same time period. Moreover, the interviewees from all the companies were selected to match in terms of job responsibilities. The geographic representation of the companies was defined by the location of the randomly selected companies. All of the CEOs were interviewed in their company settings. During all of the interviews, an interview guide was used as a helpful tool as it permitted the research categories to be followed, and to stay within the focus of the research topic and the time limit of each interview. Each interview questionnaire had a standardized open-ended format composed of semi-structured interview questions. All of the questions used during the interview were non-directed rather than directed. The decision to make all questions non-directed rather than directed was taken after the review of the current CSR literature on SMEs. A number of research findings showed that interviewees from SMEs often do not feel comfortable when using the term 'corporate social responsibility', as they either do not know what the notion implies or do not feel that the word 'corporate' best describes their company's structure. Therefore, all research questions were framed to present the issue in a non-directive way, referring to the term *enterprise culture*, proposed by Murrillo and Lozano (2006) when researching CSR in SMEs.

Discussion and conclusion

'Push' CSR factors in Bulgarian SMEs

The findings of this study suggest that the interviewed CEOs perceive CSR as their commitment responsibly to serve their local communities, environment and workforce. Educational programmes, donations to orphanages, employees' training and language courses, as well as environmental initiatives, such as the maintenance of green areas, are some of the most frequent CSR practices of the sampled companies. By exploring what drives CSR in SMEs in Bulgaria, the study contributes to the CSR literature by documenting that institutional factors on an inter-organizational and individual level of analysis play an essential role in the adaptation of CSR by SMEs in Bulgaria. The study found that institutional factors such as pressures from external stakeholders, such as industry competitors, suppliers and customers, as well as managers' personal moral values, influence CSR behaviour more than Bulgaria's CSR national strategy and EU policies, adopted recently to disseminate CSR behaviour among SMEs in the country. Some of the companies mentioning inter-organizational factors as key determinants stated:

> Our customers are our compass; they show the direction where we should go. Their preferences are what guide us when we are making decisions now and in the future... [CEO 3]

Every company that intends to be successful in the market, no matter what the characteristics of that market are, should have one major priority – to satisfy the consumers. This is not an exception in our business... [CEO 5]

Our suppliers are definitely the ones who influence the most our decisions, mainly because of the sort of wine we produce. It is very hard to find out producers of organic grape, who do not use any kind of insecticides and pesticides... [CEO 7]

These findings are consistent with what is reported by Jenkins (2006), Morsing and Perrini (2009) who identify stakeholder pressures as the key motivation for SMEs' CSR in the Western context. However, in contrast to Western countries, where stakeholder activism and market price are substantial drivers of CSR, the interview data shows that social capital and previous experience with external stakeholders is what influence business practices, such as CSR, the most in an Eastern European country in transition. In this regard one CEO explained:

... if I should prioritize these are our suppliers of high quality sorts of grapes. We operate in a region with high competition, and fewer suppliers. It is a competition for high quality grape, in many cases it is not about who is going to offer the best price, but in most cases it is about who you know and your experience with the person... [CEO 2]

The interviewed CEOs highlighted that maintaining solid relationships with their key stakeholders define to large extent their connections with the rest of their other stakeholders. The finding is consistent with the argument of Murrillo and Lozano (2006, p.237) that in SMEs, the engagement with one stakeholder implies that the company will end up moving toward the other stakeholders. One factor that explains this finding is the local concentration of SMEs in the community, observed by Russo and Perrini (2010). The majority of the interviewees said that they respond to customer pressures by providing high quality wine. The same companies' CSR initiatives are directed towards the training and retaining of their human capital. When analysing the data, a number of organizational factors were identified as influencing the extent to which a particular stakeholder influences the CSR initiatives of a company. These factors are the degree of dependence and the degree of interrelatedness that the interviewed companies experience in the value chain.

Besides inter-organizational factors such as external stakeholder pressures, many CSR practices in SMEs are encouraged by the CEOs' managerial discretion and values. These insights are in line with the argument of Spence and Schmidpeter (2003) and Murrillo and Lozano (2006) that to a large extent a company's motivation to engage in CSR is driven by the values of the leader in

Western Europe. However, the interview results contribute further to the existing literature by unpacking the importance of two variables that tend to have an impact on the leader's motivation to adopt CSR.

These are a manager's education and personal background and experience. These variables are reflected in the individual level analysis (cognitive pillar) of institutional theory (Oliver, 1997), which is embedded in the theoretical model of this study. 'When I was working and living abroad, I leant a lot just from practice. Maybe, the most important thing I learnt, and which influences how I do business today is the importance of stimulating innovation and entrepreneurial spirit within the organization ...' [CEO 2]. One of the interviewees, whose company sponsors scholarships for talented, young students also stated: 'I admire arts, when I was a teenager, I wanted to study arts, but my parents were always against. I am happy now that I can support these that have the talent but do not have the opportunity'. These observations combine to suggest that managers' personal values and experience can be motivating factors for CSR. The observations of the interview data suggested also that educational background is an essential factor in determining a company's CSR initiatives. The interview data revealed that managers who have received their education in Western countries' universities are more aware of the meanings and the practical implications of CSR. In this respect, one manager pointed out: 'I think that I hear the term CSR for first time in my business ethics classes in the university in the UK. We studied this course as a part of the curriculum' [CEO 8]. Another interviewee shared a similar view, stating: 'I think I learnt it in school for first time during the master course' [CEO 6].

In contrast to the supposition that, within the same industry, companies' strategies would be shaped by the dominance of one institutional logic accounting for isomorphic activities, this study found a co-existence of different logics within SMEs in the Bulgarian wine industry. Based on the research findings, the co-existence of different institutional logics could be seen as the interplay between inter-organizational level factors, such as pressures from customers and suppliers, and individual level factors, such as managers' individual characteristics (managers' education, previous experience and background) which can explain the various sustainable practices and stakeholder engagement initiatives within the Bulgarian wine industry.

Another interesting supposition that was not expected to result from this study is about the role of the age of the studied companies as a determinant factor which could explain to some extent the heterogeneity of co-existing institutional logics. It was interesting to observe that, of the sampled companies, those SMEs founded earlier in the first 'wave' of transition, that from a socialist to a market economy orientation, are more likely to direct their CSR practices towards the community and consider pressures from customers as the most influential factors on their CSR strategies. On the other hand, companies founded in the second 'wave' of transition, marked by Bulgaria's membership of the European Union, tend to direct their CSR activities towards their main suppliers and employees. This finding suggests that the specific date of starting up a business has an impact on the companies' CSR orientation. Furthermore, the findings of the chapter suggest the idea that an SME's present CSR activities tend to be firmly embedded in the history of the firm and its specific governance, which is often defined by a company founder's individual values and experience. However, these suppositions require future research to prove their validity and reliability further. By reviewing the social responsibility scenario in the most financially vulnerable small and medium sized companies in Bulgaria, the study seeks to contribute to the meagre literature on sustainability practice and meaning in countries in transition, as well as assist practitioners engaged in the development of national programmes for the development of effective strategy encouraging sustainability in SMEs.

References

Aguilera, R.V. and Jackson, G. (2003) 'The Cross-national Diversity of Corporate Governance: Dimensions and Determinants', *Academy of Management Review*, 28(3), 447–66.

Aguilera, R.V., Williams, C.A., Conley, J. M. and Rupp, D. E. (2006) 'Corporate Governance and Social Responsibility: A Comparative Analysis of the UK and the US', *Corporate Governance and Social Responsibility*, 14(3), 147–58.

Barlett, W. and Rangelova, R. (1997) 'Small Firms and Economic Transformation in Bulgaria', *Small Business Economics*, 9, 319–33.

Campbell, J. L. (2006) 'Institutional Analysis and the Paradox of Corporate Social Responsibility', *American Behavioral Scientist*, 49(7), 925–38.

Carroll, A. B. (1979) 'A Three-Dimensional Conceptual Model of Corporate Social Performance', *Academy of Management Review*, 4(4), 497–505.

Carroll, A. B (1999) 'Corporate Social Responsibility Evolution of a Definitional Construct', *Business Society*, 38(3), 268–95.

Ciliberti, F., Pontrandolfo, P. and Scozzi, B. (2008) 'Investigating Corporate Social Responsibility in Supply Chains: A SME Perspective', *Journal of Cleaner Production* 16(15), 1579–88.

Crane, A., Matten, D. and Spence, L. J. (2008) *Corporate Social Responsibility. Readings and Causes in a Global Context* (Abingdon: Routledge), 92–307.

Dahlsrud, A. (2008) 'How Corporate Social Responsibility is Defined: An Analysis of Definitions', *Corporate Social Responsibility and Environmental Management,* 15(1), 1–13.

Davies, I. A. and Crane, A. (2010) 'Corporate Social Responsibility in Small-and Medium-size Enterprises: Investigating Employee Engagement in Fair Trade Companies', *Business Ethics: A European Review*, 19(2), 126–39.

Del Baldo, M. (2010) 'Corporate Social Responsibility and Corporate Governance in Italian SMEs: The Experience of Some "Spirited Businesses"', *International Journal of Sustainable Society*, 2(3), 215–47.

DiMaggio, P. J. and Powell, W. W. (1983) *The New Institutionalism in Organizational Analysis* (Chicago, IL: University of Chicago Press).

Doh, J., Husted, B. W., Matten, D. and Santoro, M. (2010) 'Ahoy There! Towards Greater Congruence and Synergy between International Business and Business Ethics Theory and Research', *Business Ethics Quarterly*, 20(3), 481–502.

European Commission (2001) '*Promoting a European framework for corporate social responsibility, Green paper*' [online] Available at: <http://www.jussemper.org/Resources/Corporate%20Activity/Resources/greenpaper_en.pdf> [Accessed 20 June 2010].

Falck, O. and Heblich, S. (2007) 'Corporate Social Responsibility: Doing Well by Doing Good', *Business Horizons*, 50, 247–54.

Frederick, W. C. (1994) 'From CSR1 to CSR2: The Maturing of Business and Society Thought', *Business and Society*, 33(3), 150–64.

Fulop, G., Hisrich, R. D. and Szegedi, K. (2000) 'Business Ethics and Social Responsibility in Transition Economies', *Journal of Management Development*, 19(1), 5–31.

Gao, Y. (2009) 'Corporate Social Performance in China: Evidence from Large Companies', *Journal of Business Ethics*, 89, 23–35.

Garriga, E. and Mele, D. (2004) 'Corporate Social Responsibility Theories: Mapping the Territory', *Journal of Business Ethics*, (1–2), 51–71.

Gjølberg, M. (2009) 'The Origin of Corporate Social Responsibility: Global Forces or National Legacies?', *Socio-Economic Review*, 7(4), 605–37.

Griffin, J. J. and Weber, J. (2006) 'Industry Social Analysis: Examining the Beer Industry', *Business and Society*, 45(4), 413–40.

Husted, B. W. and Allen, D. B. (2006) 'Corporate Social Responsibility in the Multinational Enterprise: Strategic and Institutional Approaches', *Journal of International Business Studies*, 37, 838–49.

Jamali, D. and Mirshak, R. (2007) 'Corporate Social Responsibility (CSR): Theory and Practice in a Developing Country Context', *Journal of Business Ethics*, 72, 243–62.

Jamali, D., Zanhour, M. and Keshishian, T. (2009) 'Peculiar Strengths and Relational Attributes of SMEs in the Context of CSR', *Journal of Business Ethics*, 87, 355–77.

Jenkins, H. (2006) 'Small Business Champions for Corporate Social Responsibility', *Journal of Business Ethics*, 67, 241–56.

Koleva, P., Rodet-Kroichvili, N., David, P. and Marasova, J. (2010) 'Is Corporate Social Responsibility the Privilege of Developed Market Economies? Some Evidence from Central and Eastern Europe', *The International Journal of Human Resource Management*, 21(2), 274–93.

Korka, M. (2005) 'Corporate Social Responsibility in Romania: From Theory to Practice', *Transition Studies Review*, 12(1), 47–57.

Kostova, T. (1997) 'Country Institutional Profile: Concept and Measurement', *Academy of Management Best Paper Proceeding*, 180–9.

Kostova, T. and Zaheer, S. (1999) 'Organizational Legitimacy under Conditions of Complexity: The Case of the Multinational Enterprise', *Academy of Management Review*, 24(1), 64–81.

Lindgreen, A., Swaen, V. and Johnston, W. L. (2008) 'Corporate Social Responsibility: An Empirical Investigation of U.S. Organizations', *Journal of Business Ethics*, 85(2), 303–23.

Luetkenhorst, W. (2004) 'Corporate Social Responsibility and the Development Agenda: The Case for Actively Involving Small and Medium Enterprises', *Intereconomics*, 39(3), 157–66.

Matten, D. and Moon, J. (2008) ' "Implicit" and "Explicit" CSR: A Conceptual Framework for a Comparative Understanding of Corporate Social Responsibility', *Academy of Management Review*, 33(2), 404–24.

Michailova, S. (2004) 'Contextualising Fieldwork: Reflections on Conducting Research in Eastern Europe' in Marschan-Piekkari, R. and Welch, C. (eds), *Handbook of Qualitative Research Methods for International Business* (Cheltenham: Edward Elgar Publishing Limited), 365–83.

Morsing, M. and Perrini, F. (2009) 'CSR in SMEs: Do SMEs Matter for the CSR Agenda?', *Business Ethics: A European Review*, 18(1), 1–6.

Murillo, D. and Lozano, J. M. (2006) 'SMEs and CSR: An Approach to CSR in Their Own Words', *Journal of Business Ethics*, 67, 227–40.

Oliver, C. (1997) 'Sustainable Competitive Advantage: Combining Institutional and Resource-Based Views', *Strategic Management Journal*, 18(9), 697–713.

Padelford, W. and White, D. W. (2010) 'The Influence of Historical Socialism and Communism on the Shaping of a Society's Economic Ethos: An Exploratory Study of Central and Eastern Europe', *Journal of Business Ethics*, 97, 109–117.

Perrini, F. (2006) 'SMEs and CSR Theory: Evidence and Implications from an Italian Perspective, *Journal of Business Ethics*, 91, 207–221.

Russo, A. and Perrini, F. (2010) 'Investigating Stakeholder Theory and Social Capital: CSR in Large Firms and SMEs', *Journal of Business Ethics*, 91, 207–221.

Salzmann, O., Ionescu-Somers, A. and Steger, U. (2005) 'The Business Case for Corporate Sustainability: Literature Review and Research Options', *European Management Journal*, 23(1), 27–36.

Scott, W. R. (1987) 'The Adolescence of Institutional Theory', *Administrative Science Quarterly*, 32(4), 493–511.

Scott, W. R. (1995) *Institutions and Organizations* (London: Sage Publications).

Spence, L. J. (1999) 'Does Size Matter? The State of the Art in Small Business Ethics', *Business Ethics: A European Review*, 8(3), 163–174.

Spence, L. J. and Schmidpeter, R. (2003) 'SMEs, Social Capital and the Common Good', *Journal of Business Ethics*, 45, 93–108.

Tilley, F. (2000) 'Small Firm Environmental Ethics: How Deep Do They Go?', *Business Ethics: A European Review*, 9(1), 31–41.

Whitley, R. (1992) *European Business systems: Firms and Markets in Their National Contexts* (London: Sage).

Williamson, D., Lynch-Wood, G. and Ramsay, J. (2006) 'Drivers of Environmental Behaviour in Manufacturing SMEs and the Implications for CSR', *Journal of Business Ethics*, 67, 317–30.

Wood, D. J. (1991) 'Corporate Social Performance Revisited', *Academy of Management Review*, 16(4), 591–718.

Wood, D. J. and Jones, R. E. (1993) 'Stakeholder Mismatching: A Theoretical Problem in Empirical Research on Corporate Social Performance, *International Journal of Organizational Analysis*, 3(3), 229–67.

Yang, X. and Rivers, C. (2009) 'Antecedents of CSR Practices in MNCs' Subsidiary Stakeholder and Institutional Perspective', *Journal of Business Ethics*, 86(2), 155–69.

3
'Second Best' Institutions and Global Sustainability

Frederick Ahen

Introduction

In an ideal textbook world, the noble concept of sustainable development sounds less complex and more feasible to actualize. Nevertheless, the fierce scramble to appear socially responsible also involves sophisticated corporate ingenuity characterized by deviance (Cohen, 1966), which is aimed mostly at rent seeking without regard to social and environmental issues, especially in weaker institutions. Institutional theory has thus far proved very valuable in providing insights into the reasons why the rules of the international business game, with multinational companies (MNCs) as major players, are applied differently in different institutional environments, resulting in different outcomes. It is easier to identify the functions of institutions than the structure they should take in specific contexts. The available literature and conventional knowledge about institutions have mostly been developed in the West, where the judicial, socio-economic and political systems are generally formalized, stable, advanced and diverse. From theory to practice, this has led to the general assumption that the first best practices of the West should also be easily enforceable elsewhere in the developing world (Rodrik, 2008). From the start of the millennium, however, economic crises and emerging opportunities have highlighted the importance of the developing economies (DEs). First, they are potential markets notwithstanding the fundamentally different challenges they pose. Secondly, the institutional structures underpinning the rules of the game for their sustainable development are susceptible to analysis using the 'second best perspective' (Rodrik, 2008). Thirdly, both developed and developing economies, no matter their configurations as liberal market economies in Anglo-Saxon economies, or coordinated market economies in continental Europe, (Hall & Soskice, 2001; Jackson and Apostolakou, 2010), are undergoing structural modifications in their institutional underpinnings to accommodate sustainability issues. These are also due to globalization, the interconnectedness of nations' regulatory reforms, and environmental and social concerns, for example, global warming and poverty issues at the bottom of the pyramid, with reference to the pioneer work of Prahalad (2005). Fourthly, the country of origin of MNCs also affects how they handle sustainability questions in DEs.

The purpose of this chapter is to provide a new theoretical framework for analysing the institutions of DEs which are characteristically weak and transitional, using different theoretical lenses. Three events have motivated this line of reasoning. One, the relatively stable political situations and the exponential growth in the population of the youth in Africa and Asia, which provides new opportunities for businesses. Two, this young and educated middle class now has new expectations in terms of corporate responsibility (CR) and a sustainable future as they join the global chorus and demand fair play. Three, from the academic perspective, serious research aimed at explaining, interpreting and predicting the dynamic nature of markets, the nexus between the world economic and social order, as well as the extent to which these factors induce institutional change within the framework of international trade and jurisprudence, raising questions central to sustainability in DEs, has received scant attention. The rationales for furthering analysis are founded on four premises.

(1) The higher degree of corporate political power (CPP), *vis-à-vis* host countries, reduces commitment to sustainable development (Scherer and Palazzo, 2007; Hymer, 1960; Ietto-Gillies, 2002), especially in economies where there are institutional voids or weaker political and judicial structures (Campbell, 2007). This is due to MNCs' removal of competition and firm-specific advantages (Hymer, 1960).

(2) The fragmented, weak and sometimes void institutional nature of host countries gives companies a strong corporate bargaining power (CBP), especially in DEs pushing hard for foreign direct investments (FDIs) (Ietto-Gillies, 2002).

(3) In such international business environments, corporate political action (CPA) becomes an important apparatus for manoeuvring in the political circles (Mantere, Pajunen & Lamberg 2009). CPA refers to 'any deliberate firm action intended to influence governmental policy or process' (Getz, 1997, pp.32–3) and for Baron (1997, p.146) it is 'a concerted pattern of actions taken in the nonmarket environment to create value by improving overall performance [either responsibly or with deviance]'. The importance of CPA as an integral part of the corporate strategic apparatus has been highlighted by Frynas, Mellahi and Pigman (2006; cited in Mantere et al., 2009).

(4) Both collusion and rivalry can co-exist depending on the power of host countries (Pitelis, 1991). In recent years, however, questions pertaining to

CR and sustainability have been taken up by international non-governmental organizations (INGOs). Host governments' reactions are mainly rhetorical whilst local NGOs are pushed into obscurity or at most have a limited voice. This creates dependency.

We argue that supra-national organizations deserve credit for their indispensable roles. Nevertheless, INGOs and MNCs have ineffective and inefficient monitoring systems, which lack enforcement mechanisms, lack transparency, take local details for granted, and lack commitment due to stretched resources and non-binding codes, whilst their operations are mainly based on aggregate information with the 'first best' mind set (Sprote, 1990; Rashid, 2006). Further, organized scientific knowledge is not the sum of all knowledge. Knowledge of prevailing circumstances, and of time and place requires 'the man on the spot', who depends not only on aggregate statistics but context-specific information to solve sustainability problems. 'If we can agree that the economic problem of society is mainly one of rapid adaptation to changes in particular circumstances of time and place, it would seem to follow that the ultimate decisions must be left to the people who are familiar with those circumstances, who know directly of the relevant changes and of the resources immediately available to meet them' (Hayek, 1945, p.524).

We maintain that given the CPP, CBP and CPA, in the absence of powerful constellations of local NGOs and strong institutional structures, actualizing responsible actions to meet sustainability goals will be ineffective if not impossible. The focus of the debate then moves from asking what firms ought to do, to getting host country institutions right. Under appropriate conditions, it is plausible to assume that a firm's capabilities and governance systems would be aligned with specific market and institutional needs and context-bound circumstances to ensure sustainable development at the grassroots level, to paraphrase Rodrik (2008). This however should be based on knowledge from, and engagement with, local stakeholders.

Governments make reforms. Businesses do business. However these activities are pursued, society is impacted by both. It cannot be inferred here that the socio-economic quagmire of DEs, and the negative impact of certain business activities, is a historical accident, one of an unlucky spot in the global sustainability discourse. There are emerging national political and judicial processes to address such corporate governance and environmental issues. These are typically embodied in reregulation, and voluntary governance: diversifications which all have systemic effects on the macroeconomic structure to accommodate new forms of sustainable investment (World Investment Report 2010; Rodrik, 2008). The big slogan is sustainability for the core believers while the efficient market believers keep doing business as usual with CR as a by product. We are now at the crux of issues, where the analysis starts getting a little more cumbersome but also interesting. There are ample reasons to focus on CR since there is abundance of corporate irresponsibility, as with Shell in Nigeria or BP in the gulf-coast of America.

Corporate irresponsibility in DEs is not a sporadic anomaly or a mere episodic deviation from the expected industry standards, moral principles and cooperation with host government and NGOs, aimed at creating value both for the firm and its constituents. It entails systematic value destruction for the benefit of a few rent seekers. This needs to be addressed in the light of the prevailing institutions. Some organizations have a culture of denial by resorting to terminologies and a concordance of verbal techniques which help them to justify, beatify and even glorify abuses to lessen their repulsive reputation (Braithwaite, 1985a), while some companies continue to be ostensibly oblivious to their unacceptable activities. However, the growing trend towards sustainability cannot be underestimated. If this trend seems to be evident in some countries, it is simply reflective of the institutional environment. It is overwhelmingly agreed that there is a need for CR for social, economic and environmental issues (Bird, Smucker and Velasquez, 2009; Carasco and Singh, 2009; Carroll, 1991; Frederick, 1960, 1998; Freeman, 1984; Garriga and Mele, 2004; Meyer, 2004). These notions are conceptualized as corporate environmental responsibility, corporate social responsibility, corporate citizenship, corporate stakeholder engagement etc. Taxonomies along these lines, conceptualizing corporate actions in response to stakeholder demands and global challenges, especially in DEs, are manifold. Here again, given the inherent managerial mind set of taking opportunistic advantage of institutional weaknesses, the looming question is: 'Under what institutional conditions can sustainability issues be actualized?'

Methodology of analysis

The approach applied here is an introspective economic philosophical and *meta*-theoretical analysis based on Scott's (2001) three institutional pillars: normative, regulative and cultural-cognitive elements. Williamson (2000), Rodrik (2008) and Hayek's (1945) analyses, with a new lens, will help capture the questions of context, polity, mores and the nation state's links with markets and normative questions to achieve a more nuanced understanding. The spotlight then is on the voluntary nature of private governance *vis-à-vis* host country institutions.

Against this background, we argue using an analogy. If the children of my neighbours are welcomed to play in my backyard, in which I have planted roses (a private property to which I have exclusive rights of use for social and economic purposes, though that does not preclude others from admiring them), it is my responsibility to let them know that I have planted roses that are blossoming (business opportunity) and that they are not allowed to trample upon them as that would constitute a loss on my side and be subject to a settlement for damages on their side. I have to make sure that they understand and agree to the rules of the game and that they abide by them. If for any special reason they are incapable of obeying or unwilling to obey my rules, they are free to play in other backyards. If I am shy, afraid or unwilling to exercise and enforce these property rights, it does not mean that I have lost the right to complain when they trample upon the roses. They must reciprocate my kind gesture as a matter of rule. Any passer-by who cares to lament the trodden roses probably pities me. But then, again, that does not bring back the destroyed roses. It will neither get me any money back in return for the loss I have sustained due to my kindness, nor deter other children from doing the same. This is where matters stand: nations have the right and obligation to protect their own backyards. This reflection leads us to the following research questions:

(1) To what extent does the power asymmetry and political role of MNCs in DEs create socio-political and economic tensions and consequently negative social and environmental effects?
(2) Under what institutional conditions are firms more prone to sustainable development in DEs?

For our purpose, sustainable development is operationalized as today's strategic decisions, actions, innovations based on strategic ethical leadership which creates positive value for current and potential stakeholders and their environment within an institutional context but in ways which do not preclude the value creation and welfare opportunities of posterity. Any deviation from this is clearly seen as unsustainable.

There is clearly a nexus between politics, economics and society and a comprehensive analysis would be difficult without a combined review of such elements in order to put issues into proper institutional context (Sullivan, 1999). The foregoing contribution is organized as follows. First, a thorough introspective, economic philosophical analysis (Earl, 2001), with institutional theory and CR as the main units of analysis, is performed. It is followed by business and society issues in the context of DEs. We then offer the main arguments why host countries' bottom-up but cooperative role in ensuring sustainability will be the way forward in the long term.

Theoretical perspective: why institutions matter the most

Institutions are complex but they matter if we want to understand the workings of markets, societies, polity, jurisprudence, and even why managers think in a particular way and the outcome of such ways of thinking. Following North (1990), Williamson (2000) and Posner (2003) in institutional economics, institutions consist of norms, ideologies, governance etc., which shape human behaviour. Expositors of neo-institutional theory reject the rationality arguments, and we subscribe to that. Some sociologists and ethicists have focused on the normative stream, especially CSR (e.g., Carroll, 1991; Donaldson and Preston, 1995; Frederick, 1998; Freeman, 1984; Garriga and Mele, 2004), whilst organization theorists such as Douglas (1986) and Granovetter (1985) have focused on socio-cultural embeddedness, namely, norms, cultural practices and network relationships. From the sociological perspective, institutions 'consist of cultural-cognitive, normative and regulative elements that together with the associated activities and resources provide stability, order and the efficient working of markets while providing meaning to social life' (Scott, 2001, p.48; Scott, 2009). What have so far been ignored in the works of new institutional theorists are the role of supra-national institutions, INGOs, and the influence of information technologies in shaping institutions especially in DEs.

This chapter sheds light on the CR practices and the political power of organizations as Scherer and Palazzo (2007) propose, but contextualized here in DEs in the light of corporate power and responsibility towards sustainability. For Hofstede, Van Deusen, Mueller, Charles and the Business Goals Network (2002) 'institutions are the crystallizations of culture and culture is the substratum of institutional arrangements' (2002, p.800). Hence, the arduous task of differentiating between institutions and culture is useless at best (Peng and Pleggenkuhle-Miles, 2009), and we embrace this reasoning. It is argued that appropriate local institutions are the best environment for fostering sustainable practices by MNCs. They also represent the enablers and inhibitors of sound economic and social policies that lead to order in a market system. Institutions present themselves as social choices, which MNCs evaluate and adapt to or attempt to influence and reshape with their political power. Since institutions vary across national borders and societies, understanding the differences will have a great effect on the solution to underlying issues (Priem et al., 1998).

If businesses, governments and organizations continue to operate unsustainably, it simply demonstrates that the institutional environment is conducive to such practices. Where legal frameworks are weak, corruption and worthless bureaucracy take place. Where governance is out of touch with the governed, the environment and the commoners bear the brunt and are always exposed to the excessive exploitation of big businesses. Ideas, religious inclinations and ideologies matter in shaping the world view of MNCs and their perceptions of sustainability. It is apt to quote Williamson (2000) on his 'path-dependence' account of the political, economic and judicial systems of each society as 'a web of interconnected formal rules and informal constraints that together make up the institutional matrix which have led economies onto different paths of development and hence general welfare of their people'. Such differences are epitomized in the works of Putnam, Leonardi and Nanetti (1993) and Purdy, Alexander and Neil (2010). Encouraging multinationals to abide by international laws is necessary, but not the most crucial path. Strongly encouraging changes in developing nations' institutions through regulatory reforms (in nation states) which discourage corporate irresponsibility and abuse is the core issue here. This diverges from taking a crusading approach against firms' ethical performance (Weber, 2004).

Globalization-led institutional change in varieties of economies

A shift from protectionism to business friendliness now characterizes emerging economies (EEs) across the board (Wright et al., 2005). Firms' sustainable practices embedded in a day-to-day strategy implementation, which engages civil society and local constituents, are the legitimate blueprint which is devised to guide proactive and reactive responses using their dynamic capabilities. The external and internal dynamics, within which the firm operates to adapt to the externally devised regulatory reform and market changes, should aim at achieving efficiency while enhancing welfare.

Within the institutional context of DE's discourse on second best institutions, where supra-national institutions as well as NGOs play a major role (Easterly, 2006), the operational rules cannot therefore be 'one size fits all', based on some aggregate figures, as Rodrik (2008) and Hayek (1945) argue. For a comprehensive analysis see Sethi and Williams (2000) on the OECD guidelines for MNCs stipulated in 1976, and ILO tripartite declarations of principles concerning MNCs and the social policies introduced in 1997 (ILO, 2006). What is yet to be seen is how the UN Global Compact's ten principles (United Nations, 2009), aimed at aligning business with the UN agencies of labour and society, will fare. Implied here is that the technological-economic power asymmetry of corporations weighs heavily on the vulnerable host country institutions (Carasco and Singh, 2009) in ways that further worsen sustainability concerns, yet that do not explain why firms should disregard responsible practices.

Discussion

The critical roles of host country institutions

Following Scott (2009), the macro structure of the institutional environment in DEs, how such structures shape business activities, and the negative externalities they produce, are emphasized here. Berger and Luckmann (1967) and Meyer (1970) posit that social order is the result of social norms which amount to particular kinds of actors and particular ways in which they take action as they relate to each other in society. Appropriate and desirable institutions reduce, and in some cases eliminate, transaction costs for MNCs and other parties. They provide guarantees for property rights, and the enforcement of these rights ensures contractual relations (North, 1990; Posner, 2003), macroeconomic stability, and a conducive environment for accountability and voice (Easterly, 2006; Rodrik, 2008).

Some argue for special institutional arrangements to benefit existing firms aimed at stimulating economic growth (Qian, 2003), and that initial substandard labour conditions, such as sweatshops, are necessary as a spring board for emerging and developing economies (Kristof and WuDunn, 2000). This means that host countries may lower labour standards as a way of reducing costs for firms in order to attract FDIs in huge proportions. Rodrik (2008) cites the examples of Taiwan and China and, comparing them to India, concludes that resistance to foreign exploitation may perpetuate poverty, as in the case of India (Weber, 2004). The question is: 'At what cost will societies have to tolerate such exploitations and what are the potential risks for future generations?' Simply put, Will such exploitation be justifiable in the long term given the social cost? The labour standards in the affiliates and subsidiaries of MNCs may be low, given their strong bargaining power *vis-à-vis* the host government and labour unions, which may have even fewer choices.

The unilateral nature of the above leaves it open to debate. First, the changes in market and technological conditions are such that companies which do not want to risk their reputation adopt higher labour standards in order to keep the best employees and maintain credibility with stakeholders, while protecting their brand name (Douglas et al., 2001). Secondly, besides the fact that sustainable practices may be embedded in the organizational culture, they may also be motivated by the fear of expropriation by the host government (Weber, 2004; Palley, 2000).

MNC's power and the value chain in DEs

Consistent with Blalock (1989), Burt (1977) and Nebus and Ruffin (2010), I refer to power as the endowment of strategic resources, industrial technology and institutions which allow some actors to consolidate and convert their resources into influence that is exerted on another actor's decisions and actions. MNCs may affect host countries' existing institutional environments but to a large extent they adjust to the host country's informal institutions, norms, values and formal institutional structures (such as labour market laws whether enforced or not). Sustainability issues carry a bizarre twist of irony because the most money is made from the exclusive control and extraction of natural resources from extremely resource rich countries, pushing them down into the very abyss of poverty to wallow in misery and degradation.

A pittance in royalties is paid to them. Were these royalties, which are paid to governments, equitably distributed, the most fundamental human rights of health and nutrition, clean water, education, infrastructure and civil freedoms would not be such scarce commodities (Bougrine, 2006). For example, Bougrine (2006) compares Nigeria and Norway, two oil rich countries. The latter enjoys high level of sustainability and economic development, whilst the former can barely survive. While some critics may naively dismiss this as a comparison of apples and oranges, Bougrine strongly challenges conventional arguments by arguing that such evaluations are required to reveal the hidden structures which contribute to such divergence in prosperity and sustainability. These concealed elements exist because of the failed policies which MNCs and governments unilaterally, and sometimes bilaterally, have pursued in their quest to nourish and maintain the *status quo*. Again, these elements comprise the strategic positions constantly occupied by the multinationals in the value chain. This stems from the fact that the 'greater the concentration of an industry and the less powerful the labour organization linked to the industry, the higher the normal rate of profit for the industry' (Bougrine, 2006).

Following Marx (1956), profits are essential for the accumulation of capital, which in essence is the driving force of capitalism. 'In its quest to self expansion, capital always requires higher volume of super profits' (Bougrine, 2006, p.40). This in fact explains the monopolistic behaviour of MNCs, as well as their search for effective methods that will allow them to extract surplus value from the workers and nation states, and the constant need to control entire value chains. Kaplinsky (2000, p.121) defines the value chain as 'the full range of activities which are required to bring a product or service from conception through the different phases of production (involving a combination of physical transformation and input of various services), to their delivery to the final consumer and final disposal after use'. This explains why EEs are completely cut out of the valorization process. To say 'globalization' is also to suggest that that there are the globalized and the globalizers. Who governs the sustainability questions in DEs? It is some value chain keepers and their cohorts (Bougrine, 2006), deeply embedded in institutionalized corruption and inept leadership (Rodrik, 2008), supported by institutions.

Some ideologues, with their near chauvinistic defence of capitalism see sustainability, or the need to upgrade existing standards, as simple gestures of protocol and not moral obligations towards the institutions MNCs depend on to achieve their strategic corporate objectives. The polarized perspectives partly held by the EEs and DEs demand sustainability, while the capital exporters seek to defend their interests against the possible expropriation of their heavy investments and non-commitment to compensation on the basis of international law. Then again, this is where the problem lies. Some organizations even go to the extent of lobbying home country law makers, who attempt to make human right abuses punishable, all in the name of the free market (Punch, 1996; Bougrine, 2006). These are the factors which endow MNCs with so much power to evade questions of sustainability through CPA. These almost insurmountable bargaining powers are also the results of colonial hangovers, which still tend to affect the relationships between MNCs and capital importers in nation states (Easterly, 2006).

Reasons for strengthening host country institutions

Djankov et al. (2003) define institutions 'as a spectrum that runs the full gamut between private gathering (to state ownership with no room for public enforcement) to state ownership (with no room for private enterprise)' and argue that the appropriate choice depends on society's initial conditions. Though multilateral organizations usually think in terms of best practice, they ignore what happens elsewhere, informally, within the same institutions. Institutions are efficient, effective and appropriate when they operate freely but humanely without undue external interference (Ostrom, 1990). Following Ostrom (1990), the 'rules governing the use of collective goods' (host country environment and human resources) should be 'matched to local needs and conditions'.

The right of community members to devise their own rules is respected by external authorities (supra-national organizations and MNCs as political powers). By implication, 'a graduated system of sanctions' needs to be used to constrain the behaviour of firms. The implication here is that the greater the freedoms of the host country institutions to pursue welfare for all through regulatory enforcement, the better the enhancement of sustainability. A more robust role played by host nations in enforcing sustainability, rather than the INGOs' dominant positions, should be encouraged in strong collaboration with local stakeholders. This is because the local stakeholders' role has hitherto been marginal and mainly symbolic. Until now, much of the discourse on sustainability and business has put a spotlight on big businesses operating in DEs, given the inconsistency of their strategies with their sustainable practices. However, this much is factual: institutional constraints, e.g. government failures in creating a conducive environment to enhance sustainability, and the lack of transparency in setting the boundaries within which MNCs at the host country level ought to act (Sachs, 2005), are the underlying factors that have led to the perpetuation of certain practices, or the lack of amelioration.

International laws, norms and country-specific jurisprudence are all social constructs serving as facilitating tools to create the mechanism for ensuring order in international business (Addo, 1999). These laws in themselves are incapable of yielding the desired results in various contexts. This means DEs lack the properly functioning governance and the effective judiciary, which is ideally separated from the legislature in pursuit of unobstructed justice, in order to ensure appropriate law enforcement and sanctions against corporate malpractices (Posner 2003; Rodrik, 2008). In the absence of effective judicial systems, firms depend heavily on relational contracting to screen suppliers, create trust, and commit to a few suppliers as the second best means of decreasing transaction cost. These are also ways by which they escape the consequence of their actions. The same strategy would also work with local NGOs to enhance sustainable development.

Nations should therefore be free to pursue legislation that allows them to pursue economic progress as long as those policies are in the interest of their economies and do not conflict with human rights, rather than being strongly entreated to sign mere protocols which end up working top-down. That is to say, everyone should be responsible for the roses in his or her backyard. Nevertheless, it may well also be that, whilst arguments about sustainability in host countries may appear emotional, MNC managers are rational utility maximizers, who may pay little attention to anything but economic efficiency. The real shortfall in all the meaningful, and yet fluffy, codes is again that they are top-down and unenforced. The fact that many MNCs have signed the UN Global Compact, and other accords, in recent years is reassuring. Nevertheless, it is argued here that the 'backyard owners' need to act in ways that are business- and sustainability-friendly, and avoid old approaches which fail to answer the real questions about sustainability, instead of accusing MNCs. It is conjectured that to a large extent, bottom-up approaches and bilateral agreements between nation states and multinationals will bring about measures in congruence with the context-specific sustainability demands of nations. MNCs' cooperation with NGOs, local investors, diaspora communities and multilateral organizations, which are pushing to strengthen institutions in DEs, will benefit both the firms and their operational milieus.

Institutions of DEs

Every institutional environment creates incentive structures, either for a responsible or an irresponsible corporate action, although this varies in magnitude from one context to another (Campbell, 2007; North, 1990). There is a sharp contrast between the institutional environments of the developed and developing economies (Rodrik, 2008) (see Figure 3.1). In the latter, institutions are weak and are characterized by existing legislations *sans* the political will for their enforcement. International standards are in the books but they probably

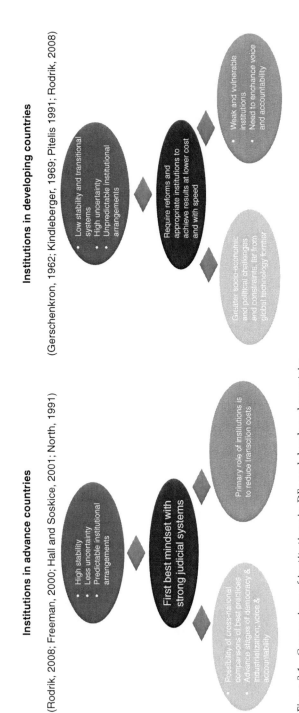

Institutions in advance countries

(Rodrik, 2008; Freeman, 2000; Hall and Soskice, 2001; North, 1991)

- High stability
- Less uncertainty
- Predictable institutional arrangements

First best mindset with strong judicial systems

Primary role of institutions is to reduce transaction costs

- Possibility of cross-national comparisons of best practices
- Advance stages of democracy & industrialization; voice & accountability

Institutions in developing countries

(Gerschenkron, 1962; Kindleberger, 1969; Pitelis 1991; Rodrik, 2008)

- Low stability and transitional systems
- High uncertainty
- Unpredictable institutional arrangements

Require reforms and appropriate institutions to achieve results at lower cost and with speed

- Weak and vulnerable institutions
- Need to enchance voice and accountability

- Greater socio-economic and political challenges and constraints, far from global technology frontier

Figure 3.1 Comparison of institutions in DEs and developed countries

mean little or nothing (Marcel, 2004; Rodrik, 2008). The existing ineffective systems work for the benefit of certain powerful rent-seeking vested interest groups, whose investments are tactically structured in ways that threaten sustainable development. In DEs, where these formalized structures are lacking, informal institutional structures and other forms of network rule the market.

We offer the following four propositions which also represent the conditions under which sustainability can be actualized in DEs:

Proposition 1. The more organized and effective the country-specific institutional framework is, the fewer the CR problems in which businesses are implicated and the more effectively sustainable practices will be enforced.

Proposition 2. Using a rival theory, in the absence of strong formal institutional structures, informal institutional structures and network collaborations with local stakeholders will be the only effective mechanism for sustainable development, since that permits accountability.

Proposition 3: Ethical responsibility and serious regulatory frameworks (consisting of graduated sanctions and incentives) will sufficiently guide the invincible hand of MNCs towards sustainable actions and decrease DEs dependency on INGOs.

Proposition 4: Meaningful CR requires the responsible use of CPP, and the adoption of bottom-up policies that allow firms to attend effectively to questions pertaining to sustainability either through divergence, convergence or cross-vergence.

Conclusions

Although some firms continue to make bold steps towards implementing sustainable programmes, there is little or no empirical evidence whether such actions are the result of pressures from enlightened and active stakeholders, with powerful constellations in certain countries, or the results of strong institutions. Consistent with Bird et al. (2009), Djankov et al. (2003) and Rodrik (2008), there is the need for second best institutions, which do not assume that what works in developed economies will work in EEs because of questions of context, circumstances and time (Hayek, 1945). The models presented so far by the UN and other agencies cannot easily be replicated in contexts where institutions are vulnerable. There are plenty of things the UN and its agencies have done right but successfully stopping corporate abuse in DEs is certainly not one of them. Countries of origin for MNCs can equally do their part through bilateral relations in terms of the way the game is played. Host countries which are capital importers should do more regulatory house-cleaning, which will allow them to alter the prevailing political and judicial culture that nourishes unsustainable practices. The efforts of supra-national organizations cannot be denied. Their actions are necessary, but not sufficient grounds for maintaining the existing top-down approach.

We espouse the strengthening of host country institutions to deal with issues in their own backyard. First, the process of handling such issues is extremely slow and the red tape based on best practice models is too cumbersome to be able to monitor and enforce correct practices by MNCs. Supra-national organizations are therefore always going to be a few steps behind events due to their presumptuous attitude, which tends to use procedural short cuts *ex ante* and assumes desirability and convergence in the long term. Convergence here refers to the 'similarity of government regulations which are implemented around the globe' (Peng and Pleggenkuhle-Miles, 2009). Those are good for cross-national evaluations but they simply do not achieve the desired results with speed and at lower social cost (Rodrik, 2008; Djankov et al., 2003). Advocates of divergence also argue that while it is possible to transplant and implement Anglo-Saxon regulations (formal rules) in other settings, it is very complex to transplant, along with the formal structures, all the informal institutional structures such as values, norms, traditions and beliefs which frame the way things unfold in the market and in industrial relations without altering the basic ownership structure and corporate governance (Bruton et al., 2004; Carney and Gedajlovic, 2001). Neither the notion of convergence nor divergence, in a strict sense, corroborates with the global market and practices (Yoshikawa and McGuire, 2008). This goes to support the arguments of Rodrik (2008) for the second best institutions or what Young, Ahlstrom, Bruton and Jiang (2008) and Peng and Pleggenkuhle-Miles (2009) call 'crossvergence' in host countries.

Secondly, very often, if no preventive action is taken in the heat of the moment, it is hardly worthwhile pursuing a case in the aftermath when so much damage has been done already. Thirdly, the magnitude of the unsustainable actions by firms, and the extent of their scope make it impossible for international organizations to function effectively. Fourthly, creating the geopolitical environment of fair relationships for DEs to act in is a way of recognizing their independence and sovereignty. Fifthly, the fragmented nature of legal frameworks, besides cultural differences across borders, has meant that, a 'one size fits all' model will not be an effective means of solving underlying corporate abuses (Rodrik, 2007). DEs can therefore model their industrial policies and investment codes on international standards which adapt to local needs, without unsolicited external influence (Ostrom, 1990).

Luo (2001) concluded that political accommodation, resource complementarity, personal relations and organizational credibility are the four main 'building blocks' upon which a firm can establish a cooperative relationship with a host government, aimed at improving ties and increasing investment returns. First, 'political accommodation' refers to the extent to which a firm responds proactively to social and environmental needs in order not to appear exploitative in the sight of government and consumers. Secondly, resource complementarity equates a firm's contribution to the governments' national development goals. Personal relations of the firm with political leaders are also important. This leads to organizational credibility, recognition or legitimacy, which refers to the firm's level of perceived integrity as viewed by governments and interest groups, as well as social and economic actors in a host country and beyond. The way forward is pluralism of academic research, which allows for different perspectives from economics, sociology, political economy and law, so as to further explore paths which will contribute to theory generation on such an important issue as sustainability within diverse institutional contexts. Host nations' regulatory institutions should be strengthened to follow international principles, as the world works towards harmonizing normative industrial standards of production, distribution and consumption, rather than leaving business-related questions of sustainability in the hands MNCs and the UN (Rodrik, 2008). For the time being, investments can flow using second best or informal approaches responsibly. Future research may focus on: (1) the elements which constitute institutions in DEs; (2) the way institutions are created, diffused, and adopted within particular nation states in DEs; (3) the dynamic and temporal dimension of the process of adaptation to new regulatory frameworks in the light of globalization, technological advancement and the imperative for sustainable practices (North, 1990); (4) the decline of old institutional structures as different forms of socio-cultural and regulatory transformations ensue; and (5) what forms of collaborations are pursued by local stakeholders and MNCs and the congruence of their activities with the sustainability needs of DEs.

References

Addo, M. K. (1999) *Sustainability Standards and the Responsibility of Transnational Corporations* (The Netherlands: Kluwer Law International Publications).

Baron, D. P. (1997) 'Integrated Strategy, Trade Policy and Global Competition', *California Management Review*, 39, 145–69.

Berger, P. K. and Luckmann, T. (1967) *The Social Construction of Reality: A Treatise in the Sociology of Knowledge* (New York: Doubleday).

Bird, F., Smucker, J. and Velasquez, M. (2009) 'Introduction: International Business Firms, Economic Development, and Ethics', *Journal of Business Ethics*, 89, 81–4.

Blalock, H. (1989) *Power and Conflict. Towards a General Theory* (Newbury Park, CA: Sage).

Bougrine, H. (2006) 'Oil: Profits of the Chain Keepers', *International Journal of Political Economy*, 35(2), 35–53.

Braithwaite, J. (1985) 'White Collar Crime', *Annual Review of Sociology*, 11, 1–25.

Bruton, G. D., Lohrke, F. and Lu, J. (2004) 'The Evolving Definition of What Comprises International Strategic Management Research', *Journal of International Management*, 10, 413–29.

Burt R. S. (1977) 'Power in Social Topology', *Social Science Research*, 6(1), 1–83.

Campbell, J. L. (2007) 'Why Would Corporations Behave in Socially Responsible Ways? An Institutional Theory of Corporate Responsibility', *Academy of Management Review*, 32(3), 946–67.

Carasco, F. E. and Singh, J. B. (2009) 'Towards Holding Transnational Corporations Responsible for Sustainability', *European Business Review*, 22(4), 432–45.

Carney, M. and Gedajlovic, E. (2001) 'Corporate Governance and Firm Capabilities', *Asia Pacific Journal of Management*, 18, 335–54.

Carroll, A. (1991) 'Corporate Social Responsibility: Evolution of a Definitional Construct', *Business Society*, 38, 268.

Cohen, A. K. (1966) *Deviance and Control* (Englewood Cliffs, NJ: Princeton Hall).

Djankov, S., Glaeser, E., La Porta, R., Lopez-de-Silanes, F. and Schleifer, A. (2003) 'The New Comparative Economics', *Journal of Comparative Economics*, 31(4), 595–619.

Donaldson, T. and Preston, L. E. (1995), 'The Stakeholder Theory of the Corporation: Concepts, Evidence, and Implications', *Academy of Management Review*, 20(1), 65–91.

Douglas, M. (1986) *How Institutions Think* (Syracuse New York: Syracuse University Press).

Douglas, S. P., Craig, C. S. and Nijssen, E. J. (2001) 'Executive Insights: Integrating Branding Strategy across Markets: Building International Brand Architecture', *Journal of International Marketing*, 9, 97–114.

Earl, P. E. (2001) 'Simon's Theorem and the Demand for Live Music', *Journal of Economic Psychology*, 22(2), 335–58.

Easterly, W. (2006) *The White man's Burden. Why the West's Efforts to Aid the Rest have Done So Much Ill and So Little Good.* (New York: Penguin Press).

Frederick, William. C. (1960) 'The Growing Concern over Business Responsibility', *California Management Review*, 2, 54–61.

Frederick, William C. (1998) 'Moving to CSR4', *Business and Society*, 37(1), 40–60.

Freeman, Richard. E. (1984) *Strategic Management: A Stakeholder Approach* (Englewood Cliffs, NJ: Prentice-Hall).

Garriga, E. and Melé, D. (2004) 'Corporate Social Responsibility Theories: Mapping the Territory', *Journal of Business Ethics*, 53(1–2), 51–71.

Getz, K. A. (1997) 'Research in Corporate Political Action', *Business and Society*, 36(1), 32.

Granovetter, M. (1985) 'Economic Action and Social Structure: The Problem of Embeddedness', *American Journal of Sociology*, 91(3), 481.

Hall, P. A. and Soskice, D. (2001) *Varieties of Capitalism: The Institutional Foundations of Comparative Advantage* (Oxford: Oxford University Press).

Hayek, F. (September 1945) 'The Use of Knowledge in Society', *American Economic Review*, 35(4): 519–530.

Hofstede, G., Van Deusen, C. A., Mueller, C. B., Charles, T. A. and the Business Goals Network (2002) 'What Goals do Business Leaders Pursue? A Study of 15 Countries', *Journal of International Business Studies*, 33, 705–803.

Hymer, S. H. (1960) *The International Operations of National Firms: A Study of Direct Foreign Investment* (Cambridge, MA: MIT Press).

Ietto-Gillies, G. (2002) 'Hymer, the Nation-State and the Determinants of Multinational Corporations' Activities', *Contributions to Political Economy*, 21, 43–54.

International Labour Organization (ILO) (2006) *Tripartite Declaration of Principles Concerning Multinational Enterprises and Social Policy* (Geneva: International Labour Organization).

Jackson, G. and Apostolakou, A. (2010) ‚Corporate Social Responsibility in Western Europe: CSR as an Institutional Mirror or a Substitute?', *Journal of Business Ethics*, 94(3), 371–94.

Kaplinsky, R. (2000) 'Globalization and Unequalization. What can be learned from Value Chain Analysis?', *Journal of Development Studies*, 37(2), 117–47.

Kristof, Nicholas D. and WuDunn, S. (2000) *Thunder from the East: Portrait of a Rising Asia* (New York: Knopf).

Luo, Y. (2001) 'Towards a Cooperative View of MNC-Host Government Relations: Building Blocks and Performance Implications', *Journal of International Business Studies*, 32, 401–19.

Mantere, S., Pajunen, K and Lamberg, J. (2009) 'Vices and Virtues of Corporate Political Activity', *Business and Society*, 48, 105–32.

Marcel, F. (2004) *Market Institutions in sub-Saharan Africa: Theory and Evidence* (Cambridge, MA: MIT Press).

Marx, K. (1956) *Capital* (Vol. I–IV) (Moscow: Progress).

Meyer J. W. (1970) 'Institutionalization', unpublished paper (Stanford University Department of Sociology).

Meyer, K. E. (2004) 'Perspectives on Multinational Enterprises in Developing Economies', *Journal of International Business Studies*, 35, 259–76.

Nebus, J. and Ruffin, C. (2010) 'Extending the Bargaining Power Model: Explaining Bargaining Outcomes among Nations, MNEs and NGOs', *Journal of International Business Studies*, 41(6), 996–1015.

North, D. (1990) *Institutions, Institutional Change, and Economic Performance* (Cambridge, MA: Harvard University Press).

Ostrom, E. (1990) *Governing the Commons: The Evolution of Institutions for Collective Action* (Cambridge University Press).

Palley, T. (2000) *Labour Standards, Economic Governance and Income Distribution. Some Cross Country Evidence, Economic Policy Paper 029* (AFL-CIO Public Policy Department).

Peng, M. W. and Pleggenkuhle-Miles, E. G. (2009) 'Current Debates in Global Strategy', *International Journal of Management Reviews*, 11(1), 51–68.

Pitelis, C. (1991) 'Beyond the Nation-State?: The Transnational Firm and the Nation-State', *Capital and Class*, April, 131–52.

Posner, R. A. (2003) *Economic Analysis of Law* (7th edn, Chicago: Aspen Publishers).

Prahalad, C. K. (2005) *The fortune at the bottom of the pyramid: Eradicating poverty through profits.* Upper Saddle River, NJ: Wharton School Publishing.

Priem, R., Worrell, D., Walters, B. and Coalter, T. (1998) 'Moral Judgment of Value in a Developed and a Developing Nation: A Comparative Analysis', *Journal of Business Ethics*, 17(5), 491–501.

Punch, M. (1996) *Dirty Business, Exploring Corporate Misconduct, Analysis and Cases* (London: Sage Publications Ltd).

Purdy, J. M., Alexander, E. A. and Neil, S. (2010) 'The Impact of National Institutional Context on Social Practices; Comparing Finnish and US Business Communities', *European Journal of International Management*, 4(3), 234–56.

Putnam, R. D, Leonardi, R. and Nanetti, R. Y. (1993) *Making Democracy Work. Civic Traditions in Modern Italy* (Princeton: Princeton University Press).

Qian, Y. (2003) 'How Reform Worked in China' in D. Rodrik (ed.), *Search of Prosperity. Analytic Narrative on Economic Growth* (Princeton, NJ: Princeton University Press).

Rashid, S. (2006) 'Watchman, Who Watches Thee? Donors and Corruption in Less Developed Countries', *Independent Review*, 10, 411–18.

Rodrik, D. (2007) *One Economics, Many Recipes; Globalization, Institutions and Economic Growth* (Princeton, NJ: Princeton University Press).

Rodrik, D. (2008) 'Second Best Institutions. Papers and Proceedings', *American Economic Review*, 98(2), 100–4.

Sachs, J. D. (2005) *The End of Poverty. Economic Possibilities of Our Time* (England: Penguin Books Limited).

Scherer, A. G. and Palazzo, G. (2007) 'Toward a Political Conception of Corporate Responsibility: Business and Society Seen from a Habermasian Perspective', *The Academy of Management Review*, 32(4).

Scott, W. R. (2001) *Institutions and Organizations* (Thousand Oaks, California: Sage).

Scott, W. R. (2009) 'Institutional Theory, Contribution to the Theoretical Research Progress' in K. G. Smith and M. A. Hitt (eds), *Great Minds in Management. The Process of Theory Development* (Oxford: Oxford University Press).

Sethi, S. P. and Williams, O. F. (2000) 'Creating and Implementing Global Codes of Conduct in Assessment of the Sullivan Principles as a Role Model for Developing International Codes of Conduct. Lessons Learned and Unlearned', *Business and Society Review*, 105(2), 169–200.

Sprote, W. (1990) 'Negotiations of UN Code of Conduct on Transnational Corporations', *German Year Book of International Law*, 33, 331–48.

Sullivan, R. (1999) *Business and Sustainability: Dilemmas and Solutions* (Sheffield: Greenleaf).

United Nations (2009) *United Nations Global Compact* bulletin available at: *http://www.unglobalcompact.org/Issues/human_rights/index.html*, accessed on 20 July 2010.

Weber, M. (2004) 'The Business Case for Corporate Social Responsibility: A Company-level Measurement Approach for CSR', *European Management Journal*, 26(4), 247–61.

Williamson, O. (2000) 'The New Institutional Economics; Taking Stock, Looking Ahead', *Journal of Economic Literature*, 38, 595–613.

World Investment Report (2010) *Investing in Low Carbon Economy* (Switzerland: United Nations Publications).

Wright, M., Filatotchev, I. Hoskisson, R. E. and Peng M. W. (2005) 'Guest Editors' Introduction Strategy Research in Emerging Economies: Challenging the Conventional Wisdom', *Journal of Management Studies*, 42(1).

Yoshikawa, T. and McGuire, J. (2008) 'Change and Continuity in Japanese Corporate Governance', *Asia Pacific Journal of Management*, 25, 5–24.

Young, M., Ahlstrom, D., Bruton, G. and Jiang, Y. (2008) 'Globalization and Corporative Governance in Emerging Economies: A Review of the Principal-Principal Perspective' *Journal of Management Studies*, 45, 196–220.

Part II

The New Challenges of ODI in China

Ling Liu

The chapters in this part focus on new challenges and opportunities for firms from emerging economies. The rapid internationalization of firms from emerging economies has captured the increasing attention of both academics and managers. Along with their rising share of commodities exports and the increasing foreign currency reserves obtained from exporting, some emerging economies, notably the BRICs, are actively engaging in capital exports and have become an important source of outward foreign direct investment. China is such a leading player that its speed of internationalization is unprecedented and its active participation in a large number of cross-border mergers and acquisitions has triggered both economic and political concerns worldwide. China was ranked fifth in generating global foreign direct investment outflows (US\$ 48 billion in 2009 (UNCTAD, 2010)), with 46 Chinese firms entering the list of Global Fortune 500 in 2010.

The surge of foreign direct investment from China is a very recent phenomenon and, therefore, unsurprisingly, studies of these Chinese MNEs are still at an early phase. Previous research has mainly focused on the determinants or motivations of outward FDI by Chinese firms (Buckley et al., 2007; Cai, 1999; Child and Rodrigues, 2005; Liu and Tian, 2008), as well as the entry strategy and the strategic asset seeking activities of Chinese MNEs (Cui and Jiang, 2009; Deng, 2009; Rui and Yip, 2008). Recent attention has increasingly been paid to the role of outward FDI in technology transfers to the home country (Zhao et al., 2010) and the role of institutional factors in the home country in shaping the international behaviour of firms (Luo et al., 2010). However, studies focusing on emerging economies in general, and Chinese MNEs in particular, remain underdeveloped. Are Chinese MNEs following the same entry strategies as their western companies when they invest in different countries? To what extent do home country and host country institutions affect the investment decisions of Chinese firms? What are their ownership advantages and disadvantages? This part aims to explore some of the issues associated with the internationalization process of Chinese firms.

Gao and Liu's chapter examines issues challenging the internationalization process of Chinese state-owned MNEs in the global market. Based on four in-depth case studies of state-owned enterprises (SOEs) in China, they take the combined approach of dynamic capability and the institution-based view to identify both internal and external challenges encountered by Chinese SOEs during their internationalization process. They find that Chinese SOEs have difficulties in effective and efficient resource configuration, as well as external sourcing and coordination. Besides these challenges, caused by internal capability deficiencies, Chinese SOEs also face challenges caused by home country institutional intervention and host country political risks.

Xu's chapter takes an historical perspective on the evolution of Sino-African political and economic relations over the past six decades. The review finds four key determining factors, that is: (1) political alliances; (2) bilateral trade; (3) aid; and (4) contractual projects that have been co-evolving to form the Chinese ODI strategy in Africa.

Li and Liu's chapter investigates export trading companies from transaction cost and institutional perspectives. In China, export trading companies have made significant contributions to exporting performance and export-led economic growth. Trading companies in China enjoy some unique characteristics that are quite different from those in developed countries. They argue that institutions in a transitional economy like China may generate additional costs in direct exporting transactions, and export trading companies play a crucial role in linking domestic producers and foreign buyers and hence reducing institutional-related costs. The conceptual framework may require further empirical analysis.

Although using different analytical approaches for their illustrative settings, the three chapters investigate the issues from the institutional perspective. They show why institutions in emerging markets are important determinants in stimulating the growth of individual Chinese firms, and how the Chinese government formulates its OFDI strategy in certain regions for the political and commercial interest of the nation.

References

Buckley, P. J., Clegg, L. J., Cross, A. R., Liu, X., Voss, H. and Zheng, P. (2007) 'The Determinants of Chinese Outward Foreign Direct Investment', *Journal of International Business Studies*, 38, 499–518.

Cai, K. (1999) 'Outward Foreign Direct Investment: A Novel Dimension of China's Integration into the Regional and Global Economy', *The China Quarterly*, 160, 856–80.

Child, J. and Rodrigues, S. B. (2005) 'The Internationalization of Chinese Firms: A Case for Theoretical Extension?', *Management and Organization Review*, 1, 381–418.

Cui, L. and Jiang, F. (2009) 'FDI Entry Mode Choice of Chinese Firms: A Strategic Behaviour Perspective', *Journal of World Business*, 44, 434–44.

Deng, P. (2009) 'Why do Chinese Firms Tend to Acquire Strategic Assets in International Expansion?', *Journal of World Business*, 44(1), 74–84.

Liu, L. and Tian, Y. (2008) 'The Internationalisation of Chinese Enterprises: The Analysis of the UK Case', *International Journal of Globalization and Technology*, 4(1), 87–102.

Luo, Y., Xue, Q. and Han, B. (2010) 'How Emerging Market Governments Promote Outward FDI: Experience from China', *Journal of World Business*, 45, 68–79.

Rui, H. and Yip, G. S. (2008) 'Foreign Acquisitions by Chinese Firms: A Strategic Intent Perspective', *Journal of World Business*, 43(2), 213–27.

UNCTAD (2010) *World Investment Report 2010: Investing in a Low-carbon Economy* (New York: United Nations).

Zhao, W., Liu, L. and Zhao, T. (2010) 'The Contribution of Outward Foreign Direct Investment to Productivity Changes within China: 1991–2007', *Journal of International Management*, 16(2), 121–30.

4
The Internationalization of Chinese State-Owned Enterprises: What Challenges Do They Face?

Lan Gao and Xiaohui Liu

Introduction

Outward foreign direct investment (ODI) from emerging economies (EEs) in general, and from China in particular, has increased substantially. China took fifth place in generating global FDI outflows with USD 48 billion in 2009 (WIR, 2010). An increasing research effort has been devoted to examining issues related to Chinese MNEs. Previous research has mainly focused on the motivations and location choices of outward FDI by Chinese firms at both country and firm levels, and the factors influencing internationalization decision-making. Yet, less attention has been paid to factors challenging or even endangering the internationalization process of these latecomers in the global market.

In the light of the growing prevalence of MNEs from EEs in global competition and the rather high rate of foreign entry failure, academics and managers have become extremely interested in understanding the factors challenging EE MNEs in achieving overseas success. Earlier research has suggested that the internationalization process can be influenced by various internal factors, such as resource commitment (Demirbag et al., 2007; Luo, 2003), control flexibility (Luo, 2003; Venaik et al., 2005), international experience (Carlsson et al., 2005; Uhlenbruck, 2004), institutional factors, including political risks (Ahmed et al., 2002; Brouthers et al., 2000), and government regulations (Child et al., 2003; Demirbag et al., 2007; Luo, 2003). However, like many aspects of international business research, the studies of this kind are overwhelmingly focused on firms from developed countries.

It is widely recognized that EE MNEs, such as China's, enter the international market with unique characteristics and facing different institutional environments compared to their counterparts from developed countries (Liu and Buck, 2009; Lu et al., 2009). They suffer from latecomer disadvantages when competing against well-established MNEs. Meanwhile, they often do not have sufficient resources, technology advantages, and modern management skills. Besides these internal weaknesses, EE MNEs are often heavily regulated and influenced by their home country institutions. Therefore, it is of theoretical significance to see whether factors identified in early studies also influence the internationalization process of EE MNEs and, more importantly, examine what new challenges face EE MNEs during their internationalization process. This chapter aims to explore these issues by studying a specific group, Chinese SOEs.

Chinese SOEs represent an ideal research setting. In 2008, 13 Chinese MNEs from various industries entered the league table of the top 100 non-financial transnational corporations from EEs and developing countries, measured by foreign assets (WIR, 2010). All 13 Chinese MNEs listed in the table are SOEs, which indicates that SOEs are the leaders in internationalization. By the end of 2008, SOEs contributed 69.6 per cent of Chinese outward FDI stock and, among the 40 largest Chinese firms by outward FDI stock, 37 were SOEs, (MOC, 2009). Although Chinese SOEs have dominated the country's outward FDI, their internationalization process was not without difficulty. For example, because of the recent unrest in Libya, Chinese firms, mainly SOEs, suffered significant investment and contract loss worth USD 18.8 billion (He and Liu, 2011). Thus, it is important to study the internationalization process of Chinese SOEs in order to help them to be better prepared and improve their post-internationalization performance.

This chapter makes several contributions to the existing literature based on a comparative case study of four Chinese SOEs. First, this study combines dynamic capability and the institution-based view to explore challenges and difficulties facing Chinese SOEs in internationalization. The combined approach helps provide new insights into the issues related to Chinese firms' internationalization. The findings from the study contribute to our knowledge of firms' overseas operations by analysing their internal dynamic capabilities within the context of the external institutional environment. Secondly, the study is among the first to examine SOEs' internationalization in terms of the alignment of firms' own capabilities and the institutional environments of both home and host countries using cross-case analysis.

The results help enhance our understanding of how internal factors and external environments help Chinese firms to deal with new challenges and overcome difficulties in their overseas operations. We extend previous International Business (IB) research by considering the role of both home country institutional intervention and host country political risk in outward FDI by Chinese SOEs. Thirdly, using the case study method, we are able to gain richer insights into the relationship between the unique characteristics of Chinese SOEs and the challenges and difficulties associated with internationalization in the context of both their home country and host countries. We also construct theoretical propositions based on case evidence which helps further advance internationalization theory by taking the unique characteristics of Chinese firms and their distinctive external environment into account.

Theoretical foundations and literature review

In order to capture the challenges caused by both internal and external factors, an approach combining the dynamic capability framework and the institution-based view has been chosen as the theoretical foundation for this study. The dynamic capability framework provides a flexible means of understanding firms' abilities to respond to a changing business environment in order to create and sustain competitive advantages. Meanwhile, the institution-based view sheds light on how firms are influenced by the institutional environments in which they operate. These two approaches complement each other and are combined to reveal the challenges that Chinese SOEs are facing during their internationalization process.

Dynamic capability

As pioneers in dynamic capability framework building, Teece et al. (1997, p.516) define dynamic capabilities as 'the firm's ability to integrate, build, and reconfigure internal and external competences to address rapidly changing environments'. Dynamic capability has been considered as the ability to generate or modify the operating or strategic routines in order to configure resources more effectively in response to a changing environment, with the aim of achieving a sustained competitive advantage. It is concerned with how firms create and access new knowledge, make investment choices, sense and seize new opportunities, reinvent business models and achieve necessary organizational transformation (Augier and Teece, 2009).

There is no consensus classification of dynamic capabilities. Dynamic capabilities have been classified from different perspectives, such as competence (Teece et al., 1997), opportunity (Augier and Teece, 2009) and resources (Eisenhardt and Martin, 2000). In this study, a resource perspective has been adopted to identify dynamic capabilities as the dynamic capability framework is considered as an extension of a resource-based view. Eisenhardt and Martin (2000) identify three categories of dynamic capabilities, namely, integration of resources, reconfiguration of resources, and the gain and release of resources. By adopting a more comprehensive approach, dynamic capabilities are disaggregated into three categories in this study: internal resource (re-)configuration; external sourcing; and coordination in order to emphasize different types of resources and incorporate competence and opportunity perspectives into the dynamic capability framework.

Resource support

The resource support of parent firms helps overseas subsidiaries in managing uncertainty and the coordination of activities, and in counterbalancing subsidiaries' vulnerability to unfamiliar institutional environments in host countries (Demirbag et al., 2007; Luo, 2003). Although parent firms will not be able to provide all the resources needed by subsidiaries, such support can certainly reduce subsidiaries' reliance on local resources, such as capital and semi-products, which will increase their competitive advantages in the host countries, especially in emerging economies (Luo, 2003). However, this is not to say that subsidiaries should entirely depend on their parent firms. A combination of resources provided by parent firms and location-specific resources acquired from host countries may provide a better balance (Demirbag et al., 2007). Child and Yan (2003) state that the quality of resource provision in host countries, especially in emerging economies, is critical in the performance of overseas subsidiaries. When investing in emerging economies, the capability to reconfigure the allocation of existing resources may well distinguish the successful firms from the unsuccessful ones. However, high power distance, which is a common characteristic of emerging economies, such as China (Hofstede, 2001), can cause serious resource-sharing difficulties (Brock, 2005).

In addition, a firm needs to commit not only financial and material resources to its internationalization, but also human resources. International experience, a key factor in overseas success, can also be allocated to overseas subsidiaries through human resource reconfiguration. At an organizational level, international experience can help overcome the negative cultural distance effects which often cause integration difficulties (Uhlenbruck, 2004). Managers with previous international experience can also help overseas subsidiaries reduce transaction costs and facilitate the identification and integration of resources (Haspeslagh and Jemison, 1991; Hitt et al., 1998, 2001). Therefore, such managers can apply and adapt the knowledge and skills learnt from previous experience to overcome difficulties and challenges during internationalization and will contribute to the improvement of post-internationalization performance (King et al., 2004).

External sourcing

Different from internal firm-specific assets, external resources are defined as resources which are used by the firm in its pursuit of growth, but over which it has no direct ownership, such as networks (e.g. Jarillo, 1989) and market opportunities (e.g. Luo, 2003; Teece, 2007). Once such resources have been identified, firms may decide to explore them directly, such as networks and market opportunities, or to acquire and integrate the resources into the firm to convert them into internal resources, such as technology and human resources.

External sourcing, which allows the firm to acquire new resources unavailable internally, has been identified as a key dynamic capability which may drive superior performance and growth (Eisenhardt and Martin, 2000; Jarillo, 1989; Teece et al., 1997). The integration of the external resources, including activities and technologies, has become increasingly important in creating strategic advantage (Teece et al., 1997). Therefore, the ability to identify and access valuable external resources has become crucial to achieving competitive advantage.

When entering a foreign market, Chinese SOEs may not have all the resources and knowledge needed for overseas operations, including finance, human resources, and local market knowledge. Hence, being able to externally source the resources needed for international expansion is important for overseas subsidiaries in order to survive in host countries.

Coordination

Coordination, representing a dimension of dynamic capability, is referred to as the ability of managers and entrepreneurs to coordinate economic activities across various parts of the firm in order to synergize internal and external resources (Augier and Teece, 2009; Eisenhardt and Martin, 2000). Firms operating in multinational markets rely extensively on intra-firm coordination across business units to achieve corporate performance (Kim and Mauborgne, 1991).

It is recognized that firms' resources and their uses are dynamic in nature (Volberda, 1996). 'Flexibility in coordinating the use of resources', combined with 'the inherent flexibility of resources available to the firm', leads to strategic flexibility (Sanchez, 1995, p.138). This in turn should help firms take advantage of existing and new strategic opportunities to address continuously changing market conditions (Uhlenbruck et al., 2003). The coordination and integration of internal and external resources enables firms to take advantage of market conditions, or even to adapt market conditions to their own interests (Augier and Teece, 2009; Chandler, 1990; Teece, 1993; Simon, 1991).

Institution-based view

The institution-based view has become an increasingly relevant and insightful tool when considering the international strategy and performance of firms from emerging economies (Hoskisson et al., 2000; Peng, et al., 2008; Wright et al., 2005). Although formal and informal institutions have been featured as 'background' conditions in traditional international business research, the deficiency of this attitude emerges in research into understanding firms' strategic behaviour and performance in developed economies (Oliver, 1997), and becomes even more striking in research concerning emerging economies

(Child and Tsai, 2005; Chung and Beamish, 2005; Narayanan and Fahey, 2005; Wan, 2005).

Early literature on outward FDI has largely focused on institutions in MNEs' host countries (Henisz and Zelner, 2005). Recently, some scholars have paid attention to the role of home country institutions in internationalization by firms from emerging economies (Luo and Tung, 2007; Witt and Lewin, 2007). However, extant IB literature seldom considers institutions in both host and home countries simultaneously (Hitt, Tihanyi, Miller and Connelly, 2006; Holburn and Zelner, 2010). Considering these two aspects together is important, since home country support may help overcome difficulties incurred in internationalization, while the institutional environments of host countries may represent both opportunities and challenges for inexperienced Chinese SOEs. We extend previous IB research by considering the role of both home country institutional intervention and host country political risk in outward FDI by Chinese SOEs.

Home country institutional intervention

The characteristics of MNEs' home countries play a role in their success, which is at least as important as the characteristics of host countries (McGahan and Victer, 2010). The institutional environment of the home country, especially emerging economies, can determine the ability and willingness of domestic firms to invest abroad (Buckley et al., 2007). However, how institutional factors and environmental dynamics in emerging economies influence their firms' internationalization has been largely overlooked in previous research (Wright et al., 2005).

Emerging economies have a different institutional and economic environment from developed countries (WIR, 2007). The former are in the process of undergoing rapid growth and industrialization, whereas the latter enjoy more stable market conditions. The institutional and economic environments of emerging economies are undergoing rapid changes, and raise challenges to indigenous firms. Previous research finds that firms from emerging economies have to deal with not only the changing economic environment, but also the changing institutional environment, which can influence their performance both directly and indirectly (Luo, 2003). The evolution of modern corporate governance in emerging economies is accompanied by new 'rules of the game', set by the government and its agents, which are also redefining their roles and developing monitoring systems according to the changing environment (North, 1990; Peng, 2004; Phan, 2001).

The institutional environment of emerging economies plays a more active role in internationalization strategies and post-internationalization performance than that in developed countries (Luo et al., 2010). On the whole, government intervention represents an important factor affecting the economic behaviour of firms from emerging economies, including China, which is in the process of transition from a centrally-planned economy to a market one. The institutional environment in China is not market-oriented, and the government has great power to influence firms' strategies through regulation, policies, and even direct state intervention. Since the implementation of the 'Go Global' strategy, the Chinese government has established a set of guidelines to promote OFDI by simplifying administrative procedures, easing capital control, informing firms' investment opportunities, and reducing political and investment risks (Buckley et al., 2008).

Host country political risks

The institutional environment for foreign investment, created by the host country government and its agents, also plays an essential role in impacting on the success of foreign subsidiaries (Pangarkar and Lim, 2003). Government policies and institutional arrangements have important implications for the survival and success of foreign investors, especially in emerging economies (Chung and Beamish, 2005; Gomes-Casseres, 1990; Hoskisson et al., 2000). Previous research indicates that the environment in which MNEs operate has a significant impact on their strategies and outcomes, and contributes to the variations in their behaviour and performance (Brouthers, 2002; Makino et al., 2004; Meyer, 2004; Peng, 2001; Uhlenbruck, 2004). Political risk has been identified as one of important factors affecting MNEs' foreign operations and performance (Ahmed et al., 2002). Political risk is determined by the actions and policies of host country governments and measured by political, policy and macroeconomic uncertainties in the prior literature (Ahmed et al., 2002; Brouthers, et al., 2000). While political risk exists more or less in every economy, it is much more in evidence in emerging economies due to the market transition and institutional conditions that prevail (Hoskisson et al., 2000; Peng, 2001). Host country governments often intervene or interfere with foreign company activities through regulations and rules (Luo, 2003). However, the frequent and unpredictable changes to these regulations and rules, especially in emerging economies, lead to environmental uncertainty and complexity (Luo and Peng, 1999). Uncertainties make subsidiaries rely even more on parent resources but weaken the contribution of the parent resources to subsidiary performance (Luo, 2003). Demirbag et al. (2007) find that a favourable managerial perception of host country political risk, which is heavily influenced by the institutional environment in which managers function (Makhija and Stewart, 2002), positively influences the perception of subsidiary performance.

Research design

The qualitative research method is very commonly applied in social and behavioural sciences and is very suitable for studying organizations, groups and individuals (Strauss and Corbin, 1990). In contrast to the explanation and control pressed by quantitative researchers, qualitative researchers pursue an understanding of the complex interrelationships among the research objects and their contexts (Stake, 1995). Due to the complex nature of this study and the objective of generating a conceptual model of a phenomenon which is yet to be comprehensively documented, the case study approach is adopted, with a view to generating a series of theoretical propositions based on a set of assumptions drawn from previous literatures and our field observations (Ghauri and Gronhaug, 2005; Yin, 2003).

Four SOEs were carefully selected for this study since multiple case study is more effective comparing to single case study: the analytical benefits from having multiple cases can be very significant, thanks to the possibility of direct replication and comparison. We follow earlier (Eisenhardt, 1989, p.537) advice to select 'polar types' to insure that 'the process of interest is transparently observable'. The first case is a white goods manufacturing company with overseas manufacturing plants in Europe, North America, Asia, Oceania and Africa. The second one is a leading telecommunication company with a global network and overseas subsidiaries in Asia, Europe and North America. The third case is a telecommunication construction company with 11 overseas subsidiaries in Asia, Africa and Europe, and the fourth is a telecommunication company with overseas subsidiaries in Asia and North America. Table 4.1 contains a list of cases examined in this research.

Semi-structured interviews were conducted in this study, which gave respondents the freedom to talk and offer their opinions and understanding of the topic. This freedom may help researchers to identify the hidden factors, which explain the issues under investigation in this exploratory study. A single respondent approach was chosen in this study. The chosen respondents all hold vital positions in their organizations, such as the head of the international department or the CEO of a key subsidiary, which guarantees a good knowledge of their firms and the internationalization process. The interview schedule is presented in Table 4.2. Each interview lasted for one to two hours. Because recording was not permitted by the interviewees, three researchers participated in the interviews, with the leading researcher focused on asking

Table 4.1   Description of cases studied

Case	Industry	Time of internationalization*	No. of overseas branches
A	Manufacturing	1994	23
B	Telecommunication	2000	5
C	Telecommunication construction	1995	11
D	Telecommunication	2000	6

Note: * The year when the first overseas subsidiary was founded.

Table 4.2 Description of interview schedule

Case	Respondent position	Interview locations	Interview date
A	Director of international business department	Beijing, China face-to-face interview	6/1/2009
B	Director of international business department	Beijing, China face-to-face interview	6/1/2009
C	Director of international department	Beijing, China face-to-face interview	8/1/2009
D	Director of international business department	Beijing, China face-to-face interview	15/1/2009

questions and the rest taking notes. We transcribed the interviews within 12 hours of their occurrence to minimize information loss. In order to triangulate, secondary data were also used in this study in order to provide more information and details to enrich the analysis, including existing academic research, websites, internal company presentations, and company annual reports.

Findings

Although all four firms have over a decade of overseas operational experience, they have encountered, and are continuously facing, many difficulties during their internationalization. The interviewees reflected on the internationalization process and admitted that SOEs should have been better prepared before investing abroad, and need to continue improving their dynamic capabilities in order to succeed in the challenging environment.

'The common problem of SOEs' international investment is a lack of awareness of difficulties and preparation of operations. Firms did not have an accurate estimation about potential difficulties, before they make the investment decisions. The fact is that SOEs' capability, especially the 'soft capability', is far behind mature international MNEs' (Interviewee A).

Resource support

Although some SOEs, such as Firm A and Firm C, had been government contractors for China's foreign aid projects in many developing countries before proceeding with their own commercial internationalization, Chinese SOEs, in general, did not have sufficient knowledge of international markets and experience of international operations when starting their overseas operations. This lack of knowledge and experience has caused huge problems during SOEs' internationalization. However, unfortunately, SOEs did not try to solve this e-problem by investing in market research and human resources, but moved ahead with their imaginary understanding of international markets. 'At an early stage, SOEs did not have international experience and international human resource stock, but understood the international market by imagination' (Interviewee A). 'We thought that if we could set the rules of the game, international investments could be done as we wish' (Interviewee C).

After experiencing the difficulties and frustrations, and reflecting on missed opportunities and losses, SOEs started to realize that they needed to invest more finance and human resources in long-term market research in order to support decision-making and later operations. All four interviewees explicitly acknowledged the importance of investing in market research. Interviewee A considered long-term market research as 'the most urgent fundamental lesson'. Interviewee B stated that 'in order to ensure the success of M&As and later operations, we must send representatives overseas to deeply learn about local situations and gather information'. 'We need to give international investment more support and unveil the mystery of international investment through long-term local research and proactive involvement', said Interviewee C. Interviewee D further echoed that 'without pre-investment market research, we do not even have the confidence in making the right investment decision, not mentioning operating in the local market'.

The benefits of investing in market research can be very significant. Before SOEs make the investment decisions, market research may help the firms to understand the real local situation, design the potential future business mode and set realistic performance targets. Meanwhile, 'through long-term local research and networking, we may bring up our own local specialists' (Interviewee B). After many years' international investment and expansion, SOEs find that, in order to understand a market, especially the local culture, consumption patterns, and traditions, they must do long-term market research by themselves to gather detailed information. 'We need at least a year or even two years to study potential markets in order to identify potential opportunities and continue investing in market research throughout the investment' (Interviewee D).

However, although SOEs have realized the importance of investing in market research, and have experienced the difficulties caused by a lack of understanding of the local markets, resource support towards this vital task is still insufficient. SOEs are very risk averse. 'SOEs normally cannot endure large pre-project exploring cost and failure experience' (Interviewee D).

Before any decision is made, managers' first concern is whether they can take responsibility for the consequences. Success or failure in SOEs is related not only to positions or job security, but also to 'face' and reputation, or even a potential future political career. 'Committing resources towards internationaliation, which is perceived as a high risk and high investment strategy, strongly challenges the principle of SOEs: don't loose the falcon until you see the hare' (Interview C). Therefore, managers, especially senior managers, are reluctant to commit finance, human resources and time to international explorative tasks, which may not be profitable in the short run. As a result, expatriate teams often receive insufficient resource support from headquarters, and feel they are 'being marginalized within the organization' (Interviewee A). This would in turn discourage their commitment to exploring the local markets. 'Expatriate teams cannot be understood by either local people of host countries or the headquarters' (Interviewee C).

External sourcing

It can be seen from the evidence presented in the previous section that SOEs sometimes, especially in the early stage of their internationalization, make investment decisions before they have done thorough market research and acquired comprehensive information about the potential market or potential business partners. Under these circumstances, SOEs have to overcome the difficulties caused by the internal incapacity through external sourcing, because fixing the problems by conducting market research, and training their own local specialists can be both resource and time consuming. 'Because of the high costs associated with training our own stuff, sometimes, we try to recruit staff externally' (Interviewee D).

Without the knowledge of local employees, it will cost expatriate teams much more to settle into the local market, in terms of finance and time: 'From paying rent deposit to paying governments commission according to local convention, no matter how big or small the issue is, it is extremely difficult for the expatriate teams to work efficiently' (Interviewee C). Overseas subsidiaries should rely more on local employees, and it has been proved to be easier to solve local conflicts through local employees, especially in emerging and developing markets, where conventions rather than legislation guide ways of doing business.

In developed countries, complicated legal systems and the range of legislation in place also cause extra difficulties and create challenges for SOEs. In these markets, SOEs often have to bring in local managers or specialists to help with executing investment projects. 'We invited western managers to help us with initiating some projects in developed countries. But these people were not retained by the firm to help with later operations' (Interviewee D).

Although SOEs have started to rely on local recruits to settle in local markets better, there is a lack of a sustainable mechanism to retain these valuable human resources. Foreign employees often find that they are unable to 'fit in' to the organization, and it is very difficult for them to climb up the career ladder to senior management positions. The reason behind this is deeply embedded in the SOEs' culture. 'In SOEs' culture, there is very deep belief of *zijiren* (family members; one of our own)' (Interviewee A). In overseas subsidiaries, only expatriate teams are considered as *zijiren*. Local employees, especially foreigners who are non-ethical Chinese, are treated as outsiders and are not completely trusted. 'The lack of real trust in professional managers and local employees has significantly slowed down our overseas expansion because training our own local specialists is very time consuming' (Interviewee D).

Besides the lack of trust in international recruits, SOEs also have concerns about acquiring information through agencies, such as investment banks. 'It is very difficult for them to make a sell by repeating the history stories even if they have very attractive projects in some cases. We do not trust investment bankers and their stories one hundred per cent' (Interviewee B). This is understandable now that investment banks have been discredited by the global financial crisis.

Coordination

The complicated organisational structure of SOEs represents a big challenge to efficient intra-firm coordination. A nationwide SOE normally consists of a national headquarters, several regional headquarters and many provincial subsidiaries. If an SOE operates in several industries or sectors, the structure can get even more complicated. Subsidiaries in different industries or sectors can be financially independent but commercially linked. Strategies are often set by different departments within the headquarters. The difference between similar strategies caused serious confusion and conflicts during the execution stages among subsidiaries, while the overlapping of strategies also caused misallocation or even waste of resources. 'It has been an inherited problem (from government ancestors) that each department does things in its own way' (Interviewee A). 'Because of the lack of coordination among departments, nobody wants to compromise and follow others' lead, which results in very low management and execution efficiency' (Interviewee D).

Compared to the tangled condition in headquarters, coordination between headquarters and overseas subsidiaries is no better. Chinese SOEs have not developed a very efficient management system to operate at international levels, as echoed by Interviewee B: 'Even the very simple and effective management mode is still under development'. The headquarters responds only passively to overseas subsidiaries' requests, rather than proactively plan the global operation as a whole.

Meanwhile, the burden of having to coordinate different departments at headquarters has cost expatriate managers too much time and energy, which could have been devoted to international expansion. 'This process generates a huge amount of communication and internalization cost, and also makes the expatriate teams very frustrated. Besides the frustration and difficulties, the representatives are very easy to be edged because of the unsystematic information and misunderstanding' (Interviewee C).

Home country institutional intervention

The Chinese government and its agents, especially the SASAC (State-owned Assets Supervision and Administration Commission of the State Council) and the MOC (Ministry of Commerce), are involved in the whole internationalization process of SOEs. The government has the authority to approve investment projects, set regulations for overseas operation and evaluate firm performance. All international investment projects proposed by SOEs that are under the supervision of the SASAC are subject to the MOC's review. For these investment projects, the MOC needs to contact the Chinese embassies or consulates in host countries for suggestions and information. Embassies and consulates need to provide information about the social security and economic development of host countries, the bilateral trade between China and the host country, and other necessary information. The MOC will issue 'a green or red light' to the proposed projects accordingly, based on the review.

After the projects are approved, SOEs still do not have the full autonomy to undertake their international operations. The SASAC has set many regulations in order to strictly control and monitor SOEs' operations, especially the allocation of finance resources. 'SOEs' finance resources are all under strict control of the government. From investment perspective, SOEs do not have much money at their command' (Interviewee A). Besides the control of capital investment, the government even has detailed guidelines for daily operations, such as the out-of-pocket expense claim standard. However, the standard is neither set by people who understand the real situation, nor has it been keeping up-to-date. 'According to this standard, employees cannot even afford accommodation and subsistence' (Interviewee C).

The government has clear requirements for the financial performance of SOEs' internationalization. It does not tolerate any failure, or even setback, of overseas investments. Especially after the finance crisis, financial performance has become the sole evaluation indicator of overseas success. Other value adding contributions of international investments have been neglected. 'In the past, one international investment is evaluated according to a flexible, feasible, explainable and rational system, which contains many indicators, including politics, economics, diplomacy, finance and future development. Now, it is different' (Interviewee B). 'Using financial performance as the sole evaluation indicator is very short sighted' (Interviewee D). Since the political and career future of SOEs' senior managers are often decided by the SASAC rather than their firms, the performance requirement is like 'a sword hanging over managers' heads' forcing them to focus solely on generating financial returns rather than the long-term development of their firms. As a result, sometimes 'no decision is the best decision' (Interviewee A). By doing so, managers can completely avoid the risks associated with international investments. However, the firms would miss out on all the experience which could have been accumulated during internationalization and might lead to future development.

Host country political risks

When entering a foreign market, SOEs have encountered a very different institutional environment. 'There are too many laws and regulations in developed countries. The legislation in these countries is very complicated' (Interviewee D). SOEs are not in a position to win the host country government over for any special treatment. This is very different from the domestic institutional environment where SOEs are often protected and preferentially treated. Some SOEs, such as Firm B and Firm D, are even involved in building industry regulations at home. The adaptation from being a regulator to being regulated has caused SOEs some disorientation and represents a great challenge.

Besides the formal institutional differences, such as the legal system, industry regulations and accounting standards, the informal ones, such as culture and underlying rules, also require SOEs' attention. 'For example, in Africa, without local government support, projects with the investment over US\$ 10 million are hardly able to succeed' (Interviewee C). In such cases, SOEs need to commit to major network building with local governments in order to get official support or approval. 'SOEs international investments need to win the support of domestic and foreign governments in order to ensure the success of investment and operations' (Interviewee A).

The unfamiliarity of host country institutions can be overcome by knowledge accumulation. In comparison, the unstable political environment of some emerging and developing countries poses an uncontrollable risk for Chinese SOEs. 'For some countries, especially in Africa, after the change of regimes the policy may take a U-turn to change from "for China" to "against China"' (Interviewee A). This unstable political environment poses an enormous challenge to Chinese SOEs' operations and the safety of existing investment. It also causes concerns about future investment.

Challenges of the internationalization of Chinese SOEs

In the previous section, we categorized the case findings into the six aspects of dynamic capability and the institutional theory, including resource support, external sourcing, coordination, home country institutional intervention and host country political risks. These six aspects are directly related to SOEs' internationalization process. Our findings show that SOEs are facing enormous challenges and difficulties throughout their internationalization process, including initiation, execution, operation and evaluation.

A lack of international market knowledge is the first hurdle on SOEs' way to internationalization. Although all the four firms studied have realized the importance of investing in market research in order to gather sufficient information about local markets to support decision-making and operations, there is still limited resource support towards this task. The risk-averse culture embedded in SOEs has prevented managers from committing resources, including finance, human resources, and time towards market research because of the non-profit generating characteristic of this explorative task. As a result, at the top, managers can hardly make any confident decision about internationalization because of insufficient information about foreign markets; while at the front line, expatriate teams are discouraged from taking on any opportunity because of the insufficient resource support. This leads to the following proposition.

Proposition 1: Insufficient resource support can increase the risk of internationalization and delay SOEs' overseas expansion.

There are mainly two types of resources that SOEs desperately need during their internationalization: knowledge and human resources. The former includes market information, local regulations, host country culture and technology; while the latter includes managers with rich international management experience and local market expertise. Knowledge acquisition can be achieved by recruiting qualified personnel in the international labour market. Chinese SOEs do recruit managers with local knowledge and international investment experience to help with initiating overseas investment. However, SOEs often do not have the authority to retain these valuable human resources for long-term operations. Very few foreign managers can be promoted to senior positions in Chinese SOEs because of trust issues. As for frontier employees, although SOEs realize that they should rely more on local employees to understand the local market and solve conflicts, there is a lack of real trust in any foreign employees inside the organization. This distrust has resulted in wasted human resources and low commitment.

Proposition 2: Chinese SOEs have not yet developed an effective human resource management mechanism to retain the valuable personnel recruited internationally.

Chinese SOEs have not been unknown for their bureaucracy, over-staffing and low efficiency. These inherited characteristics come from their root, the Chinese government, and do not make a positive contribution to the highly effective and efficient coordination needed for internationalization. The complex organizational structure of Chinese SOEs increases these pitfalls and creates more difficulties for their internationalization. The lack of coordination among different business departments leads to overlapping or conflicting strategies and confusion in operations. Meanwhile, expatriate managers have to spend much of their time and energy in communicating with different departments in the headquarters, which has caused resource waste and low efficiency.

Proposition 3: The lack of intra-firm coordination will cause SOEs difficulties in achieving effectiveness and efficiencies in internationalization.

One of the key characteristics of Chinese SOEs is their close relationship with the government. Born as a part of the government, Chinese SOEs have been feeding on government resources and enjoying favourable treatment and protection throughout their development. At the same time, Chinese SOEs are not truly independent enterprises like their western counterparts but are under the direct supervision and control of the Chinese government. The line 'manager' of SOEs, the SASAC, is directly responsible to the State Council, and has the authority and responsibility to involve itself in SOEs' decision-making, resource allocation and performance evaluation. However, the regulations set by government officials to guide the internationalization of SOEs are often out-of-date and unrealistic. SOEs have to operate under the constraints imposed by the SASAC in the already challenging international market. Besides operational constraints, the performance of SOEs is also under supervision of the SASAC. Because of the high priority given to financial performance by the SASAC, other aspects of long-term development, such as marketing, team building, and technology, have been put at the bottom of the priority list of managers. It is foreseeable that this short-term orientation will cause problems in the long run as SOEs need more than money to succeed in the international market.

Proposition 4: Severe home country institutional intervention will constrain Chinese SOEs' internationalization expansion.

Chinese SOEs are subject to different political risks in developed and developing countries. In developed countries, Chinese SOEs cannot bargain any favourable treatment from local governments. They have to fight for their positions in open competition regulated by well-established legislation which is unfamiliar to Chinese SOEs. This is a difficult adjustment because of the superior position enjoyed by SOEs at home. Furthermore, because of the special relationship between SOEs and the Chinese government, there is discrimination against SOEs for national security reasons in some western countries, such as the bill pending in the US to block Chinese SOEs from receiving Pentagon contracts.

In comparison, in many developing countries, Chinese SOEs may gain local government support by networking. However, the unstable political environment in some countries, such as the recent unrest in Libya and Egypt, can cause serious safety problems to both expatriates and investments. Chinese SOEs may have to endure enormous consequential finance loss. Even in some countries with relatively stable political environments, the government's attitude towards Chinese investors can make a U-turn as a result of the change of a regime after a general election.

Proposition 5: Host country political risks will cause concerns and difficulties in Chinese SOEs' internationalization.

Conclusion

We have systematically investigated the impact of SOEs' internal dynamic capabilities and external institutional environments on their internationalization process. Our findings highlight various challenges and difficulties facing Chinese SOEs in their overseas operations. In particular, we find that Chinese SOEs lack the capability to provide sufficient resource support towards internationalization, retain valuable human resources acquired externally, and effectively coordinate different business units during their internationalization process. Besides the internal deficiency, both home and host institutional environments can cause difficulties for Chinese SOEs' internationalization.

The findings from the study have theoretical, practical and policy implications. In terms of theoretical implications, the study indicates that the institutional contexts of both host and home countries are more than background conditions and represent both opportunities and difficulties in firm internationalization. It implies that future research on EE MNEs should simultaneously take the distinctive home country environment and host county institutions into account.

This study has several practical implications. First, Chinese SOEs should, and could, have been better prepared for their internationalization. Top managers in Chinese SOEs have started to realize the importance of resource support, external sourcing, and coordination in the performance of internationalization. However, this realization has not yet been converted into reality. Chinese SOEs should modernize their organizational structure and management ideology in order to be better positioned in the international market. Secondly, Chinese SOEs should communicate with the SASAC in order to bargain for more autonomy, especially in daily operations. Thirdly, although host country political risks are out of the control of individual firms, SOEs could use financial tools, such as insurance and hedge funds, to protect their overseas investments and minimize financial loss.

A number of important political implications can also be derived. The Chinese government should give SOEs more freedom in their operations by loosening up its control on SOEs, in order to enable them to function as modern enterprises. Furthermore, the performance evaluation standards set by the SASAC should be more comprehensive rather than solely focused on short-term financial returns while ignoring the long-term development of the firm. Although there are many challenges on the way to achieve successful internationalization, it does not mean that Chinese SOEs should turn away from internationalization. On the contrary, SOEs should use the process as an opportunity to improve their competitive capabilities.

References

Ahmed, Z. U., Mohamad, O., Tan, B. and Johnson, J. P. (2002) 'International Risk Perceptions and Mode of Entry: A Case Study of Malaysian Multinational Firms', *Journal of Business Research*, 55, 805–13.

Augier, M. and Teece, D. J. (2009) 'Dynamic Capabilities and the Role of Managers in Business Strategy and Economic Performance', *Organization Science*, 20(2), 410–21.

Brock, D. M. (2005) 'Multinational Acquisition Integration: The Role of National Culture in Creating Synergies', *International Business Review*, 14(3), 269–88.

Brouthers, K. D. (2002) 'Institutional, Cultural and Transaction Cost Influences on Entry Mode Choice and Performance', *Journal of International Business Studies*, 33(2), 203.

Brouthers, L. E., Brouthers, K. and Werner, S. (2000) 'Perceived Environmental Uncertainty, Entry Mode Choice and Satisfaction with EC-MNC Performance', *British Journal of Management*, 11(1), 183–95.

Buckley, P. J., Clegg, L. J., Cross, A. R., Liu, X., Voss, H. and Zheng, P. (2007) 'The Determinants of Chinese Outward Foreign Direct Investment', *Journal of International Business Studies*, 38(4), 499–518.

Buckley, P. J., Cross, A. R., Tan, H., Voss, H. and Liu, X. (2008) 'Historic and Emergent Trends in Chinese Outward Direct Investment', *Management International Review*, 48(6), 715–48.

Carlsson, J., Nordegren, A. and Sjoholm, F. (2005) 'International Experience and the Performance of Scandinavian Firms in China', *International Business Review*, 14(1), 21–40.

Chandler, A. (1990) *Scale and Scope* (Cambridge, MA: Belknap Press).

Child, J., Chung, L. and Davies, H. (2003) 'The Performance of Cross-Border Units in China: A Test of Natural Selection, Strategic Choice and Contingency Theories', *Journal of International Business Studies*, 34(3), 242–54.

Child, J. and Tsai, T. (2005) 'The Dynamic between Firms' Environmental Strategies and Institutional Constraints in Emerging Economies: Evidence from China and Taiwan', *Journal of Management Studies*, 42(1), 95–125.

Child, J. and Yan, Y. (2003) 'Predicting the Performance of International Joint Ventures: An Investigation in China', *Journal of Management Studies*, 40(2), 283–320.

Chung, C. C. and Beamish, P. W. (2005) 'The Impact of Institutional Reforms on Characteristics and Survival of Foreign Subsidiaries in Emerging Economies', *Journal of Management Studies*, 42(1), 35–62.

Demirbag, M., Tatoglu, E. and Glaister, K. W. (2007) 'Factors Influencing Perceptions of Performance: The Case of Western FDI in an Emerging Market', *International Business Review*, 16(3), 310–36.

Eisenhardt, K. M. (1989) 'Building Theories from Case Study Research', *Academy of Management Review*, 14(4), 532.

Eisenhardt, K. M. and Martin, J. A. (2000) 'Dynamic Capabilities: What are They?', *Strategic Management Journal*, Special Issue: The Evolution of Firm Capabilities, 21(10/11), 1105–21.

Ghauri, P. N. and Gronhaug, K. (2005) *Research Methods in Business Studies* (London: Prentice Hall).

Gomes-Casseres, B. (1990) 'Firm Ownership Preferences and Host Government Restrictions: An Integrated Approach', *Journal of International Business Studies*, 21(1), 1–22.

Haspeslagh, Philippe C. and Jemison, D. B. (1991) *Managing Acquisitions, Creating Value through Corporate Renewal* (New York: The Free Press).

He, X. and Liu, X. (2011) *http://world.people.com.cn/GB/57506/14700664.html*, accessed on 22 May 2011.

Henisz, W. J. and Zelner, B. A. (2005) 'Legitimacy, Interest Group Pressures, and Change in Emergent Institutions: The Case of Foreign Investors and Host Country Governments', *Academy of Management Review*, 30(2), 361–82.

Hitt, M., Harrison, J. S. and Ireland, R. D. (2001) *Mergers and Acquisitions: A Guide to Creating Value for Stakeholders* (Oxford, UK: Oxford University Press).

Hitt, M., Harrison J., Ireland R. D. and Best A. (1998), 'Attributes of Successful and Unsuccessful Acquisition of U. S. Firms', *British Journal of Management*, 9(1), 91–114.

Hitt, M. A., Tihanyi, L., Miller, T., and Connelly, B. (2006) 'International Diversification: Antecedents, Outcomes, and Moderators', *Journal of Management*, 32(6), 831–67.

Hofstede, G. (2001) *Culture's Consequence: Comparing Values, Behaviours, Institutions, and Organisations Across Nations* (2nd edn, London, New Delhi, Thousand Oaks: Sage Publications).

Holburn, G. L. F. and Zelner, B. A. (2010) 'Policy Risk, Political Capabilities and International Investment Strategy: Evidence from the Global Electric Power Industry', *Strategic Management Journal*, 31(2), 1290–315.

Hoskisson, R. E., Eden, L., Lau, C. M. and Wright, M. (2000) 'Strategy in Emerging Economies', *Academy of Management Journal*, 43(3), 249–67.

Jarillo, J. C. (1989) 'Entrepreneurship and Growth: The Strategic Use of External Resources', *Journal of Business Venturing*, 4(2), 133–47.

Kim, W. C. and Mauborgne, R. A. (1991), 'Effectively Conceiving and Executing Multinationals' Worldwide Strategies', *Journal of International Business Studies*, 4(3), 419–48.

King, D. R., Dalton, D. R., Daily, C. M. and Covin, J. G. (2004) 'Meta-Analyses of Post-Acquisition Performance: Indications of Unidentified Moderators', *Strategic Management Journal*, 25(2), 187–200.

Liu, X. and Buck, T. (2009) 'The Internationalization of Chinese firms: Two Case Studies from Lenovo and BOE', *Journal of Chinese Economic and Business Studies*, 7(2), 167–81.

Lu, J., Xu, B. and Liu, X. (2009) 'The Effects of Corporate Governance and Institutional Environments on Export Behaviour in EEs: Evidence from China', *Management International Review*, 49, 455–78.

Luo, Y. (2003) 'Market-Seeking MNEs in an Emerging Market: How Parent-Subsidiary Links Shape Overseas Success', *Journal of International Business Studies*, 34(3), 290.

Luo, Y. and Peng, M. W. (1999) 'Learning to Compete in a Transition Economy: Experience, Environment, and Performance', *Journal of International Business Studies*, 30(2), 269–95.

Luo, Y., and Tung, R. L. (2007) 'International Expansion of Emerging Market Enterprises: A Springboard Perspective', *Journal of International Business Studies*, 38(4), 481–98.

Luo, Y., Xue, Q. and Han, B. (2010) 'How Emerging Market Governments Promote Outward FDI: Experience from China', *Journal of World Business*, 45(1), 68–79.

Makhija, M. V. and Stewart, A. C. (2002) 'The Effect of National Context on Perceptions of Risk: A Comparison of Planned Versus Free-Market Managers', *Journal of International Business Studies*, 33(4), 737–56.

Makino, S., Isobe, T. and Chan, C. M. (2004) 'Does Country Matter?', *Strategic Management Journal*, 25(10), 1027–43.

McGahan, A. M. and Victer, R. (2010) 'How Much Does Home Country Matter to Corporate Profitability', *Journal of International Business Studies*, 41(1), 142–65.

Meyer, K. E. (2004) 'Perspectives on Multinational Enterprises in Emerging Economies', *Journal of International Business Studies*, 35(4), 259.

MOC (2009) *2008 Statistical Bulletin of China's Outward Foreign Direct Investment* (Beijing: MOC).

Narayanan, V. K. and Fahey, L. (2005) 'The Relevance of the Institutional Underpinnings of Porter's Five Forces Framework to Emerging Economies: An Epistemological Analysis', *Journal of Management Studies*, 42(1), 207–23.

North, D. C. (1990) *Institutions, Institutional Change and Economic Performance* (Cambridge: Cambridge University Press).

Oliver, C. (1997) 'Sustainable Competitive Advantage: Combining Institutional and Resource-based Views', *Strategic Management Journal*, 18: 679–713.

Pangarkar, N. and Lim, H. (2003) 'Performance of Foreign Direct Investment from Singapore', *International Business Review*, 12(5), 601–24.

Peng, M. W. (2001) 'Business Strategies in Transition Economies', *Academy of Management Review*, 26(2), 311–13.

Peng, M. W. (2004) 'Outside Directors and Firm Performance during Institutional Transitions', *Strategic Management Journal*, 25(5), 453.

Peng, M. W., Wang, D. Y. L. and Jiang, Y. (2008) 'An Institution-Based View of International Business Strategy: A Focus on Emerging Economies', *Journal of International Business Studies*, 39(5), 920.

Phan, P. E. (2001) 'Corporate Governance in the Newly Emerging Economies', *Asia Pacific Journal of Management*, 18(2), 131–6.

Sanchez, R. (1995) 'Strategic Flexibility in Product Competition', *Strategic Management Journal*, 16(2), 135–59.

Simon, H. A. (1991), 'Organisations and Markets', *Journal Economic Perspectives*, 5, 25–44.

Stake, R. E. (1995) *The Art of Case Study Research* (Thousand Oaks, California: Sage).

Strauss, A. and Corbin, J. (1990) *Basics of Qualitative Research: Grounded Theory Procedures and Techniques* (Newbury Park, CA: Sage).

Teece, D. J. (1993), 'The Dynamics of Industrial Capitalism: Perspectives on Alfred Chandler's Scale and Scope', *Journal Economic Literature*, 31, 199–225.

Teece, D. J. (2007) 'Explicating Dynamic Capabilities: The Nature and Microfoundations of (Sustainable) Enterprise Performance', *Strategic Management Journal*, 28, 1319–50.

Teece, D. J., Pisano, G. and Shuen, A. (1997) 'Dynamic Capabilities and Strategic Management', *Strategic Management Journal*, 18(7), 509–33.

Uhlenbruck, K. (2004) 'Developing Acquired Foreign Subsidiaries: The Experience of MNEs in Transition Economies', *Journal of International Business Studies*, 35(2), 109.

Uhlenbruck, K., Meyer, K. E. and Hitt, M. A. (2003) 'Organizational Transformation in Transition Economies: Resource-Based and Organizational Learning Perspectives', *The Journal of Management Studies*, 40(2), 257.

Volberda, H. W. (1996) 'Toward the Flexible Form: How to Remain Vital in Hypercompetitive Environments', *Organization Science*, 7(4), 359–74.

Venaik, S., Midgley, D. F. and Devinney, T. M. (2005) 'Dual Paths to Performance: The Impact of Global Pressures on MNC Subsidiary Conduct and Performance', *Journal of International Business Studies*, 36: 655–675.

Wan, W. P. (2005) 'Country Resource Environments, Firm Capabilities, and Corporate Diversification Strategies', *Journal of Management Studies*, 42(1), 161–82.

WIR (2007) *World Investment Report 2007: Transnational Corporations, Extractive Industries and Development* (New York: United Nations).

WIR (2010) *World Investment Report 2010: Investing in a Low-Carbon Economy* (New York: United Nation).

Wright, M., Filatotchev, I., Hoskisson, R. E. and Peng, M. W. (2005) 'Strategy Research in Emerging Economies: Challenging the Conventional Wisdom', *Journal of Management Studies*, 42(1), 1–33.

Yin, R. K. (2003) *Case Study Research: Design and Methods* (3rd edn, Thousand Oaks, California: Sage).

5
The Formation of Chinese Outward FDI Strategy in Africa: A Historical Perspective

Yue Xu

Introduction

In the past decade, China has posited Africa as one of the most important regions for carrying out its 'go global' strategy (Gu, 2005, p.8). The share of Chinese outward direct investment (ODI) flow to Africa increased from 2.62 per cent in 2003 to 9.82 per cent in 2008 (MOFCOM, 2009). Compared with Asia, Africa enjoyed a relatively small but strong growth rate of Chinese ODI flow (OECD, 2010). By the end of 2008, Africa has become the second largest recipient of Chinese ODI. Relative to a long-term low inflow of FDI from the global market to Africa (Naudé and Krugell, 2007), China's proactive ODI strategy in the region is currently the subject of unprecedented attention (Large, 2008; Carmody, 2008; Carmody and Taylor, 2009).

Africa emerged as a key destination of Chinese ODI through several development periods. According to Hong and Sun (2006), the top three regions by the end of 1991, which attracted the most Chinese ODI flows were North America, Oceania and Asia. Five years later, the top three locations were Asia, Latin America and Africa. By the end of 2002, the top three host regions were Asia, Africa and North America. The African region has become more important since 2003 and both ODI flow and stock have increased consistently until the end of 2008 (when there was an interruption due to the impact of the financial crisis).

Although FDI to developing countries had been extensively studied, 'there is a dearth of research on the factors that affect FDI to Africa' (Asiedu, 2006, p.65). The question of what caused the recent growth episode of Chinese ODI in Africa is still under-explored (Large, 2008). Taylor (2009, p.182) suggests that China's engagement with Africa is grounded in pragmatism. Based on existing historical studies (e.g. Cheru and Obi, 2010; Taylor, 2009; Large, 2008; Rotberg,

2008; Taylor, 2006), this chapter takes an historical perspective to review the evolution of Sino-African political and economic relations that shape the development of Chinese ODI in the region. The result of this review suggests four key determining factors that have been influentially co-evolving with the development of Chinese ODI in Africa. These four factors are: (1) political alliances; (2) bilateral trade; (3) aid; and (4) contractual projects.

This chapter has two main parts. The first part recalls key Sino-African political and economic activities based on six stages. The second part explains the formation of Chinese ODI strategy in Africa. In this part, four determining factors identified from the first part are discussed. It highlights ODI motives and processes indicating the co-evolution of activities in the four dimensions. Finally, the chapter is concluded by discussing risks for future Chinese investors in Africa.

Evolution of China's engagement in Africa

Stage 1: 1949–1955

When The People's Republic of China (China) was established in 1949, its government firmly allied itself with the Soviet Union. As Larkin (1971, p.15) records, any contract between Chinese Communist and non-Asian delegates had to be through a Moscow-financed front organization. However, such foreign policy didn't mean China's international relations was totally dependent on the Soviet Union. In 1954, China formed a set of 'Five Principles of Mutual Coexistence'[1] to guide its foreign policy conduct. These principles were formally unveiled at the Bandung Conference[2] and were later expanded by China to deal with all non-Communist developing world countries, including African countries.

Before the Bandung Conference of 1955, China had very little contact with Africa, primarily because most African countries remained under colonial administration. These countries had not formed the nationalist organizations that later played an important role in gaining national independence. It was at the Bandung Conference that China first made tentative links with the African countries, including Egypt, Ethiopia, the Gold Cost (Ghana), Liberia, Libya, and Sudan. The Bandung Conference marked the start of a definite interest by China in Africa. Trade with Africa was initiated after that although limited to those countries that obtained independence. At the conference, Chinese Premier Minister Zhou Enlai, extended an open invitation to all the Egyptian delegates to visit Beijing. On 22 August 1955, China and Egypt signed a trade agreement and, on 30 May 1956, Egypt became the first African country to establish relations with Communist China. Through Egypt, China began directing further diplomatic efforts in Africa (Taylor, 2006, p.20).

Stage 2: 1956–1965

In its early establishment, China was eager to gain more support for securing international recognition as the sole legitimate government with respect to Taiwan. This need was considered in China's foreign policy towards Africa (Hughes, 2006). The result was that by 1965, 17 of 38 African states had recognized the legitimacy of the Chinese government (Cheru and Obi, 2010, p.55). In the same period, African countries needed China's support in gaining independence. In 1961, the Afro-Asian Solidarity Fund Committee met for the first time in Conakry, Guinea. The aim of this organization was to provide support for African liberation organizations. China became a member and a Chinese delegate was elected Vice-Chairman of the committee (Brzezinski, 1964).

China's aid policy in Africa started in 1956, after the Bandung Conference of 1955. The original 'Five Guiding Principles' were replaced by China's 'Eight Principles of Economic and Technical Aid', which were announced by Chinese Premier Minister Zhou Enlai on 15 January 1964 during his visit to fourteen African countries. From 1956 to 1965, China provided all forms of economic assistance to support the newly independent African countries. The assistance was provided on a grant basis despite the fact that China was also struggling with limited resources.

Economically, China became more involved in Africa, starting with North Africa, particular Algeria and Egypt, and then adding other North African countries such as Ethiopia, Morocco, Sudan and Tunisia (Taylor, 2006, p.21). During the late 1960s, African countries formed an FDI policy by which investors from the West were required to include some significant undertakings that would bring positive effects and reduce negative effects in the host markets. China has traditionally presented itself as a developing country and, to African countries, this means China should be more welcome as a collaborator because Chinese operations are more likely to provide appropriate models and offer more instructive experience in the conditions of underdevelopment (Cheru and Obi, 2010, p.28).

Stage 3: 1966–1977

From May 1969, China began to send its ambassadors to all countries with which it had diplomatic relations. Such an aggressive diplomatic strategy finally resulted in major political gains. In 1971, China secured a seat in the UN with the support of 26 African countries (Cheru and Obi, 2010, p.56). However, China's interest and influence in Africa suffered a great setback because of the domestic upheaval caused by the Cultural Revolution (1966–1976). The number of foreign delegations visiting China was 116 in 1966, 53 in 1967, and 12 in 1968 (Taylor, 2006, p.33). The situation began to recover after July 1977 when the Communist Party of China (CPC) Chairman, Hua Guofeng, asked the International Department of the CPC and the Ministry of Foreign Affairs to study relations between Chinese and African governments.

China was ideologically motivated to provide further support to national liberation movements in Africa. This ideology prompted China to provide state-to-state aid, most notably to Tanzania (Yu, 1970). Chinese aid to Africa grew from a low of US$ 428 million in 1966 to nearly US$ 1.9 billion in 1977 (Cheru and Obi, 2010, p.55). From 1970 to 1976, China made more aid commitments to Africa than the Soviet Union did (Taylor, 2006). By the end of the 1970s, 44 of the 50 independent African countries had officially recognized China as sole legitimate government of Taiwan and the mainland (Strauss, 2009, p.781).

In this period, Sino-African trade relations had been unstable. The total trade volume increased initially, dropped and then resumed but only reached $720 million by 1977 (Rotberg, 2008, p.25). To repair the damage caused by the Cultural Revolution, China embarked on an active African policy. The case of the TanZan rail project in 1969 signalled China's comeback in Africa. It was China's biggest aid commitment and was the largest single offer of assistance made in that period. Taylor (2006) argues the implications of the project are in several aspects. First, it showed that despite the turmoil of the Cultural Revolution, China's commitment to Africa was unchanged. Secondly, it showed China's commitment to reducing Moscow's influence in Eastern and Southern Africa, mainly Tanzania and Zambia. Thirdly, it signalled the leading position of China in supporting the national liberation struggle in Africa.

Stage 4: 1978–1989

Since 1978, China's foreign policy had shifted to 'a more circumspect advocating of stability and dialogue' (Taylor, 2006, p.50). From 1978 to 1990, more than 230 delegations from sub-Saharan countries visited China (Rotberg, 2008). In 1979, Chinese Premier Minster Li Xiannian visited Africa representing the most senior official to tour African since Zhou Enlai's tour. In 1982, Chinese Premier Minister Zhao Ziyang visited 11 African countries to give China greater manoeuvrability in Africa. However, generally speaking, Chinese engagement in the African continent dwindled in this period, partially because the need to use the alliances for anti-Soviet purposes had passed (Taylor, 2009). This attitude changed after the Tiananmen Square events when the supportive attitude of developing countries, including African countries, became important to China in countering the isolation endured at the hands of the West (Taylor, 2006, p.63).

The shift of China's strategy from a command economy to globalization also began to influence the central goals and objectives of developmental assistance from China to poor countries (Cheru and Obi, 2010). Aid policy was adjusted, resulting in 'Four Principles on Sino-Africa Economic and Technological Cooperation' announced in 1983 (Cheru and Obi, 2010, p.56). Taylor (2006, p.61) says that in this period, Chinese aid policy was to cultivate as many allies as possible in Africa and to maintain those friendship already in existence through lower-level aid projects. The form of aid was also adjusted, so that instead of granting spectacular aid, as in the past, China provided assistance to those states that needed it.

Chinese investment in the African continent dwindled also because of the failure of economic development in Africa. Africa's simple structure of trade could not satisfy the needs of China. In the meanwhile, China gradually joined the global market and increasingly developed other channels of trade. The overall fall in trade volumes after 1980 did not pick up until 1986 (Rotberg, 2008). During this period, the Third World experienced a debt crisis, which was partially affected in most African countries. The IMF/World Bank (WB) had to apply structural adjustment programmes and instruments to the region.

From the early 1980s, Africa started to experience a process of marginalization, expressed by an increase in debts. Although Africa was undergoing structural adjustment due to Western pressure, lots of foreign investors withdrew their investment. By contrast, China gradually began to make direct investments. For example, a Togo sugar plant was developed, based on Chinese aid, in 1987. Later, the enterprise was taken over and became a combination of China's assistance and joint investment cooperation. This model was gradually spread to other China-aided enterprises (Rotberg, 2008).

Stage 5: 1990–1999

In the 1990s, China had more frequent visits by senior figures from Africa. For example, Chinese Vice President Zhu Rongji paid his first visit to Africa in 1995 which kicked off the new 'Africa boom' in China (Rotberg, 2008, p.24). Chinese President Jiang Zeming visited Africa four times and, in 1996, put forward five suggestions for the strengthening of Chinese–African relations. Meanwhile, African countries accelerated the process of multi-party democracy and the liberalization of the economy under the watchful eyes of the IMF and the World Bank. Market forces were allowed greater freedom in the revitalization of African economies (Cheru and Obi, 2010).

To obtain IMF financial support, African countries have to accept close observation and the adjustment of their political and economic policies. Taylor (2009) argues that, compared with support from the IMF, African countries may prefer alliances with China because of its less constrained, or unconditional, assistance. In 1995, the working conference on foreign aid was held and the State Council of China introduced new policies on foreign aid, whose aim was to encourage more qualified Chinese corporations to participate in overseas economic cooperation and technical assistance projects (Zhang, 2007).

This is the stage at which China experienced a rapid development under the liberalized policy. In the 1990s, African economic reform programmes convinced China that the macroeconomic situation in the region was taking a favourable turn for Chinese commerce (Taylor, 2009). China, with the growth of other Asian economies such as India, became the driving force for African economic development (Ndulu et al., 2007). Between 1989 and 1997, Sino-African trade increased by 431 per cent (Taylor, 2006, p.71). To promote trade, China places no tariffs on the 25 poorest African states (Taylor, 2009, p.21). As part of China's encouragement to further develop Sino-African trade, China has established 11 Investment Development and Trade Promotion Centres in Africa since 1995.

Contractual projects were used as a typical mode of entry for Chinese ODI. For example, the four largest projects during this period were generated this way. They were the 100 million RBM oil exploitations projects in Sudan, two textile factories in Tanzania and Zambia, a railway renovation project in Botswana, and a cement factory project in Zimbabwe (Cheru and Obi, 2010, p.58). In the meantime, China has sought to take advantage of African economic development and encourage joint ventures and economic cooperation at multiple levels (Taylor, 2006, 2009).

Stage 6: 2000–present

In recent decades, Chinese–African relations have been characterized by summit diplomacy, equality, co-development, and cooperation. Such a relationship cannot be found in Africa's relations with any other country (Rotberg, 2008). Since 2000, 4 Ministerial Conferences have been held – in 2000, 2003, 2006 and 2009 – based on the Forum of China-African Cooperation (FOCAC). The first summit was held on 10–12 October 2000 in Beijing and marked a milestone in promoting the China–Africa strategic relationship. The forum was attended by 80 ministers from 44 African countries. The meeting has essentially strengthened Sino-African relationships in three ways, that is, political, economic (especially on economic assistance), and with respect to the ongoing strategy. An immediate effect from the strengthened relations was revealed by the fact that African countries played a pivotal role in securing China's membership of the World Trade Organization (WTO) in 2001 and in China's successful bid for the 2008 Olympic Games.

These Ministerial Conferences addressed the political and economic order to be set up across developing countries in facing new challenges from globalization, what is called the 'new type of strategic partnership', which means south-south cooperation in response to the ideology that globalization offers more benefits to the Western world (Taylor, 2009, p.17). After three summits, President Hu Jintao started his 'eight countries, twelve days' visit to Africa in February 2007. The outcome of FOCAC reflected the increased importance of

China's leadership in Africa, as President Hu Jintao remarked on his visit of South Africa: 'Africa is the continent with the largest number of developing countries and China is the biggest developing country' (Taylor, 2009, p.15).

China's aid policy has been further adjusted in line with its changed economic development. After the summits in 2006 and 2009, aid support became immense. Governmental and business circles shifted to favour straight 'commercial' relations or other 'practical' forms of economic support to Africa (Cheru and Obi, 2010, p.26). Aid with more economic purposes is reflected in China's need for resources. For example, China arranged a $3 billion oil-backed credit line to rebuild Angola's shattered infrastructure in 2002 (Rotberg, 2008).

This is the period in which China moved closer to a market economy where profits, not political agendas, drove most of the economic and trade activities (Rotberg, 2008). The saturation of export markets and a rapid increase in the cost of importing raw materials into China, made Africa increasingly important to China's economy (Taylor, 2009). In the summer of 2006, Chinese Premier Minister Wen Jiabo toured seven African countries. They had a combined trade volume of over $38 billion, representing 52.2 per cent of total Chinese–African trade in 2007 (Rotberg, 2008, p.51). China has greatly increased its oil imports from Africa and they account for 30 per cent of its annual oil imports in 2005 (Rotberg, 2008, p.39). The bilateralism is shown by increased trade and a fall in tariffs on both sides (Rotberg, 2008).

Rapid trade development developed alongside Chinese ODI in Africa. By the end of 2000, Chinese companies had established 499 companies in Africa with a total contractual investment of $900 million, of which $680 million was Chinese capital (Taylor, 2006, p.70). Independent Chinese enterprises are assisted by the Chinese government through 'tied' financial agreements and soft loans attached to specific projects within Africa. The Chinese are viewed as being highly efficient in delivering rapid results through their projects in Africa. Cheru and Obi (2010, p.28) comment that Chinese firms are prepared to go to geographical areas and sectors in Africa where most Western investors are not prepared to take business (or personal) 'risks'. According to Gu (2009), China's accumulated investment in Africa rose from $982.7 million in 2002 to $13.5 billion at the start of 2007.

FDI, through special economic zones (SEZs), emerged also in this period. At the 2006 summit, the Beijing Action Plan (BAP) was formed. China announced its intention of developing between three and five SEZs on the African continent. These SEZs are intended to serve as enclaves for Chinese investment in key African states (Rotberg, 2008). Later, they were established as the Zambian Mining Hub, Indian Ocean Rim Trading Hub, Tanzanian Logistic Hub, Nigeria Gateway to West Africa and the Manufacturing Hub in Egypt. Davies (2010) comments that SEZs promote a clustering effect in African economies so they are attractive to African states that want to move away from simple resource extraction by investors.

Integrated Chinese ODI model

Key influential factors

Based on this historical review of Sino-African political and economic relationships, and as noted in the Introduction, four factors have emerged which have had an influential impact on Chinese ODI. They are: (1) political alliances; (2) bilateral trade; (3) aid; and (4) contractual projects.

First, the history of Sino-African relations can be viewed as a process of pursuing political alliances by both sides. China's policy in Africa was initially part of its anti-hegemonic agenda. This policy was fully promoted at the Bandung Conference in 1955. Africa is part of China's foreign relations with the Third World. Its foreign policy for Africa features a wider approach to 'non-aligned', 'developing' or 'Southern' countries (Large, 2008). Yu (1970) highlights interesting arguments about this over whether there is a Chinese model in dealing with foreign relations with African countries, and whether it is dangerous for African countries to accept such a model and become politically over-dependent on China.

Secondly, the history of Sino-African relations can be viewed as a process of trade development. Asiedu (2002) argues that openness to trade will promote FDI into Africa. The Sino-African trade relationship is characterized by an unbalanced trade structure. Industrial restructuring in post-independence African economies usually started with an expansion of light industry, typically the clothing and textile industry. These two sectors account for 4.7 per cent of total exports from sub-Saharan African countries (Taylor, 2009, p.66). But, the Chinese government has used multiple methods to support the competitiveness of Chinese exporters, such as free capital, direct and indirect subsidies, and incentives. China is, therefore, able to compete with the lowest-cost producing countries. China's main African imports are from oil-producing states and oil clearly dominates the profile of Africa's exports to China (about 70 per cent) (Taylor, 2009, p.37). This situation has been caused by several factors. First, robust economic growth stimulated a huge upsurge in China's demand for oil. Secondly, China's domestic supply of oil declined. In addition, decentralization and liberalization of its energy sectors did not improve production efficiency. For energy security, hunting external sources became inevitable.

Thirdly, the history of Sino-African relations is recorded in the economic aid provided by China to African countries, although Chinese aid figures are not available to the public. Generally, China offers aid in three forms: grants; zero-interest loans; and, since 1995, low-interest 'concessional' loans with subsidized interest rates. Brautigam (1998, p.8) argues that China's 'largely unexamined' foreign aid programme 'has as deep a history and as broad a range of experience as any established in the West'. Rotberg (2008, p.202) argues that China's aid programme has, over half a century, taken forward its security and socialism, its Third World leadership, as well as cooperation for mutual benefit, and the gearing up for going global. The aid programme continues and will be further expanded in the latest stage of new developments. At the 2006 FOCAC, Chinese President Hu Jintao pledged to double China's aid to Africa by 2009. He also promised to offer $3 billion in preferential loans and $2 billion in preferential export buyers credits, and set up a $5 billion fund to support investment by Chinese firms in African economies (Brautigam, 2008).

Fourthly, the history of Sino-African relations is accompanied by China's involvement in large projects. Those projects often started from aid programmes with strong government involvement. For example, Wen Jiaobao, in his 2006 tour to Africa, claimed that China has offered Africa more than $44 billion in aid over the past 50 years to finance 900 infrastructural projects (Rotberg, 2008, p.52). It is not unusual for some of the aid-led projects to be associated later with other entry strategies, such as mergers and acquisitions or joint ventures. Taylor (2009, pp.22–3) observes that after some aid-led projects were completed, Chinese firms would set up branch offices of their home companies, and might then establish joint ventures to look at potential profitable business.

Internationalization process

The historical review suggests that Chinese foreign investors in Africa have been driven by two main motives. These motives are resource-seeking and market-seeking. Both motives also interact with China's trade relations with African countries.

Resource extraction is generally presented as the primary motivating dynamic behind the current Chinese engagement in Africa (Downs, 2004). Increased oil import triggers more direct investment in the oil sector. According to Taylor (2009) the competitiveness of Chinese oil companies comes from several areas. First, Chinese oil investors try to avoid direct competition by going to places for oil where the U.S. and European companies are not present. Secondly, since most of them are state-owned, there is less pressure to pay an investment return to shareholders and they may enjoy a lower cost of management. Thirdly, special government policies allow these companies to commit large amount of funds and labour in resource-rich countries, as well as the finances to acquire exploration and development rights,.

Market-seeking is manifest in China's ODI. Brautigam (2003, p.459) finds that, in around 1970, Chinese investors, originally from South East Asia, established export-oriented manufacturing firms in the duty-free export processing zone (EPZ) in Mauritius. By 1982 there were more than 115 EPZ firms, and 59 per cent of the capital invested in the EPZ came from Hong Kong Chinese. As a result, the Chinese overseas network makes Mauritius a destination for Hong Kong capital. These Asian capitalists created strong connections with local capital, invested in joint ventures, and formed part of a successful export-oriented industrialization.

Africa is a highly heterogeneous group of forty-seven countries, each having different sized economies, populations and surface areas. Rotberg, (2008, p.80) points out that China's African strategy follows 'trade and aid' packages in which 'China puts [a] lucrative package of investment and development on the table in exchange for [a] continuous flow of African resources'.

In accordance with the stage process of internationalization (Vernon, 1966; Johanson and Vahlne, 1977; Melin, 1992), trade and aid activities moderate the risk caused by the liabilities of being foreign (Zaheer, 1995). China's economic assistance plays the role of building up trust, opening market information, and securing commercial deals. Economic assistance can be viewed as the cost of building up a 'relational asset' (Dunning, 2002) for a long-term benefit. Particularly for the aid approach, China offers a different strategy from previous Euro-American partners. China does not claim an interest, at least not directly. Rotberg (2008, p.81) comments that China's aid policies have 'no strings attached' and are 'non-interference'. China allows SOEs to internationalize first. SOEs act as the agency (Buckley et al., 2007) to strengthen political relationships. Because of their state ownership, they can bear cost flexibly. This option is not available to many other Western investors. Jenkins and Thomas (2002, p.53) recognize that investors' 'African perception', which is the belief that instability has spread through most African countries, causes a low FDI inflow in the region. China's trade-aid packages prove to be more effectively and easily adopted to counter the impact of such perception.

However, the negative effect of the trade and aid packages is recognized. The first issue is the spill-over effect of Chinese ODI. FDI supplies capital and provides spill-overs of foreign technology and know-how to host economies. However, the current investment focus cannot sufficiently prove a positive spill-over effect to African economies. For example, Taylor (2009) finds that Chinese light industry products are taking over African markets. These industries are characterized by lower technology and intensive labour, therefore they have a low entry barrier. The domestic market players find it hard to compete with the imported product's price and hard to export the same products since more Chinese entrepreneurs set up similar businesses and compete in providing cheap products. So, market penetration through export has impeded the growth of indigenous African firms. Another issue is corruption in African countries. Poorer regulatory quality and lower control of corruption are prominent problems in African countries. Cuervo-Cazurra and Genc (2008) argues that when both developed country MNEs and developing country MNEs invest in the least developing countries, the latter may have a competitive advantage because they may have the capability for managing poor institutional environments. Indeed, such capabilities of Chinese investors may be potential competitive advantages. But criticism of Chinese investors, particularly, of those oil companies that are engaging in Africa, is often linked to the potential for making corruption worse in the host country (Taylor, 2009, p.164). Haglung (2009) adds that Chinese SOE resource-seekers pursue excessive cost-cutting and segregated management practices, neglecting Africa's local environmental and social concerns.

Conclusions

The historical review of Sino-African relations suggests China's growing presence in Africa is a process of translating various traditional ties into a commercial relationship. History suggests political alliances used to, and may continue to, dominate China's engagement in Africa. Therefore, it is perhaps too simple to use 'trade and aid' packages to describe China's Africa strategy. It is obvious that the 'historical friendship' between China and Africa represents an 'outdated ideological approach' (Taylor, 2009, p.46). Sino-African relations have dramatically shifted as a result of Chinese international commercial strategies in Africa since 2000.

For the African countries, the issue of FDI spill-over effect is of concern. Taylor (2009, p.182) argues China has an African policy but Africa doesn't have a China policy. There is no official African Union (AU) view on Sino-African ties, whether positive or negative, with respect to their downsides. Since China prefers bilateral dealings, it is difficult to construct a single 'China Policy' in Africa. It turns out that African may have little actual negotiating power over China (Taylor, 2009, p.182). The issue of energy will always be sensitive to the international community, given that one third of the world's oil-rich economies are in Africa (Rotberg, 2008, p.89) and China is seeking various resources (mainly oil) in Africa (Taylor, 2009, p.37). The tensions surrounding China's exports to Africa may call more attention to this: people realize that Africa has become China's market, but not the reverse, because the trade structure for African products is dominated by natural resources.

For Chinese investors, the issue of a regional economic bloc should be considered. From the 1990s to the 2010s, a joint African approach has been gradually adopted by the African regional economic bloc. African countries want to rely on their own will and capacity in unison with their regional economic communities, or with the AU as a whole, to formulate, negotiate and monitor developmental terms and requirements for investors within Africa (Cheru and Obi, 2010, p.25). China's engagement with Africa is grounded in pragmatism and so it is up to each African state to negotiate how and where it takes shape.

China may have had experience of dealing with key African countries, but the development of regional institutions may create a more complex environment for Chinese ODI.

The main purpose of this chapter is to address history as the root and background of Chinese ODI. In the review process, the author has come across arguments making the tendentious criticism of China as 'colonist' and 'imperialist'. Such argument is unavoidable but beyond the capacity and purpose of this chapter. Rather, this chapter attempts to demonstrate the multiple historical effects on the formation of Chinese ODI strategy in Africa. It is obvious that strategic relationships between China and African countries will be influenced by the legacy of history. It will be interesting to see how much each historical dimension affects future Chinese ODI strategy as the China–Africa relationship grows in depth, scale and complexity in coming years.

Notes

1. The 'Five Principles of Mutual Coexistence' are: (1) mutual respect for each other's territorial integrity; (2) non-aggression; (3) non-interference in each other's internal affairs; (4) equality and mutual benefit; and (5) peaceful coexistence (cited in Taylor, 2006, p.18).
2. The Bandung Conference was a meeting of Asian and African countries in Bandung, Indonesia, between 18 April and 24 April 1955. During this conference, the 'Five Principles of Mutual Coexistence' was initially adopted to govern relations between China and India. Later, they were applied to relations with all states.

References

Asiedu, E. (2002) 'On the Determinants of Foreign Direct Investment to Developing Countries: Is Africa Different', *World Development*, 30(1), 107–19.

Asiedu, E. (2006) 'Foreign Direct Investment in Africa: the Role of Natural Resources, Market Size, Government Policy, Institutions and Political Instability', *World Economy*, 29(1), 63–77.

Brautigam, D. (1998) *Chinese Aid and African Development: Exporting Green Revolution* (London: Macmillan Press).

Brautigam, D. (2003) 'Close Encounters: Chinese Business Networks As Industrial Catalysis in Sub-Saharan Africa', *African Affairs*, 102, 447–67.

Brautigam, D. (2008) *China's African Aid Transatlantic Challenges* (Washington, DC: The German Marshall Fund of the United States), 1–32.

Brzezinski, Z. (1964) *Africa and the Communist World* (Stanford, California: Stanford University Press).

Buckley, P. J., Clegg, L. J., Cross, A. R., Li, X., Voss, H. and Zheng, P. (2007) 'The Determinants of Chinese Outward Foreign Direct Investment', *Journal of International Business Studies*, 38, 499–518.

Carmody, P. (2008) 'Exploring Africa's Economic Recovery', *Geography Compass*, Vol. 2 No. 1, pp. 79–107

Carmody, P. and Taylor, I. (2009), *Flexigemony and Force in China's Geoeconomic Strategy in Africa: Sudan and Zambia Compared* (Institute for International Integration Studies), 1–21.

Cheru, F. and Obi, C. (2010) *The Rise of China and India in Africa: Challenges, Opportunities and Critical Interventions* (London: Zed).

Cuervo-cazurra, A. and Genc, M. (2008) 'Transforming Disadvantages into Advantages: Developing-Country MNEs in the Least Developed Countries', *Journal of International Business Studies*, 39(6), 957–79.

Davies, M. (2010), *How China Is Influencing Africa's Development* (Paris: OECD), 1–32.

Downs, E. S. (2004) 'The Chinese Energy Security Debate', *The China Quarterly*, 177, 21–44.

Dunning, J. H. (2002) 'Relational Assets, Networks, and International Business Activities' in Contractor, F. J. and Lorange, P. (eds), *Cooperative Strategies and Alliances* (Amsterdam: Pergamon), 569–93.

Gu, X. (2005) 'China Returns to Africa', *Treads East Asia*, 9, 1–20.

Gu, J. (2009) 'China's Private Enterprises in Africa and the Implications for African Development', *The European Journal of Development Research*, 21(4).

Haglund, D. (2009) 'In it for the Long Term? Governance and Learning among Chinese Investors in Zambia's Copper Sector', *The China Quarterly*, 199, 627–46.

Hong, E. and Sun, L. (2006) 'Dynamics of Internationalization and Outward Investment: Chinese Corporations' Strategies', *The China Quarterly*, 187, 610–34.

Hughes, C. R. (2006) *Chinese Nationalism in the Global Era (Politics in Asia)* (London: Routledge).

Jenkins, C. and Thomas, L. (2002), *Foreign Direct Investment in Southern Africa: Determinants, Characteristics and Implications for Economic Growth and Poverty Alleviation* (CASE/Oxford and Crefsa, London of School of Economics), 1–60.

Johanson, J. and Vahlne, J. E. (1977) 'The Internationalization Process of the Firm: A Model of Knowledge Development and Increasing Foreign Market Commitment', *Journal of International Business Studies*, 4, 20–9.

Large, D. (2008) 'Beyond "Dragon in the Bush": The Study of China-Africa Relations', *African Affairs*, 107(462), 45–61.

Larkin, B. D. (1971) *China and Africa, 1949–1970: The Foreign Policy of the People's Republic of China* (Los Angeles: University of California Press).

Meilin, L. (1992) 'Internationalization as a Strategy Process', *Strategic Management Journal*, 13, 99–118.

MOFCOM (2009), *2008 Statistical Bulletin of China's Outward Foreign Direct Investment*, available at: http://hzs2.mofcom.gov.cn/, accessed 2010).

Naudé, W. A. and Krugell, W. F. (2007) 'Investigating Geography and Institutions as Determinants of Foreign Direct Investment in Africa Using Panel Data', *Applied Economics*, 39(10), 1466–4283.

Ndulu, B., Chakraborti, L., Lijane, L., Ramachandran, V. and Wolgin, J. (2007) *Challenges of African Growth: Opportunities, Constraints and Strategic Directions* (Washington, DC: World Bank).

OECD: *China's Outward Direct Investment* (chapter 3), available at: http://www.oecd.org/dataoecd/28/10/40283257.pdf (accessed 2010).

Rotberg, R. I. (2008) *China into Africa: Trade, Aid, and Influence* (Washington, DC: Brookings Institution Press).

Strauss, J. C. (2009) 'The Past in the Present: Historical and Rhetorical Lineages in China's Relations With Africa', *The China Quarterly*, 199, 777–95.

Taylor, I. (2006) *China and Africa: Engagement and Compromise* (London: Routledge).

Taylor, I. (2009) *China's New Role in Africa* (Boulder, Colorado: Lynne Rienner).

Vernon, R. (1966) 'International Investment and International Trade in the Product Cycle', *Quarterly Journal of Economics*, 80, 190–207.

Yu, G. T. (1970) *China and Tanzania: A Study in Cooperative Interaction* (California: University of California).

Zaheer, S. (1995) 'Overcoming the Liability of Foreignness', *Academy of Management Journal*, 341–63.

Zhang, H. (2007) 'China's Aid to Africa: Oil Oriented or Not?', *World Economic Research*, 10, 76–88.

6
The Exporting Trading Companies from China: An Institution-based View

Jia Li and Ling Liu

Introduction

Exporting is the foreign market entry mode most commonly adopted by firms in order to grow and develop in international markets, thanks to its lower costs, risks, and resource commitment. The existing studies in this field look at a range of issues from export-related barriers and strategies, to determinants of performance (Katsikeas et al., 2009). There is also complementary literature on: import-related stimuli (Katsikeas, 1998); importing problems (Katsikeas and Dalgic, 1995); relationships between the export and importer (Leonidou and Kaleka, 1998); and international and global purchasing activities (Leonidou, 1999). Being the 'merchant' between domestic manufacturers and foreign buyers, trading companies play a significant role in global business (Jones, 1998), supporting manufacturers' exports (Peng and Ilinitch, 1998) and purchasing companies' imports (Quintens, Matthyssens and Faes, 2005). The study of trading companies remains underdeveloped (Jones, 2000; Peng et al., 1998); in particular, the study of trading companies based in transition economies. The differences, in exporters' characteristics and in the exporting channel from developed and developing countries (Das, 1994; Tesfom et al., 2004), plus the heterogeneity of trading companies logically suggests to a new trial of trading companies from one emerging economy, like China, which has the reputation of a distinct business mode and environment.

Transition economies are found in countries and regions where formal and informal institutions are comprehensively and fundamentally changing, particularly from a centrally-planned to a market-based economy (Peng, 2003, p.275). In contrast to developed economies, with stable and matured institutions, transition economies unavoidably go through a special period of mixed institutions (Nee, 1992), where institutional constraints (Child and Yuan, 1996), institutional voids (Miller et al., 2009), the uncertainty of institutional change (Child and Tse, 2001), misalignment between institutional supply and firm demand (Witt and Lewin, 2007), and reaction between this institutional environment and organizations (Peng, 2003) jointly construct a distinctive institutional environment.

One of the consequences of institutional transition is that it may generate massive institutional barriers leading to additional transaction costs for firms engaging in the market place, whilst it may also offer considerable opportunities for others. This may be particularly true in the case of market exchange in international markets where domestic manufacturers and foreign buyers interact with each other.

China is one of the most representative of transition economies (Hoskisson et al., 2000) and shares the same institutional problems as others. However, its large population, dramatic economic growth and distinctive political economy, calls for a special consideration in international business, especially from the institutional perspective (Child, 2009). Though China has adopted a programmatic approach to reform, so as to avoid political and social instability, uncertainty remains high for both domestic and international firms doing business in China (Child and Tse, 2001). The institutional void inherited from an economy formerly centrally-planned still leaves many constraints for domestic firms (Child and Yuan, 1996). Their behaviour, decisions, and strategy have been affected heavily by a misalignment that leads to high transaction costs (Child and Yuan, 1996; Witt and Lewin, 2007).

Child and Tse (2001) argue that the lack of intermediate institutions in China – such as legal, finance, distribution, and management systems – to support business operations, may generate opportunities for those firms which are able to reduce transaction costs and increase efficiency. As a result, trading companies' economic activities and characteristics fall under the influence of such institutional conditions.

This article uses exporting trading companies (ETCs) in China to examine the interaction between institutions and organizations, especially in the context of a transition economy. The first section reviews theoretical literature about trading companies. The second section develops a conceptual framework and propositions. The third section illustrates how formal and informal institutions in China increase direct transaction costs for domestic manufacturers and foreign buyers, and how ETCs manage to reduce these additional transaction costs through creating and organizing an indirect market. The final section is the conclusion.

The theoretical explanation of trading companies

Transaction cost economics (TCE) approach
Coase (1937) initially describes transaction costs as the missing part of neoclassical economics and as the reference for the boundary of the firm. Williamson

(1985, 1988, 1996, 1979) further systematically builds up TCE as a paradigm for analysing economic organizations, including the basic unit of analysis (transaction), the three denotations of transactions (Frequency, uncertainty and asset specificity).

TCE answers the question why trading companies can exist in international business – they can lower the transaction costs of international trade (Peng, 1998a; Peng and York, 2001a; Roehl, 1983; Trabold, 2002). Casson (1998) believes TCE to be the first and most important theory on trading companies, as transactions between producers and consumers could not happen without control of costs. He states that international trade involves numerous transactions and contracting issues among sellers, buyers and intermediaries, which contain large amounts of risk and uncertainty, as well as great information asymmetry due to the operation of different time, location and culture. Each of them is related to transaction costs. Moreover, the vertical integration into the distribution channels has been broadly discussed in the TCE field (Williamson, 1985), though most of the discussion is from the perspective of manufacturers (Peng, 1998a).

By using three transaction characteristics – frequency, uncertainty and durability – Roehl (1983) analyses the JGTCs' product characteristics and non-transaction functions. Peng et al. (1998) and Peng and York (2001) integrate TCE and agency theory, and argue that the U.S. exporting intermediaries' performance relies on the manufacturer's 'make-or-buy' decision, which is decided by the comparison between the transaction costs saved by ETCs and the resulting agent costs.

Institutional theory approach

North (1990, p.3) indicates that 'institutions are the rules of the game in a society or, more formally, are the humanly devised constraints that shape human interaction'. Scott (2008, p.33) concludes there are three general pillars – regulatory, normative, and cognitive – of institutions. These institutions contain informal constraints, like norms, cultures and ethics, and formal constraints, such as laws, regulations, rules, and so forth (Peng, 2006b).

The institution-based view, have has been prevailing in recent literatures of on IB (International Business) (Peng et al., 2008), especially in research studies exploring the transactions across nations (Henisz and Swaminathan, 2008). However, applying the institutional perspective to the analysis of trading companies is more rare. Hessels and Terjesen (2010) argue that the SMEs' decision as between direct or indirect exporting is determined by the level of globalization of the domestic institutional 'field', including competitors, customers, suppliers, and so on. From an institutional approach, Ma (2006) advises exporters to choose state-owned import intermediaries in transition markets in order to pursue advantages and resources from uneven institutional arrangements.

However, there are two limitations to the existing analysis of ETCs. First, inadequate attention has been paid to foreign buyers or importers: equally important stakeholders in business (Perdue and Summers, 1991; Quintens et al., 2005). In fact, the use of intermediaries or trading companies is a common method by which international purchasers, particular where they are small, can engage with simple products or products with a lower purchasing risk or in unfamiliar markets. One study of American purchasers (Ciancarelli, 1999) reported at least 13 per cent use trading companies during international purchases (Quintens et al., 2005). Thus it's hard to make the decision of use of trading companies without purchasers' stake.

Another limitation to existing studies of trading companies is that there is inadequate consideration of institutional factors. Peng (2006, 2001) argues that existing theories in IB emerged from western countries with sound marketing institutions and it is necessary to pay more attention to the way institutional factors are applied in emerging markets. The institution-based view has increasingly become the most important supplement to existing theories in IB (Peng, Wang and Jiang, 2008). It's extremely important for this study, since institutions greatly affect transaction costs analysis. The next section will provide an integrated model of transaction costs economics and institutional theories to analyse the ETCs' role in transition economies.

An integrative model of TCE and IT

The TCE perspective

The comparative approach to different transactions and governance structures is the main method within the TCE framework (Williamson, 1985, 1996). Markets, firms and hybrid modes, as different structures for organizing transactions, incur different degrees of cost, 'the superior efferent one can form' (Williamson, 1985, p.86). The competition does not only happen between market and firm, but among different markets as well. These markets with varying government structures entail different costs. They are made by different firms, namely, market-makers (Anderson and Gatignon, 2008; Casson, 1982; Spulber, 2003, 1999, 1996). Spulber (1999, p.256) indicates that 'through pricing and market-making activities, the most efficient market microstructure produces the greatest gains from trade net of transaction costs'. He further explains that the 'economies of scale and scope', 'coordination economies' and the identity of third parties help these market-makers to reduce the transaction costs. In addition, Foss and Foss (2005) also say that, 'While transaction costs are a major source of value dissipation, reducing such dissipation may create value.' Firms creating more efficient markets with lower transaction costs can outperform others.

The market is defined as 'a group of buyers and sellers of a particular good or service'. (Mankiw, 2008, p.66). In the exporting market, there are normally three main groups of players: sellers (manufacturers), buyers, and trading companies (brokers and resellers) (Casson, 1998; Peng, 1998). They consist of two basic markets, direct markets and indirect markets (Spulber, 2003). The former is created and operated by manufacturers and buyers; whereas the latter involves intermediaries, such as trading companies. From the perspective of manufacturers or buyers, either direct markets or indirect markets incur transaction costs; they will choose whichever has the lowest costs. From the trading companies' point of view, they have to reduce the transaction costs of the indirect market, including themselves, in order to survive and acquire the value postulated by Spulber et al. Consequently, among these different markets created by ETCs, the most efficient one with the lowest transaction costs will win.

The IT perspective

Institutions provide stable structures for human interaction to reduce uncertainty (North, 1990). Coase (1998) states that 'the costs of exchange depend on the institutions of a country: its legal system; its political system; its social system; its educational system; its culture; and so on'. Therefore, institutions affect firms' decisions and strategy through ruling, or 'signalling which conduct is acceptable', and 'constraining the range of acceptable action' (North, 1990). This influences the uncertainty of environment, opportunism and the resulting transaction costs (Peng, 2006), or through influencing the disequilibrium of product and factor markets and resource acquirement (Peng, 2001b). On the other hand, individuals and organizations push for institutional change through innovation, strategy, and so on (Peng, 2003; Scott, 2008, pp.76–7).

In particular, the institution-based view is extremely significant for studies of transition economies (Peng, 2005). These transition economies, like China and Russia, retain some institutions from the previous centrally-planned economy, and lack the sound and complete institutions of a market economy, which leads to institutional voids and conflicts. The direction and speed of transition and reform in these markets are unclear. The emerging economic agents are unfamiliar with market mechanisms. All of these institutional conditions jointly increase transaction costs for domestic and foreign companies (Child and Tse, 2001; Hoskisson et al., 2000; Meyer, 2001).

Therefore, based on our model of an exporting market with three parties and our institution-based view, we argue that when these economies are experiencing institutional transition from a centrally-planned economy to a market-based economy, formal and informal institutions add transaction costs to the direct market between domestic manufacturers and foreign buyers (see Figure 6.1).

Proposition 1: The institutional transition increases the additional transaction costs of domestic manufacturers' direct export.

Proposition 2: The institutional transition increases additional transaction costs for foreign buyers' direct import.

Meanwhile, domestic and foreign companies in transition economies usually manage to use more adaptive strategies to response to these institutions (Peng, 2003). In addition, this institutional transition also offers business opportunities for some companies. Child and Tse (2001) argue that the lack of intermediate institutions in China, such as legal, finance, distribution, and management systems, which can support business operations, may generate opportunities for those firms who are able to reduce transaction costs and increase efficiency. Those companies, like trading companies, with more contact and cooperation with advanced international firms, are more likely to obtain these opportunities in these transitional economies.

Therefore, we propose that ETCs in transition economies effectively reduce the transaction costs related to institutions by offsetting these negative institutional effects and establishing more efficient trading institutions in the indirect market which centres on them (see Figure 6.1).

Proposition 3: Through organizing a more efficient indirect exporting market, ETCs in transition economies are able to reduce institution-related transaction costs for domestic manufacturers.

Proposition 4: Through organizing a more efficient indirect exporting market, ETCs in transition economies are able to reduce institution-related transaction costs for foreign buyers.

In the next section, China's exporting system and export trading companies (ETCs) will illustrate, as an example, how formal and informal institutions increase direct transaction costs for domestic manufactures and foreign buyers, and how ETCs manage to reduce these additional transaction costs through creating and organizing an indirect market.

Institutional transition for China's ETCs

Compared with a handful of studies on exporting intermediaries from the US and the EU, and on some general trading companies from Japan and Korea, trading companies or exporting trading companies from China are still mysterious. There are two reasons: the first one is underdeveloped research about China. Recently, academic interest has started to shift to emerging markets and to China, especially as they continue their brilliant economic performance

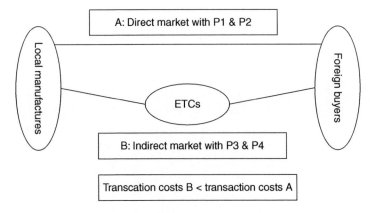

Figure 6.1   Adapted from Spulber (2003)

Note: P1, P2, P3 and P4 refers to proposition 1, 2, 3 and 4 respectively.

whilst other developed economies are in continuous downturn. But, the studies about China are still unstructured and lack sound theories (Peng, 2005).

The second reason is the lack of data on the trading companies sector, due to their character as service firms and their uncertain separation from manufacturers in the whole exporter dataset (Peng and Ilinitch, 1998). For instance, there is no statistic on trading companies or ETCs in China's official annual statistical report (made by custom, national bureau of statistics or other department). In this sector, the two main institutional conditions of China's exporting market and ETCs – the export authority and the reselling system – are used to illustrate how they increase the transaction costs of export in the direct market.

China's trading companies and export authority

From 1949–1977, 12 state-owned trading companies were established in different product categories. They had a monopoly of all imports and exports in China (Young et al., 1998). Each of them took charge of one specific category of products and was exclusively licensed to export or import that category of product. For example, China Minerals Corporation Import (China Minmetals Corporation now) and China National Silk and Export Corporation were established in 1950 and 1951 (respectively), and exclusively process the import and export of minerals and silk. By 1978, these state-owned trading companies had grown to 11 headquarters and 130 subsidiaries in major cities in China (Fu, 2008). But only the headquarters, and several subsidiaries in some trading ports, had an import/export authority, while the majority of subsidiaries only took responsibility for purchasing domestic products for export. The establishment of these trading companies' headquarters and subsidiaries, and the grant of import/export authority are the role of the Ministry of Trade of PRC (Ministry of Commerce now) (Fu, 2008).

From 1978–1993, the central government began the reform of the planned economy by gradually adding marketing economic factors. Local governments are allowed to establish province-owned trading companies or take over some local subsidiaries that belonged to previous state-owned trading companies. These new trading companies are authorized to import/export some products by government authority. But these authorities are still limited to specific classes of product. In particular, there have been two kinds of export authority in China from then on. One is called a trading authority, and is specifically issued to the trading companies to trade products or service offered by others, such as manufacturers. Another one is specially named as a manufacturer's export authority, and allows some manufacturers to export their own products (Ma and Li, 2003; MFTEC, 2001). Up to 1993, there were only 4000 trading companies with the trading authority to operate an import/export business, and 2000 Chinese manufacturers and 160,000 foreign investment companies with the authority to export their own products. All these local companies are state-owned (Liu, 2007).

In 1994, the central government issued the first Foreign Trade Law of the PRC. It formally introduced a series of regulations on exporting, including the compulsory approval system for an exporting authority to go through MOFCOM (Ministry of Commerce) and an alternative agency system for other companies and organizations without exporting authority (NPCSC, 1994). Meanwhile, the shareholding reform of state-owned trading companies begin to take effect (Fu, 2008), which made them act as economic organizations, rather than government organizations. In addition, a new registration system for authority to export was attempted experimentally in five special economic zones and with 1000 larger state-owned manufacturers. But, until 1998, there were only 8335 trading companies with the authority to operate an import/export business, and 9526 Chinese and foreign investment manufacturers with the authority to export their own products (Fu, 2008).

After China's accession to the WTO in 2001, the government gradually lowered the barriers to market access, including the export market. In 2004, the Foreign Trade Law of the PRC was revised (NPC, 2004) and the approval system for import and export authority was gradually replaced by a registration system. Private firms and individuals were finally allowed to enter into international trade (Fu, 2008).

In particular, the foreign wholly-owned trading companies were initially allowed in 2004 (MOFCOM, 2004; SETC, 1999). The joint venture style of trading companies are less common. In 1997, the first three Sino-foreign trading companies were approved (Fu, 2008). Until 2002, there were only five Sino-foreign trading companies (Ma and Li, 2003).

Although the Chinese government had allowed private firms to obtain export authority from 2004, the procedure was still complicated for them. To apply for export authority, a firm had to register with many government authorities, including the local Administration of Industries and Commerce, the Taxation Bureau (which is important for a product with export tax rebates), the Administration of Foreign Exchange (foreign exchange is controlled in China), Customs (including e-port, on-line customs, and so on), Bureau of Quality and Technical Supervision, the bank, and so on.

Generally, in China, the 'export authority' had for many years been exclusively available to trading companies (whether state-owned or in other ownership) and some large manufacturers. According to statistics, in 1986 the exporting undertaken by trading companies made up 94.4 per cent (FDI manufacturers 5.6 per cent) of the total amount in China and was still 34 per cent (FDI manufacturers 47.9 per cent) in 2000 (Yao and Chen, 2001).

The reselling system in China's export market

Under this 'export authority', a special 'reselling system' had been developed in China's export market. The reselling system means that ETCs first buy the ownership of products from domestic manufacturers through a buying contract, and then sell them to foreign buyers through a selling contract. From 1949 to 1978, this system was compulsory for all domestic manufacturers and ETCs under government regulation. From 1979, with the reform of the foreign trade system in China, the central government experimentally promoted the 'agency system', which allows ETCs to represent manufacturers without export authority (through an agency contract) to contract with buyers (through a selling contract).

However, the related laws, such as the Civil Law General Principles of PRC and Contract Law of PRC, fail to identify clearly the obligations, rights and principal-agent relationship for ETCs and manufacturers in an agency contract. The main problems are that the ETCs, as the agent, take more of, and even the full, risk during the transaction, since the agency contract is not properly protected under domestic laws and the selling contract only appears under the agent's name. In addition, the commission fee for brokerage is only 1–3 per cent in practice, which is far less than the profit from a normal export transaction. So, both business tradition and reason enable most ETCs to use the reselling system in practice in China. Moreover, given the complicated and time consuming foreign exchange and tax rebates systems run by government authorities, the manufacturers are willing to accept this reselling system to reduce the time it takes to turn around capital. Thus, until 1986, the amount of export by agency system only made up 6.3 per cent of the total amount (in 1990 it was 7.29 per cent; in 1991 it was 5.1 per cent; in 1992 it was 1.2 per cent;

in 1993 it was 3.7 per cent: in 1994 it was 1.41 per cent; in 2000 it was 4.4 per cent) (Xu, 2000; Yao and Chen, 2001).

China's institutions, domestic manufacturers and ETCs' role

Coase (2008) believed that 'what are traded on the market are not, as is often supposed by economists, physical entities, but the rights to perform certain actions, and the rights which individuals possess are established by the legal system'. Formal institutions, like law and regulation, and informal institutions, like norms, 'enable social actors and action, conferring licenses, special powers, and benefits to some types of actors' (Scott, 2008, p.52). Thus institutions lead to different costs for the same transaction by different organizations.

In China, the 'export authority', as a formal institution in the export market, had been the exclusive authority for trading companies and some large manufacturers. Many domestic manufacturers could not trade directly with foreign buyers, lacking an exporting authority, until recently. But the current complicated appliance procedure also bewilders many manufacturers. Meanwhile, these manufacturers have adapted themselves to the previous trading pattern, with informal institutions, receiving orders from trading companies, and with a lack of trade-related functions and channels. The reselling system that has operated until now increases the confusion.

In addition, the lack of export-related resources, especially financial resources, worries manufacturers. Ahmed et al. (2008) suggest that financial inhibitors are the main obstacles for exporters and non-exporters in this emerging market. The inadequate support from local financial systems and from government (such as tax concessions), and the nature of the financial payment system in exporting, such as the risky and slow payment terms, jointly harass these exporters. In China, most exporters are private firms, SMEs or micro-enterprises, and township and village enterprises, with limited export-related resource (such as brand, reputation, finance, human capital, experience, channels, and so on). These emerging private firms are usually small and under-capitalized, without access to formal financing, private credit or even raw materials: all these are dominated by state-owned banks, SOE and large manufacturers in China. The lack of concern about their needs during the issue of regulations makes private firms more vulnerable, whilst local government prefers to offer benefits and priority to those large firms, which contribute more tax (Nee, 1992). In particular, the system of tax rebates and foreign exchange controls in China, which adds to the involvement of administrations and banks, not only increases exporters' administrative costs, but slows their capital turn around.

Moreover, the trade show is considered one of the most efficient methods to transact business between exporter and foreign buyer (Ling-yee, 2007). They are extremely important to China's exporters, because of the brief history of China's firms' internationalization and the large number of 'stay at home' exporters (Peng and Chen, 2009). However, these trade shows present high institutional barriers to domestic manufacturers. For instance, Canton fair, organized by the Ministry of Commence (MOFCOM), is the largest, the most representative and the oldest trade fair in China, beginning in 1957, (Canton Fair, 2010). Due to the inertia of economic planning policy, authority to attend is formally only given to larger exporters with a certain export size. Others have to buy access through their personal network or on the black market at a high cost. Thus, the ETCs and larger manufacturers with higher exports than small manufacturers have privileges in obtaining the authority to attend. In addition, other expenses (travel, advertising, and so on) related to a trade fair are also extremely high for a normal exporter. In general, these formal institutional barriers in China increase the additional transaction costs for domestic manufacturers' direct exporting. In turn, the ETCs are able to find some efficient methods for bypassing or offsetting these transaction costs.

Firstly, ETCs are able to take advantage of 'economies of scale and scope', due to a 'larger volume of transactions than individual buyers and sellers' (Spulber, 1999). Since they own more manufacturers and buyers, and process more exporting deals than individual manufacturers and buyers, China's ETCs are able to achieve economies of scale and scope, and then reduce the costs generated by institutional barriers per deal. For instance, the complicated and costly application and annual renewal of the export authority is more economic for ETCs with their many transactions than for manufacturers.

Secondly, in the long history of monopoly, China's ETCs accumulated considerable intangible assets (knowledge, experience, and so on) related to exporting, which can reduce transaction costs. Roehl (1998) indicates that JGTCs' experience and knowledge, based on experience, help them to greatly increase transaction efficiency and information assets. China's ETCs construct sound relations with buyers and good reputation in some industries. Most state-owned trading companies inherit their previous company name and product brand. All of them have become sunk costs for their economies of scale. In addition, some ETCs are still state-owned or acquire connections with state-owned trading companies, such as registration as subsidiaries of SOE. These connections help them to obtain some privileges, such as a free ticket for Canton fair, or to lower some administrative fees by paying back 'management fees' or sharing some part of their profits with state-owned trading companies.

Finally, the withdrawal of government and planning institutions generated a large pool of manufacturers encompassing many previously struggling manufacturers as well as small and medium-sized private manufacturers. But the present unsound institutional conditions in China, such as in the financial markets, fail to support efficient intermediate institutional support for struggling manufacturers in export markets. In particular, the high level of uncertainty over institutional transition in China, like the exchange rate and interest rate, and the uncertainty of international trade itself increases manufacturers' transaction costs. Some of them refuse to, or lack the resources to commit to, other parts of exporting transactions rather than simple manufacturing. Meanwhile long-term isolation from the export operation also increases these domestic manufacturers' asymmetric information and uncertainty about foreign buyers and exporting transactions. In turn, due to those experiences and information about international trade and foreign buyers, ETCs could take more risks and involve themselves generally in the entire exporting process, such as R&D, material purchasing, financing, brand establishment and maintenance, etc. They are willing to spend more resources on the establishment of trustful networks with forwarders, banks, and government administrations. In turn, the more functions the ETCs undertake, the more organizations participate in each export transaction, the more likely China's ETCs are to achieve economies from coordination (Spulber, 1999) and reduce the transaction costs in each part of an exporting deal. In general, China's ETCs offer domestic manufacturers a single more efficient, feasible and low-risk domestic transaction, instead of an international transaction, which incurs more resources and commitment, and involves higher risk-taking in current institutions.

China's institutions, foreign buyers and ETC's role

Importing or international purchasing is becoming popular for increasing numbers of firms due to the uniqueness of their products, more choice, and lower costs but with a better quality than domestic products, reliable suppliers, and so on (Leonidou, 1999). However, there are still some barriers, which can become large obstacles for an importer. These barriers cross from internal firm-level, external environments to domestic and foreign ones (Birou and Fawcett, 1993; Katsikeas and Dalgic, 1995; Leonidou, 1999). The institution-related factors, such as environmental uncertainty, affect exporter-importers inter-organizational relationships (Matanda and Freeman, 2009).

For instance, the Asian developing countries, such as Japan initially, then the Asian tigers, currently China, have been the most important importing location due to their lower price and strong productivity. However, different local institutions and business modes also make the importer's supplier-selection decision difficult (Deng and Wortzel, 1995).

Importing, like other business activities in China, also faces many institution-related challenges. The most important one is related to the 'quality' problem, enforcement of contracts, and monitoring costs for importers. The cost of enforcement (or monitoring) contracts is one important sub-cost in transaction costs theory (Furubotn and Richter, 2005, p.25), and closely related to international trade in practice (Peng, 1998a). The existing literatures on international purchasing and importing indicate that the quality and timely delivery of products became the most pressing problems for the purchaser's supplier selection decision (Kannan and Tan, 2002; Katsikeas and Dalgic, 1995; Leonidou, 1999). In China this issue is more significant. According to the China Purchasing Development Report of 2010 (LFRC, 2010), the 'unreliable supplier' and 'on-time delivery' are listed as first and third in the list of challenges for foreign purchasers about sourcing in China (the second is increasing operational costs). Moreover, research into international purchasing offices (IPOs) in China indicates that one main function of these IPOs is to control quality (Nassimbeni and Sartor, 2006). This indirectly suggests that the 'quality' of products is the main problem for importing from China. Thus these issues about quality and enforcement of contract significantly increase importers' monitoring costs in enforcing contracts, and even influence suppliers' selection.

There are two institution-related conditions that contribute to and increase these problems. The first is about formal institutions, for example, China's current legal system and enforcement, while the latter one relates to informal institutions and the individual's and organizations' attitude to habits of contracting and obligation in Chinese society (Luo, 2002), which are different from other societies. Coase (2008) argues that the legal system is important in a world of positive transaction costs, especially for enforcement costs. Although improving, the legal system in China is still imperfect for foreign companies, with 'inadequate protection of intellectual property, and insufficiently transparent legal and regulatory processes' (Child, 2009). Obviously, this weak legal system will also encourage opportunism in the import and export markets in China.

Furthermore, the informal institutions in China also increase this situation. The absence and inappropriateness of formal commercial law in the history of China fails to build a strong spirit of contract and obligation (Luo, 2002). All these are crucial for the transaction costs of international trade, since it is costly for exporters and importers from different countries to monitor each other's behaviours closely after contracting. In particular, most of the contracting activities in exporting and importing, not only with buyers and sellers, but with forwarders, shipping companies and other related organizations, are usually through fax, email and even orally by telephone, and without complete contracts and legal documents. These norms of international trade, formed in western marketing economies with a sound legal system, greatly reduce transaction costs for each organization but require individuals to display a spirit of contract and obligation. However, a transition economy like China, without these institutional conditions, has higher costs for the firms involved, especially the foreign buyers. In addition, when accidents happen between production and contractual enforcement, and a modification between manufacturers and buyers is required, the negotiation and enforcement costs are even higher. Unfortunately, with incomplete contracts and 'bounded rationality' in design, production, time, exchange rates, shipping costs, etc, this condition is quite common in an export deal, especially for the first transaction for a product.

So, the legal system in China fails to protect the enforcement of exporting contracts well. Meanwhile, China's informal institutions, such as individuals' and companies' spirit of contractual obligation, are different from international trading institutions and increase enforcement costs. All these formal and informal institutions in China jointly increase foreign buyers' transaction costs.

Thus, ETCs are able to solve these problems, and reduce transaction costs in a new indirect market. ETCs, as a neutral third party, have more incentive and capability than manufacturers and buyers to monitor the quality of products (Spulber, 1999, p.23). In terms of China, there are two things which enhance these incentives and capabilities.

The reselling system in China enables ETCs to take the whole responsibility, rather than partial responsibility, for coordinating each part in a transaction and monitoring the quality, time and other related issues within the contract. They sometimes even put higher and stricter terms to manufacturers than buyer asks, in order to avoid risk and uncertainty, such as a frequently changing foreign exchange rate, to offer a better service for buyers and improve their reputation, such as sending the goods in advance.

Because they have had a monopoly for a long time in undertaking export business in China, ETCs have accumulated great deal of knowledge of the quality of products and manufacturers. In particular, some of these trading companies, especially the SOEs, have been engaged in a specific product category for many decades, and even employ personnel who used to work in related manufacturers as quality control staff. Thus, these experienced ETCs have less asymmetric information than foreign buyers in term of the quality of product, schedule of production, supply of raw material, and manufacturers' capability. They are even able to identify the best qualified manufacturers for a specific export order, before the transaction, based on their previous cooperation. In particular, their geographic closeness to manufacturers enables ETCs to identify manufacturers with lower costs. ETCs usually send their own quality control staff to the factory to monitor the production progress and product quality. Certainly, the same culture also helps them to negotiate with these domestic manufacturers better than foreign buyers. As a result, China's ETCs are able to organize an export transaction more efficiently than foreign buyers' indirect transactions.

Conclusion

This article examines China's exporting system and exporting trading companies (ETCs) and illustrates how specific formal and informal institutions increase the direct transaction costs for domestic manufacturers and foreign buyers, and how ETCs interact with both and manage to reduce these additional transaction costs in international markets.

Institutions have the reputation of easing transaction costs for economic organizations (Peng, 2006). In a transitional economy, however, the uncertainty of speed and direction of institutional transition, the unsound marketing institutions, and conflict with a formerly centrally-planned economy, give rise to additional costs for economic transactions. One of the consequences of institutional transition is that it may generate massive institutional barriers leading to additional transaction costs for firms engaging in the market place. To some extent, the lack of intermediate institutions may generate considerable opportunities for those firms who are able to reduce transaction costs and increase efficiency (Child and Tse, 2001). By constructing a three party export market model from an institution-based perspective, we argue that when transitional economies are experiencing institutional transition from a centrally-planned economy to a market-based economy, formal and informal institutions increase additional transaction costs in the direct market between domestic manufacturers and foreign buyers.

In transition economies, some firms are able to undertake effective pragmatic strategies to offset those costs generated from institutions (Peng and Heath, 1996). China's ETCs, through offering domestic manufacturers and foreign buyers more efficient trading institutions, offer a logical choice for a export/import channel decision for manufactures and importers, especially when they are confronted with institutional barriers in these transitional economies. For example, China's ETCs offer domestic manufacturers one efficient, feasible and low-risk domestic transaction, instead of an international transaction, which incurs more resources and commitment, and higher risk-taking in current institutions. The reselling system in China enables ETCs to take the whole responsibility of coordinating with each party in one transaction, and to monitor the quality, time and other related issues for the contract, hence reducing costs for foreign importers.

Finally, the experience of ETCs in China carries implications for other transitional economies. The ETCs, as the intermediary economics organizations, are able to strengthen the efficiency of marketing exchange, fulfil some important but missing functions within the emerging market, and ease the problems generated by institutional transition and reform. Therefore, those policy makers who would engage in export-oriented economic development should offer these ETCs some supportive incentive policies. In addition, they also need to pay more attention to these informal exporting institutions, created and operated by ETCs, which reflect the practical needs of market and economic organizations, when they reform or create formal institutions. Deng Xiaoping, the Chinese reformer and politician, said that reform in China should 'cross a river by feeling for the stones'. We believe that these institutions, created and operated by marketized companies, are just such stones.

References

Ahmed, Z. U., Julian C. C. and Mahajar A. J. (2008) 'Export Barriers and Firm Internationalisation from an Emerging Market Perspective', *Journal of Asia Business Studies*, 3(1), 33–41.

Anderson, E. and Gatignon, H. (2008) 'Firms and the Creation of New Markets', in Ménard, C. and Shirley, M. M. (eds), *Handbook of New Institutional Economics* (Heidelberg: Springer Berlin).

Birou, L. M. and Fawcett, S. E. (1993) 'International Purchasing: Benefits, Requirements, and Challenges', *Journal of Supply Chain Management*, 29(2), 27–37.

CantonFair (2010) *About Canton Fair* (Canton).

Casson, M. (1982) *The Entrepreneur: An Economic Theory* (Totowa, NJ: Rowman & Littlefield Pub Inc.).

Casson, M. (1998) 'The Economic Analysis of Multinational Trading Companies' in Jones, G. (ed.), *The Multinational Traders* (London: Routledge).

Child, J. (2009) 'China and International Business' in Rugman, A. M. (ed.) *Oxford Handbook of International Business* (Oxford: Oxford University Press).

Child, J. and Tse, D. K. (2001) 'China's Transition and Its Implications for International Business', *Journal of International Business Studies*, 32(1), 5-21.

Child, J. and Yuan, L. (1996) 'Institutional Constraints on Economic Reform: The Case of Investment Decisions in China', *Organization Science*, 60–77.

Ciancarelli, A. (1999) 'More Companies Source Globally', *Purchasing*, 126(2), 20–21.

Coase, R. H. (1937) 'The Nature of the Firm', *Economica*, 4(16), 386–405.

Coase, R. H. (1998) 'The New Institutional Economics', *American Economic Review*, 88(2), 72–4.

Coase, R. H. (2008) 'The Institutional Structure of Production', in Ménard, C. and Shirley, M. M. (eds), *Handbook of New Institutional Economics* (Berlin, Heidelberg: Springer-Verlag).

Das, M. (1994) 'Successful and Unsuccessful Exporters from Developing Countries: Some Preliminary Findings', *European Journal of Marketing*, 28(12), 19–33.

Deng, S. and Wortzel, L. H. (1995) 'Importer Purchase Behavior: Guidelines for Asian Exporters', *Journal of Business Research*, 32(1), 41–7.

Foss, K. and Foss, N. K. (2005) 'Resources and Transaction Costs: How Property Rights Economics Furthers the Resource Based View', *Strategic Management Journal*, 26(6), 541–53.

Fu, Z. (2008) *The 30 years of China's Foreign Trade* ('Zhong guo dui wai mao yi 30 niang') (Beijing: China Financial & Economic Publishing House).

Furubotn, E. G. and Richter, R. (2005) *Institutions and Economic Theory: The Contribution of the New Institutional Economics* (Ann Arbor: University of Michigan Press).

Henisz, W. and Swaminathan, A. (2008) 'Institutions and International Business', *Journal of International Business Studies*, 39(4), 537–39.

Hessels, J. and Terjesen, S. (2010) 'Resource Dependency and Institutional Theory Perspectives on Direct and Indirect Export Choices', *Small Business Economics*, 34(2), 203–20.

Hoskisson, R. E., Eden L., Lau, C. M. and Wright, M. (2000) 'Strategy in Emerging Economies', *The Academy of Management Journal*, 43(3), 249–67.

Jones, G. (1998) 'Multinational Trading Companies in History and Theory', in Jones, G. (ed.), *The Multinational Traders* (London: Routledge).

Jones, G. (2000) *Merchants to Multinationals: British Trading Companies in the Nineteenth and Twentieth Centuries* (USA: Oxford University Press).

Kannan, V. R. and Tan, K. C. (2002) 'Supplier Selection and Assessment: Their Impact on Business Performance', *Journal of Supply Chain Management*, 38(4), 11–21.

Katsikeas, C. S. (1998) 'Import Stimuli and Import Development', *Management International Review*, 215–37.

Katsikeas, C. S. and Dalgic, T. (1995) 'Importing Problems Experienced by Distributors: The Importance of Level-of-Import Development', *Journal of International Marketing*, 3(2), 51–70.

Katsikeas, C. S., Leonidou, L.C. and Samiee, S. (2009) 'Research into Exporting: Theoretical, Methodological, and Empirical Insights', in Kotabe, M. and Helsen, K. (eds), *The Sage Handbook of International Marketing* (London: Sage Publications Ltd).

Leonidou, L. C. (1999) 'Barriers to International Purchasing: The Relevance of Firm Characteristics', *International Business Review*, 8(4), 487–512.

Leonidou, L. C. and Kaleka, A. A. (1998) 'Behavioural Aspects of International Buyer-Seller Relationships: Their Association with Export Involvement', *International Marketing Review*, 15(5), 373–97.

LFRC (2010) *China Purchasing Development Report* (Hong Kong: Li and Fung Research Centre & China Federation of Logistics & Purchasing).

Ling-yee, L. (2007) 'Marketing Resources and Performance of Exhibitor Firms in Trade Shows: A Contingent Resource Perspective', *Industrial Marketing Management*, 36(3), 360–70.

Liu, Y. (2007) *The Reform of China's International Trade System* ('Zhong Guo Wai Mao Ti Zhi Gai Ge De Jin Cheng Xiao Guo Yu Guo Ji Bi Jiao') (Beijing: University of International Business and Economics Press).

Luo, Y. (2002) 'Partnering with Foreign Firms: How Do Chinese Managers View the Governance and Importance of Contracts?', *Asia Pacific Journal of Management*, 19(1), 127–51.

Ma, X. (2006) 'Beyond Transaction Cost Determinants: An Integrated Framework for Export Intermediary Selection in Emerging Economies', Relationship between Exporters and Their Foreign Sales and Marketing Intermediaries, 23.

Ma, K. and Jun, Li (2003) *China Business* (Beijing, China: China International Press).

Mankiw, N. G. (2008) *Principles of Economics* (Mason, OH: South-Western Publication).

Matanda, M. J. and Freeman, S. (2009) 'Effect of Perceived Environmental Uncertainty on Exporter-Importer Inter-organisational Relationships and Export Performance Improvement', *International Business Review*, 18(1), 89–107.

Meyer, K. E. (2001) 'Institutions, Transaction Costs, and Entry Mode Choice in Eastern Europe', *Journal of International Business Studies*, 357–67.

MFTEC (ed.) (2001) *Regarding the Provisions for the Control of Enterprises Power to Engage in Import and Export Business* (China: Ministry of Foreign Trade and Economic Cooperation of the People's Republic of China.

Miller, D., Lee, J., Chang, S. and Le Breton-Miller, I. (2009) 'Filling the Institutional Void: The Social Behavior and Performance of Family vs Non-family Technology Firms in Emerging Markets', *Journal of International Business Studies*, 40(5), 802–17.

MOFCOM (2004) *Measures for Administration on Foreign Investment in Commercial Fields* (China: The Ministry of Commerce of the People's Republic of China).

Nassimbeni, G. and Sartor, M (2006) 'International Purchasing Offices in China', *Production Planning & Control*, 17(5), 494–507.

Nee, V. (1992) 'Organizational Dynamics of Market Transition: Hybrid Forms, Property Rights, and Mixed Economy in China', *Administrative Science Quarterly*, 37(1).

North, D. C. (1990) *Institutions, Institutional Change and Economic Performance* (Cambridge: Cambridge University Press).

NPC (ed.) (2004) *Foreign Trade Law of The People's Republic of China of 2004* (Congress, Standing Committee of the National People's) (Beijing).

NPCSC (ed.) (1994) *Foreign Trade Law of PRC of 1994* (Standing Committee of the National People's Congress) (California).

Peng, M. W. (1998) *Behind the Success and Failure of US Export Intermediaries: Transactions, Agents, and Resources* (Westport, CT: Quorum Books).

Peng, M. W. (2001) 'The Resource-based View and International Business', *Journal of Management*, 27(6), 803–29.

Peng, M. W. (2003) 'Institutional Transitions and Strategic Choices', *The Academy of Management Review*, 28(2), 275–96.

Peng, M. W. (2005) 'Perspectives – from China Strategy to Global Strategy', *Asia Pacific Journal of Management*, 22(2), 123–41.

Peng, M. W. (2006) *Global Strategy* (Cincinnati: Thomson South-Western).

Peng, M. W. and Chen, H. (2009) 'Strategic Responses to Domestic and Foreign Institutional Pressures in the Chinese Toy Industry', *International Studies of Management and Organization*, Available online at: http://www.utdallas.edu/~mikepeng/pdf/Peng ChenToys0808ISMOR3.pdf

Peng, M. W. and Heath, P. S. (1996) 'The Growth of the Firm in Planned Economies in Transition: Institutions, Organizations, and Strategic Choice', *The Academy of Management Review*, 21(2), 492–528.

Peng, M. W. and Ilinitch, A. Y. (1998) 'Export Intermediary Firms: A Note on Export Development Research', *Journal of International Business Studies*, 29(3), 609–20.

Peng, M. W., Ilinitch, A.Y. and Hill, C. (1998) 'Entrepreneurs as Agents in Export Trade: A Resource-Based Perspective' (Working Paper).

Peng, M. W., Wang, D. Y. L. and Jiang, Y. (2008) 'An Institution-based View of International Business Strategy: A Focus on Emerging Economies', *Journal of International Business Studies*, 39(5), 920–36.

Peng, M. W. and York, S. A. (2001) 'Behind Intermediary Performance in Export Trade: Transactions, Agents, and Resources', *Journal of International Business Studies*, 32(2), 327–46.

Perdue, B. C. and Summers, J. O. (1991) 'Purchasing Agents' use of Negotiation Strategies', *Journal of Marketing Research*, 28(2), 175–89.

Quintens, L., Matthyssens, P. and Faes, W. (2005) 'Purchasing Internationalisation on Both Sides of the Atlantic', *Journal of Purchasing and Supply Management*, 11(2–3), 57–71.

Roehl, T. (1983) 'A Transactions Cost Approach to International Trading Structures: The Case of the Japanese General Trading Companies', *Hitotsubashi Journal of Economics*, 24, 119–35.

Roehl, T. (1998) 'Is Efficiency Compatible with History? Evidence from Japanese General Trading Companies?' in Jones, G. (ed.), *The Multinational Traders* (Routledge).

Scott, W. R. (2008) *Institutions and Organizations: Ideas andIinterests* (Sage Publications, Inc.).

SETC (ed.) (1999) 'Experimental Measures for Foreign-funded Commercial Enterprises' (China, State Economic and Trade Commission of the People's Republic of China).

Spulber, D. F. (1996) 'Market Microstructure and Intermediation', *The Journal of Economic Perspectives*, 10(3), 135–52.

Spulber, D. F. (1999) *Market Microstructure: Intermediaries and the Theory of the Firm* (Cambridge, UK: Cambridge University Press).

Spulber, D. F. (2003) 'The Intermediation Theory of the Firm: Integrating Economic and Management Approaches to Strategy', *Managerial and Decision Economics*, 24(4), 253–66.

Tesfom, G., Lutz, C. and Ghauri, P. (2004) 'Comparing Export Marketing Channels: Developed Versus Developing Countries', *International Marketing Review*, 21(4/5), 409–22.

Trabold, H. (2002) 'Export Intermediation: An Empirical Test of Peng and Ilinitch', *Journal of International Business Studies*, 33(2), 327–44.

Williamson, O. E. (1979) 'Transaction-Cost Economics: The Governance of Contractual Relations', *Journal of Law and Economics*, 22(2), 233–61.

Williamson, O. E. (1985) *The Economic Institutions of Capitalism: Firms, Markets, Relational Contracting* (New York: The Free Press).

Williamson, O. E. (1988) 'The Logic of Economic Organization', *Journal of Law, Economics, and Organization*, 4(1), 65.

Williamson, O. E. (1996) *The Mechanisms of Governance* (New York: Oxford University Press).

Witt, M. A. and Lewin, A. Y. (2007) 'Outward Foreign Direct Investment as Escape Response to Home Country Institutional Constraints', *Journal of International Business Studies*, 38(4), 579–94.

Xu, H. (2000) *The Agency System in UK and US* ('Ying mei dai li fa yan jiu') (Beijing: China Law Press).

Yao, J. and Chen, G. (2001) 'A Troublesome Agency System: Export Procurement and Agency Systems Would Go Hand in Hand in post-WTO China's Foreign Trade Activities', *International Trade*, 12.

Young, S., Hood, N. and Lu, T. (1998) 'International Development by Chinese Enterprises: Key Issues for the Future', *Long Range Planning*, 31(6), 886–93.

Part III

The New Forms of International Small Businesses

Olli Kuivalainen and Simon Harris

The chapters in this part focus on international new ventures (INVs) and so-called born-global firms. In their seminal article, Oviatt and McDougall (1994) define an INV as '...a business organization that, from inception, seeks to derive significant competitive advantage from ... the sale of outputs in multiple countries' (p.49). What drives our interest in these types of firms? Born-global firms are a new breed of international organization. They are different from their earlier counterparts, having internationalized early and rapidly and having not stayed in the home markets for long before commencing international operations (for example, Cavusgil and Knight, 2009; Oviatt and McDougall, 1994). These firms, however, are extremely important from a public policy perspective in being a source of high value jobs, economic growth and exports (Wright et al., 2007). There is both academic and managerial interest in the phenomenon but the theories and frameworks for understanding it are still deficient or remain at an early phase of development (Keupp and Gassmann, 2009).

The phenomenon of born-globals and INVs began to gain wider interest both in academia and in the business literature of the late 1980s. Jones, Coviello and Tang (2011) note that *venture-type* research is one of the oldest international entrepreneurship research streams. For example, McDougall (1989) distinguished between international and domestic new ventures, and other early scholars focused on the early and rapid internationalization of small and medium-sized enterprises (SMEs) (for example Jolly et al., 1992). A parallel track that labelled rapidly internationalizing firms as 'born-globals' evolved over the subsequent decade (for example, Knight and Cavusgil, 1996, 2004; Rennie, 1993). These firms can be seen as more or less equivalent to the global start-ups which form one type of the INVs in the typology of Oviatt and McDougall (1994).

This research has focused on issues such as the speed of their entry into international markets after their foundation, reflected in the growth of their foreign sales to total sales ratio and the scale and scope of their operations (see, for example, Jones et al., 2011; Kuivalainen et al., 2007; Zahra and George, 2002). It has also extensively studied determinants or drivers of these types of firm and of their early internationalization behaviour. Externally, for example, the development of communication and transportation technologies has facilitated the formation of born-global firms (see, for example, Knight and Cavusgil, 1996). Internally, these firms have been seen to be entrepreneurial, possessing a mindset and specific skills that help them address entry barriers such as liability of newness. Bell (1995) found that the commitment of management was important in the rapid process of internationalization and in their making important related strategic decisions, while Knight and Cavusgil (1996) propose that the most distinctive feature of born-global firms is that they are managed by entrepreneurial visionaries who do not care where their customers are located.

Reflecting how these firms have tended to be defined, however, there are a number of important areas concerning the phenomenon that have remained under-explored. First, as Zahra and George's (2002) review of international entrepreneurship research argued, while we know a lot about the initial internationalization of INVs and born-global firms, we know little about what happens to them after the initial steps in the internationalization process. Even now, few studies have focused on this issue and this observation remains valid. There is very little empirical research to inform us whether early and rapid internationalization does, in fact, lead to long-term survival and success (see for example Kuivalainen et al., 2007; Wright et al., 2007).

Secondly, research in this area has focused on the outward process of internationalization rather than the inward process that has often complemented it in practice although a few exceptions naturally do exist in the extant research (see, for example, Knudsen and Servais, 2007). One of the reasons for this situation is the way these firms have often been defined. The scale of the internationalization dimension in the widely-used INV or born-global firms definitions (see e.g. Knight and Cavusgil, 2004; Oviatt and McDougall, 1994 and as quoted above) can be implicitly found ('the sale of outputs', i.e. sales) but, unfortunately, this definition relates only to outward internationalization. Consequently, the focus of most of the born-global studies has been on the determinants behind the early internationalization, on the speed with which they commence international operations, and on the foreign sales to total sales ratio.

Thirdly, we know little about how the external networks of these firms, or the international value chains that develop and evolve over time, despite the early advocacy of this by Oviatt and McDougall (1994). The development of entrepreneurial networks has been of great interest in entrepreneurship (e.g. Hite and Hesterley, 2001; Larson and Starr, 1993) but is only now coming to the attention of international business research (Kontinen and Ojala, 2010).

The fourth area, which we would especially like to highlight here, concerns our knowledge of the international management processes of the entrepreneurs and of their firms, and about the internal developments and changes in the operational modes within these businesses as they grow beyond their initial stages to become multinational enterprises in their own right. Here, the picture remains rather obscure to academics, managers and public policy makers alike. This is especially surprising because it is this, *a priori*, that would appear to be central to their success, and thereby to their performance in financial, business, growth and employment terms. There is therefore a strong argument that international entrepreneurship research interest should now turn to how these entrepreneurial firms are organized, managed and led as they eventually develop to become small multinational enterprises.

The framework presented in Table III.1 looks at international entrepreneurship research by presenting questions to define what has been the main objective of each research sub-domain, to highlight those areas where we see the greatest gaps in our knowledge. We believe that the biggest gap is in the area of how INVs and born-global firms manage and structure their internationalization, and why they do it in the way they do. The reason why this gap may have arisen is that internationalization research, in each of the three streams of the internationalization process research, the network research, and the INV/born-global research, has mostly taken a perspective that is external to the firm, and has not seen the changes within these firms, when they operate internationally, to be within their focus.

For example, while it has often been acknowledged that capabilities and resources are important, we know rather little about how entrepreneurs develop or acquire them, where they come from, and how they change as the firm grows. Here, the integration of theoretical frameworks from the rich heritage of strategic management research may help (see, for example, Verbeke, 2003; Rugman, 2008), where the resource-based view of the firm and its development and evolution into the knowledge-based view and the dynamic capability perspective may be of particular value (see e.g. Teece et al., 1997; Teece, 2007; Weerawardena et al., 2007). While recognizing the importance of networks of relationships, research has not been concerned with how entrepreneurs develop and use them, and what their strategies and actions are in doing so.

So we advocate that international entrepreneurship research should now address the forms, strategies and operations of INVs in the future as well as their evolution (see also Jones et al., 2011; Zettinig and Benson-Rea, 2008). One way forward, as advocated in some chapters here, would be to study how strong customer and partner orientation shapes the development of firms and the value of their networks over the long run. Here one possible research interest could be micro-multinationals, internationalized SMEs operating with a number of complex entry modes and having different value chain activities in a number of

Table III.1   The areas of focus of the international entrepreneurship research and the possible gaps which should be addressed

Perspective Focus	'External business aspects' perspective	'Internal management aspects' perspective
Who: Who the firms and the entrepreneurs are	The early IE research: Oviatt and McDougall (1994); Knight and Cavusgil (2004); Johanson and Valhne (1977) etc.	Subsequent IE research and entrepreneurship research as well (e.g. Andersson & Flouren, 2011)
What: The conditions and contextual factors that lead to IE firms of different types	Much subsequent IE research (see Jones et al., 2011)	More limited research but there is research about the determinants such as global mindset (e.g. Nummela et al., 2004).
How: How the firms internationalize	Network approach / Uppsala linked internationalization process associated research / INV, born-global and born again-global pathway research (e.g. Bell et al., 2003)	There are multiple studies which focus on capabilities needed to begin international operations rapidly (see e.g. Zahra et al., 2000; Karra et al., 2008). As yet research has paid little attention to the resources and capabilities that need to be accessed mobilized and coordinated to make internationalization work sustainably over time.
Why: Why the firms do it the way that they do	Network approach / Uppsala linked internationalization process associated research and INV/BG research Johanson and Valhne (2009).	As yet research has paid little attention to the internal aspects of firms that lead some firms to internationalize one way or another or not at all.

countries (see, for example, Dimitratos et al., 2003). The entrepreneurs' underlying motivations, particularly their resource combinations, specific contexts of experience, and management and decision processes influence how the firms configure their operations, choose the scale and scope of their ambitions, and define their internationalization strategy; but, here we have little knowledge. Further, it is important to know how entrepreneurial dynamism is maintained as the firms rapidly become larger multinational enterprises with more complex global operations. It is for this reason that we argue that a useful research focus now is in the management processes that are so important to making international entrepreneurial firms work effectively and develop.

The chapters in this part provide a glimpse of how INVs grow and implement their strategies. Nummela and Saarenketo tell us how an international new venture changes its strategy and its form over time; and in this chapter they focus on its operation mode change. The chapter provides us with important information about how the form of the INV changes in the course of time, and why these changes take place.

Hagen and Zucchella investigate how two entrepreneurial ventures have grown internationally by utilizing the internet as a main sales channel in their operations. The key driver of their growth has been the set of organizational capabilities and the firms' ability to exploit opportunities embedded in global e-business. McDonald and Park study the resources of the SMEs that were behind their early internationalization. The value of the value networks of the firms is proven in the development of their foreign knowledge competencies, for example. This result naturally supports the importance of networks in the internationalization of INVs (see e.g. Chetty and Campbell-Hunt, 2003; Coviello and McAuley, 1999).

Finally, Sigfusson and Harris complement these chapters by focusing on why international entrepreneur managers might build and manage their relationships by utilizing the cyberspace and Web 2.0, and how this can enable them to conduct their international business successfully. For an INV, the internet offers various possibilities as a sales channel, marketing tool and information source and, as is emphasized here, as a networking tool that offers a vehicle for eventual internationalization (see e.g. Loane, 2006).

In summary, the idea behind this part is to provide evidence especially on how international new ventures conduct international business successfully – the gap in our research that Zahra and George (2002) highlighted. While not exhaustive, the chapters in this part offer both academics and business practitioners ideas about 'how to make the internationalization process a success after the initial internationalization' and 'what kinds of resources and capabilities are needed to do this?'

References

Bell, J. (1995) 'The Internationalization of Small Computer Software Firms: A Further Challenge to "Stage" Theories', *European Journal of Marketing*, 29(8), 60–75.

Bell, J., McNaughton, R., Young, S. and Crick, D. (2003) 'Towards an Integrative Model of Small Firm Internationalisation', *Journal of International Entrepreneurship*, 1, 339–62.

Cavusgil, S. T. and Knight, G. (2009) *Born Global Firms: A New International Enterprise* (New York, NY: Business Expert Press, LLC).

Chetty, S. and Campbell-Hunt, C. (2003) 'Explosive International Growth and Problems of Success amongst Small to Medium-sized Firms', *International Small Business Journal*, 21(1), 5.

Coviello, N. E. and McAuley, A. (1999) 'Internationalization and the Smaller Firm: A Review of Contemporary Empirical Research', *Management International Review (MIR)*, 39(3), 223–56.

Dimitratos, P., Johnson, J., Slow, J. and Young, S. (2003) 'Micromultinationals: New Types of Firms for the Global Competitive Landscape', *European Management Journal*, 21(2), 164–74.

Fletcher, M. and Harris, S. (2011) 'Knowledge Acquisition for the Internationalization of the Smaller Firm: Content and Sources', *International Business Review*, 20 (forthcoming).

Hite, J. M. and Hesterly, W. S. (2001) 'The Evolution of Firm Networks: From Emergence to Early Growth of the Firm', *Strategic Management Journal*, 22(3), 275–86.

Jack, S., Moult, S., Anderson, A. R. and Dodd, S. (2010) 'An Entrepreneurial Network Evolving: Patterns of Change', *International Small Business Journal*, 28(4), 315–37.

Johanson, J. and Vahlne, J. E. (1977) 'The Internationalization Process of the Firm – A Model of Knowledge Development and Increasing Market Commitments', *Journal of International Business Studies*, 8(1), 23–32.

Jolly, V. K., Alahuhta, M. and Jeannet, J. P. (1992) 'Challenging the Incumbents: How High Technology Start-ups Compete Globally', *Journal of Strategic Change*, 1(1), 71–82.

Jones, M. V., Coviello, N. and Tang, Y. K. (2011) 'International Entrepreneurship Research (1989–2009): A Domain Ontology and Thematic Analysis', *Journal of Business Venturing*, 26(6) 632–59.

Karra, N., Phillips, N. and Tracey, P. (2008) 'Building a Born Global Firm: Developing Entrepreneurial Capabilities for International New Venture Success', *Long Range Planning*, 41(4), 440–58.

Keupp, M. M., and Gassmann, O. (2009) 'The Past and the Future of International Entrepreneurship: A Review and Suggestions for Developing the Field', *Journal of Management*, 35(3), 600–33.

Knight, G. and Cavusgil, S. T. (1996) 'The Born Global Firm: A Challenge to Traditional Internationalization Theory', *Advances in International Marketing*, 8, 11–26.

Knight, G. and Cavusgil, S. T. (2004) 'Innovation, Organizational Capabilities, and the Born-Global Firm', *Journal of International Business Studies*, 35(2), 124–41.

Knudsen, M. P. and Servais, P. (2007) 'Analyzing Internationalization Configurations of SME's: The Purchaser's Perspective', *Journal of Purchasing & Supply Management*, 13, 137–51.

Kontinen, T. and Ojala, A. (2010) 'Network Ties in International Opportunity Recognition of Family SMEs', *International Business Review*, 20(4), 440–53.

Kuivalainen, O., Sundqvist, S. and Servais, P. (2007) 'Firms' Degree of Born-Globalness, International Entrepreneurial Orientation and Export Performance', *Journal of World Business*, 42(3), 253–67.

Larson, A. and Starr, J. A. (1993) 'A Network Model of Organisation Formation', *Entrepreneurship Theory and Practice*, 17(2), 5–15.

Loane, S. (2006) 'The Role of the Internet in the Internationalisation of Small and Medium Sized Companies', *Journal of International Entrepreneurship*, 3, 263–77.

McDougall, P. P. (1989) 'International Versus Domestic Entrepreneurship: New Venture Strategic Behavior and Industry Structure', *Journal of Business Venturing*, 4(6), 387–400.

Nummela, N., Saarenketo, S., and Puumalainen, K. (2004) 'A Global Mindset – A Prerequisite for Successful Internationalization?', *Canadian Journal of Administrative Sciences*, 21(1), 51–64.

Oviatt, B. M. and McDougall, P. P. (1994) 'Toward a Theory of International New Ventures', *Journal of International Business Studies*, 25(1), 45–64.

Rennie, M. W. (1993) 'Global Competitiveness: Born Global', *McKinsey Quarterly*, 4, 45–52.

Rugman, A. (2008) 'Redefining Global Strategy: Crossing Borders in a World Where Differences Still Matter', *Journal of International Business Studies*, 39(6), 1091–93.

Teece, D. J. (2007) 'Explicating Dynamic Capabilities: The Nature and Microfoundations of (Sustainable) Enterprise Performance', *Strategic Management Journal,* 28, 1319–50.

Teece D. J., Pisano G. and Shuen, A. (1997) 'Dynamic Capabilities and Strategic Management', *Strategic Management Journal,* 18, 509–33.

Verbeke, A. (2003) 'The Evolutionary View of the MNE and the Future of Internalization Theory', *Journal of International Business Studies,* 34(6), 498–504.

Weerawardena, J., Sullivan Mort, G., Liesch, P. W. and Knight, G. (2007) 'Conceptualizing Accelerated Internationalization in the Born Global Firm: A Dynamic Capabilities Perspective', *Journal of World Business,* 42(2), 294–306.

Wright, M., Westhead, P. and Ucbasaran, D. (2007) 'Internationalization of Small and Medium-sized Enterprises (SMEs) and International Entrepreneurship: A Critique and Policy Implications', *Regional Studies,* 41(7), 1013–29.

Zahra, S. A. and George, G. (2002) 'International Entrepreneurship: The Current Status of the Field and Future Research Agenda' in M. A. Hitt, R. D. Ireland, S. M. Camp and D. L. Sexton (eds), *Strategic Entrepreneurship: Creating a new Mindset* (Oxford: Blackwell).

Zahra, S. A., Ireland, R. D. and Hitt, M .A. (2000) 'International Expansion by New Venture Firms: International Diversity, Mode of Market Entry, Technological Learning, and Performance', *Academy of Management Journal,* 43(5), 925–50.

Zettinig, P. and Benson-Rea, M. (2008) 'What Becomes of International New Ventures? A Coevolutionary Approach', *European Management Journal,* 26(6), 354–65.

7
Switching Operation Mode – A Strategic Approach

Niina Nummela and Sami Saarenketo

Introduction

International business researchers have been interested in the choice of a company's foreign operation mode since the 1960s (Hymer 1960, 1976), and there is good reason to conclude that this has become an established field of research (Benito et al., 2010; Werner 2002). Therefore, one might question whether there is really a need for another study on the subject. However, a review of the literature shows that, surprisingly, despite the quantity of prior research on the topic, it seems to be rather biased. For example, researchers seem to have concentrated their efforts on studying the company's entry into a foreign market and the operation mode chosen, and to have paid significantly less attention to what happens after the entry has been made (Canabal and White 2008; Brouthers and Hennart 2007; Welch et al., 2007; Harzing, 2002).

Foreign entry mode choice has been investigated from several theoretical viewpoints, including *internalization and transaction costs* (e.g. Anderson and Gatignon, 1986; Buckley and Casson, 1976; Kogut and Singh, 1988), *eclectic* (Dunning, 1981), and *knowledge-based* (Kogut and Zander, 1993) theories (e.g. Welch et al. 2007), and many of these might also be appropriate when trying to understand subsequent changes of operation mode. However, most of them have been developed based on empirical studies conducted among large, multinational enterprises (Schwens, 2010). Our understanding of the foreign operation modes of small and medium-sized enterprises, and the decision-making related to them, is much more limited. In our opinion, choice or change of foreign operation mode is a strategic decision, and thus it should be evaluated more broadly – instead of a market level investigation it should be studied on a company level and linked with company strategy. This kind of holistic approach would be very appropriate when studying the changes of operation modes in small and medium-sized companies.[1]

Given the aspect of change and the dynamics of operation modes (Clark et al., 1997; Petersen et al., 2000; Petersen and Welch, 2002), it is very unfortunate that only a few studies on foreign operation modes have had a longitudinal research design (Benito et al., 2009). And yet, longitudinal studies would add to our understanding not only of the choice of entry mode but also the relation of entry mode choices to later changes of operation modes (Canabal and White, 2008; Brouthers and Hennart, 2007).

Consequently, there seems still to be an opportunity for a novel contribution related to foreign operation modes, particularly from the viewpoint of small and medium-sized enterprises and applying a longitudinal research design. This study aims to describe the internationalization process of an international new venture, a small software firm, from the viewpoint of the foreign operation modes used. It takes a holistic perspective and approaches the process from the perspective of strategic decision-making.

The remainder of this chapter is structured as follows. In the following section, we will review previous research on foreign operation modes and the internationalization of small high-tech firms. The subsequent section describes the research design of the study as well as data collection and analysis. Next, the findings of the study are reported and, then, a discussion of their interpretation is offered. We conclude the chapter with suggestions for future research.

Literature review

Foreign operation mode is commonly defined as an institutional arrangement that makes it possible for a company to offer its products on foreign markets (cf. Root, 1994). Although the literature often refers to operation mode, we should actually use the term as a plural, and discuss operation modes and mode combinations or packages, because companies use multiple operation modes simultaneously (Benito and Welch, 1994; Clark et al., 1997; Petersen and Welch, 2002; Benito et al., 2009). Change of operation mode refers here to the adjustment of the initial entry mode to serve the market in an optimal way (Benito et al., 1999). According to prior knowledge, there may be several reasons for changing the operation mode, including, for example, desire for increased control in the market, performance of the local operator, reassessment of the market situation, changes in the foreign market, and changing internal conditions (Petersen et al., 2000; Benito et al., 1999). It is noticeable here, that the majority of drivers for change have been external, particularly market-related factors. Internal, organization-bound factors have aroused significantly less interest; for example, the role of top management has been largely ignored (Herrmann and Datta, 2006, 2002) although there have been suggestions for studying the composition of top management and its role (Canabal and White, 2008).

In the case of international new ventures, the key strategic decision – to go international – is made very early in the company life cycle, maybe at the time of its founding (Autio et al., 2000), or even before the company legally exists. Later, other strategic decisions include the choice of country and entry mode (Andersen 1993, 1997). These decisions are strongly intertwined in SMEs (Papadopoulos, 1987). Additionally, among software firms, the entry mode choice is entwined with the product strategy and the service model chosen (Ojala and Tyrväinen, 2006).

Researchers appear to agree that in order to reduce resource constraints and the risks involved, international new ventures often choose low-commitment entry modes (Aspelund et al., 2007). This is in line with the findings of Mullins and Forlani (2005): high-growth successful companies are very risk-averse, particularly when investing their own money. After all, later change of entry mode may be costly, risky and laborious (Pedersen et al., 2002; Petersen and Welch, 2002; Petersen et al., 2000; Calof and Beamish, 1995).

Previous studies (for example, Petersen et al., 2000) suggest that international operation mode decisions are likely to have a 'lock-in' effect that impedes the firm's ability to change. For example, having selected franchising as the operation method in a particular market, the firm may find it very difficult to terminate the franchising arrangement even though conditions change and make the mode unfavourable for the firm. Research has shown that when firms make operation mode decisions, they hardly ever consider, or plan for, future mode options, in spite of evidence that operation mode changes are quite common. While most of the studies regarding this 'lock-in' effect are conducted among the larger corporations, which more naturally experience path dependency and structural inertia, there is reason to assume that international new ventures may also grow to be 'mode myopic' (cf. Benito et al., 2009). In the case of small software firms, the dominating entry mode is exports (Bell, 1995) and it is very probable that many of these firms stick to this mode and sub-optimize their operations in the market.

In sum, most firms operating internationally will sooner or later experience switches of operation mode and, therefore, it is important to examine this phenomenon from the strategic decision-making perspective. While the existing research has often adopted a cross-sectional static perspective and external issues are predominantly used as explanatory factors of mode changes, we aim to make a contribution by taking a holistic and longitudinal approach to the topic.

Research design

This research is a longitudinal single case study. The case study approach allows for the obtaining of a deeper understanding of the phenomenon under scrutiny (see Ghauri, 2004; Yin, 2003; Eisenhardt, 1989). Conducting research on organizational change and processes in a holistic and comprehensive way is often best approached by using a longitudinal research design (e.g. Pettigrew, 1990; Van de Ven, 1992; Pettigrew et al., 2001). Given our interest in the internationalization process and, particularly, the changes in the foreign operation mode, a single case study approach was regarded as the most appropriate one.

The selection of the case is a crucial decision in the research process and should therefore be made after careful consideration and critical evaluation of the alternatives. Random selection is neither necessary nor desirable, and theoretical sampling is recommended (Eisenhardt and Graebner, 2007). This involves choosing cases that are likely to replicate or extend the emergent theory (Eisenhardt, 1989). The theoretical qualifications of the case must also be kept in mind, in other words how well they fit the conceptual categories, and the extent of their explanatory power (Eisenhardt, 1989; Smith, 1991). The company chosen as the case for this study is a small software company. As a small international new venture it provides the necessary contrast to the companies previously studied, and yet its history is long enough to offer fertile material for longitudinal research design.

The study utilizes process data – data collected at multiple points of time – to produce process theory, that is, understanding patterns in the changes of foreign operation mode through events (Langley, 1999). Thus, our study could be regarded as an exploratory one, because such studies seem to be quite exceptional among previous researches into internationalization process (e.g. Welch and Paavilainen-Mäntymäki, 2010).

Case study is a research strategy which typically uses multiple data sources to investigate a phenomenon (Piekkari et al., 2009). Also, in this study, data triangulation (cf. Denzin, 1978) was used to capture a complete, holistic picture of the subject matter. It is assumed here that the use of multiple types of data and methods will uncover something that might have been neglected in a simpler research design. (cf. Jick, 1979). Additionally, we think that the combination of different types of data increases the validity of our findings (typically considered as a weakness of case studies (e.g. Eisenhardt, 1989; Lincoln and Guba, 1985; Jick, 1979).

In line with the recommendations of Huber and Power (1985), we gathered the data for the research in face-to-face interviews with the most knowledgeable informant available, the CEO of the case company. Our investigation is based on the perception of the owner-manager, who is at the nucleus of the internationalization process, which in small firms is very much driven by the entrepreneur or the top management team (e.g. Loane et al., 2004; Manolova et al., 2002; Holmlund and Kock, 1998). In the interviews, the owner-manager was asked to look back and describe the company's internationalization. All the interviews were tape-recorded and transcribed in full in order to increase the reliability of the data. The interview data was triangulated with internal company documents and secondary data, such as articles in the popular press and company accounts.

The case company: Wipeaway

WipeAway [2] is a data security company founded in 1997, and its first commercial product was launched in 1999. The product has global potential as the number of leasing computers will increase considerably, and this will highlight the problem of data security further. Additionally, regulation encouraging attention to data security will be introduced in several countries.

The company is privately owned, but the ownership structure has changed during its history. For the three first years, the owners were the co-founders of the company but, in 2000, a venture capital organization acquired a minority of the shares. Later, some of the company's international partners gradually purchased shares in the company. At the moment, the two key owners are the CEO (one of the founders) and the head of their German partner firm. The latter also acts as the Chairman of the Board.

WipeAway is an international new venture; it has targeted international markets since its inception. Its international growth ambitions have been explicitly documented from very early on, as this excerpt from the company's business plan from year 2000 shows: 'Due to global need for the XXX software, WipeAway considers all the countries its market. However due to limited resources will concentrate to major European (Scandinavia, Germany, Great Britain and Ireland) and American markets. Because XXX can be localized relatively easy, WipeAway will make localized version of product if it can find good partners for the other markets also.'

After launching the first product in 1999 the company started growing rapidly. The company became quite soon the market leader in its home market. As the operations on the domestic market seemed to proceed smoothly, the company started looking for additional markets abroad. Also, the investors realized the potential of international markets and encouraged the management to move in that direction.

First contacts with international customers were made indirectly, following the domestic customers. For example, the company contacted the local subsidiary of a multinational company and tried to get a 'foothold' in the company. The underlying idea was to continue to make further approaches to customers within the company network. Next, direct contacts with foreign customers were also made. This was the task of an export manager based at headquarters. Customers were approached at various events, starting with a trade fair in Amsterdam in 1999. The first export deals were closed with Swedish customers in the same year.

However, the management soon realized that a home-based strategy was not going to be efficient enough; they needed to get closer to customers. Consequently, they began to select countries similar to the home market as target markets. These target markets consisted of Scandinavia and Northern Europe (particularly the Benelux countries and Germany). Other countries were not excluded but, given the limited resources of the company, the focus of activities was on the selected countries. After the selection of the market, they created country-specific strategies for each target market, and also named one person from the company as responsible for the market. Next, they focused on creating effective partnerships with the dealers in the target markets.

Encouraged by the investment of the venture capitalist, in 2000 the management started negotiations in several countries, including Australia, Hungary, Ireland, Portugal Spain, the UK and the US, and simultaneously conducted market research into Germany and Japan. The partner selection proceeded quite rapidly. Soon WipeAway had a global partner network covering four continents. The dealer network in Western Europe was quite dense, with partners in Austria, Belgium, Cyprus, Denmark, France, Germany, Greece, Hungary, Ireland, Italy, Luxembourg, the Netherlands, Norway, Spain, Sweden and Switzerland. The main world markets, such as North America and Japan were also covered, as well as the fast growing Asian countries.

At the same time, the company learned its first lessons in internationalization the hard way: closer co-operation with the partners revealed various problems and, in several cases, the partner had to be changed. Some of the processes were also very time-consuming and frustrating. The management soon realized that the partner network was not manageable and, by the end of year 2001, the company's financial situation had become alarming. Radical measures had to be taken, some of the recently recruited people had to be dismissed, and the strategy had to be reassessed.

Year 2002 became a watershed for the internationalization strategy of the company: instead of geographic spread, the emphasis was placed on profitable growth. 17 countries, altogether, were excluded from the budget of 2003 and, in order to improve the efficiency of the remaining partnerships in Scandinavia, Benelux, Germany, Japan and the UK, a new steering model was introduced. This 'franchising' model was based on the idea that all the partners would operate under the WipeAway brand. The partner companies were named accordingly (for example, WipeAway UK, WipeAway Italy etc.), even though they remained independent companies. The partners who committed to this business model received support through education and motivation, as well as 50 per cent of the profits. By the end of 2004, the model was implemented and seven international WipeAway offices operated around the world (Asia, AustralAsia, Germany, Italy, US West, US East, UK). In 2004, the company announced that, with the exception of minority ownership in their

German partner company, the company had no interest in establishing foreign subsidiaries since the franchising model seemed to work so well. The growth through partnerships and the franchising model continued in 2006–2007 with the establishment of a third office in the US and offices in France, Sweden and Canada.

However, parallel to the franchising operation, the company continued to sell directly to some customers, mainly in Scandinavia and the Benelux countries This was expected to reduce as the franchising model expanded to new countries. In addition to changes within operation mode, the original focus on public sector organizations and large, listed companies was formulated as five main customer segments: large companies; public sector; recycling centres; leasing companies; and financial institutions.

The next major turning point was in 2010, when the company introduced a new vision for developing the WipeAway Group. In fact, the development into a 'micro-multinational' company had already been taking shape for some years. Foreign direct investments had already started in 2002, when the company acquired a minority of the shares of its German partner company. The development continued with other majority ownerships of partners in Sweden and France, as well as some 'green field' investments as a result of establishing subsidiaries in the UK and the US. The most recent additions to the group were subsidiaries opened in Italy and Japan in 2010 and the company also has plans to expand into other countries (for example, Spain). Today WipeAway is an international company with two offices in the home market and nine international offices, of which seven are its subsidiaries. The group has roughly 70 employees, who represent approximately 15 nationalities, Finns being in a minority.

Although the focus of international expansion has recently been on the establishment of subsidiaries, the company has not completely abandoned other foreign operation modes. Direct sales and in-house exports continue to selected customers, although the export personnel at the headquarters act also as key account managers for the subsidiaries. Additionally, the company still has resellers in more than 30 countries, and new partnerships have been started, particularly in emerging markets such as Slovenia, Poland and Romania. In two countries, the WipeAway offices still operate on the franchising model but the situation is expected to change.

In terms of foreign operation mode, two critical strategic decisions can be identified. In 2001, drastic action was needed, and taken, in order to save the company, and a part of this strategy was the introduction of a new business model in international operations. The management was very committed to the 'franchising model' and saw it then as a solution for long-term operations. Consolidation towards a group developed gradually, as the company progressively increased its control in international markets. According to the CEO, the main motivation for changing operation mode, from the once efficiently functioning 'franchising' model to wholly- or majority-owned subsidiaries, has been the desire to increase the company's control of international operations, and also increase the commitment of their representatives in the market. Besides these rather typical reasons for mode change (cf. Welch et al., 2007), the change is partly due to the change of ownership and top management. In particular, the role of the current Chairman of the Board was decisive in this development. Naturally, also, positive cash flow was a necessary prerequisite for this, as well as a considerable attitudinal change.

Discussion and conclusions

The main motivation for this study was to examine the foreign operations modes of an international new venture, especially from the perspectives of 'operation mode switching and packaging'. This is important because it is evident that sooner or later a good number internationally active small firms will experience a switch (Welch et al., 2007). While some earlier studies have pointed out the reasons for mode switching, it is noteworthy that the focus has been predominantly on external factors. Yet hardly any studies have approached the issue from a strategic decision-making perspective.

A single-case study naturally has its limitations but in our opinion several interesting conclusions can be drawn from the case. First, it confirms some of themes that have already been addressed by other researchers. For example, it shows that foreign operation modes are really used as combinations of several modes, 'mode packages' (Benito et al., 2009), and also confirms that changes in this portfolio of operation modes may be implemented gradually.

However, one case can also be powerful in challenging a prevailing understanding and assumptions of how processes are initiated and developed. This case highlighted the fact that the choice of operation mode is not always a decision made for each market independently – on the contrary, it was a decision concerning the whole business model and strongly driven by company strategy. The mode choice is implemented, then, market-by-market, but the timing of the change of operation mode is determined by market-related factors, particularly the partner, and also the economic situation in the target market. After all, during an economic downturn investments are less expensive.

In line with earlier research (for example Welch et al., 2007), it may be concluded from this case that desire for control and commitment may be the key drivers behind mode change, but that both of them should be interpreted more broadly than previously. For a small firm, the change of foreign operation mode is a tool for managing its international growth – it wants to monitor and control its value network which has spread geographically, and it wants to do it as efficiently as possible. Adopting a full-control operation mode instead of a shared control mode is just a sign of this. In general it has very little to do with individual markets.

Furthermore, the case provides interesting new information about the drivers of foreign operation mode change. Although there are a few studies which indicate that the top management and the manager's personal characteristics may have an impact on the foreign entry mode choice (Herrmann and Datta 2002, 2006; Musteen et al., 2009), studies on the role of top management in later mode changes is practically non-existent. Our case suggests that the changes in ownership and the role of key shareholders and management might offer attractive avenues for further research. Additionally, complementing the findings of this study by increasing the number of cases and providing a cross-case analysis would validate the conclusions further. Finally, one of the next steps could also be a more in-depth examination of mode switching behaviour across the two broad categories of operation modes, i.e. full control v. shared control mode.

Notes

1. Our knowledge of this linkage in SMEs is insufficient but from the context of MNCs we know that the international corporate strategy may be a powerful explanatory factor for the entry mode choice (Harzing, 2002).
2. In order not to reveal the identity of the case company, a fictitious name was used in the chapter.

References

Andersen, O. (1993) 'On the Internationalization Process of Firms: A Critical Analysis', *Journal of International Business Studies*, 24(2), 33–46.

Andersen, O. (1997) 'Internationalization and Market Entry Mode: A Review of Theories and Conceptual Frameworks', *Management International Review*, 37(2), 7–42.

Anderson, E. and Gatignon, H. (1986) 'Modes of Foreign Entry Mode: A Transaction Costs Analysis and Propositions', *Journal of International Business Studies*, 17(3), 1–26.

Aspelund, A., Madsen, T. K. and Moen, Ø. (2007) 'A Review of the Foundation, International Marketing Strategies, and Performance of International New Ventures', *European Journal of Marketing*, 41(11/12), 1423–48.

Autio, E., Sapienza, H. J. and Almeida, J. G. (2000) 'Effects of Age at Entry, Knowledge Intensity, and Imitability on International Growth', *Academy of Management Journal*, 43(5), 909–24.

Bell, J. (1995) 'The Internationalization of Small Computer Software Firms. A Further Challenge to "Stage" Theories', *European Journal of Marketing*, 29(8), 60–75.

Benito, G. R. and Gripsrud, G. (1992), 'The Expansion of Foreign Direct Investment: Discrete Rational Location Choices or a Cultural Learning Process?', *Journal of International Business Studies*, 23(3), 461–76.

Benito, G. R. G. and Welch, L. S. (1994) 'Foreign Market Servicing: Beyond Choice of an Entry Mode,' *Journal of International Marketing*, 2(2), 7–27.

Benito, G. R. G., Pedersen, T. and B. Petersen (1999), 'Foreign Operation Methods and Switching Costs: Conceptual Issues and Possible Effects', *Scandinavian Journal of Management*, 15(2), 213–29.

134 *The New Forms of International Small Businesses*

Benito, G. R. G., Petersen, B. and Welch, L. S. (2009) 'Towards More Realistic Conceptualizations of Foreign Operation Modes', *Journal of International Business Studies*, 40(9), 1455–70.

Benito, G. R. G., Petersen, B. and Welch, L. S. (2010) 'Mode Combinations and International Operations: An Empirical Investigation', *Proceedings of the 36th EIBA Conference*, 9–11 December 2010, Porto.

Brouthers, K. D. and Hennart, J. F. (2007) 'Boundaries of the Firm: Insights from International Entry Mode Research', *Journal of Management*, 33(3), 395–425.

Buckley, P. J. and Casson, M. (1976) *The Future of Multinational Enterprise* (New York: Holmes and Meier Publishers).

Calof, J. L. and Beamish, P. W. (1995) 'Adapting to Foreign Markets: Explaining Internationalization', *International Business Review*, 4 (2), 115–31.

Canabal, A. and White, G. O. (2008) 'Entry Mode Research: Past and Future', *International Business Review*, 17(3), 267–84.

Clark, T., Pugh, D. S. and Mallory, G. (1997) 'The Process of Internationalization in the Operating Firm', *International Business Review*, 6(6), 605–23.

Denzin, N. K. (1978) *The Research Act: A Theoretical Introduction to Sociological Methods* (New York: McGraw-Hill).

Dunning, J. H. (1981) 'Toward an Eclectic Theory of International Production: Some Empirical Tests', *Journal of International Business Studies*, 11(2), 9–31.

Eisenhardt, K. M. (1989) 'Building Theories from Case Study Research', *Academy Management Review*, 14(4), 532–50.

Eisenhardt, K. M. and Graebner, M. E. (2007) 'Theory Building from Cases: Opportunities and Challenges', *Academy of Management Journal*, 50(1), 25–32.

Gartner (2008) 'Gartner Says More than 1 Billion PCs in Use Worldwide and Headed to 2 Billion Units by 2014', *www.gartner.com*, 23 June 2008, accessed 18 January 2011.

Ghauri, P. (2004) 'Designing and Conducting Case Studies in International Business Research' in Marschan-Piekkari, R. and Welch, C. (eds), *Handbook of Qualitative Research Methods for International Business* (Cheltenham: Edward Elgar), 109–24.

Hart, S. J. (1991) 'A First-time User's Guide to the Collection and Analysis of Interview Data from Senior Managers' in Smith, N. C. and Dainty, P. (eds), *The Management Research Handbook* (London: Routledge), 190–203.

Harzing, A. W. (2002) 'Acquisitions Versus Greenfield Investments: International Strategy and Management of Entry Modes', *Strategic Management Journal*, 23, 211–27.

Herrmann, P. and Datta, D. K. (2002) 'CEO Successor Characteristics and the Choice of Foreign Market Entry Mode: An Empirical Study', *Journal of International Business Studies*, 33(3), 551–69.

Herrmann, P. and Datta, D. K. (2006) 'CEO Experiences: Effects on the Choice of FDI Entry Mode', *Journal of Management Studies*, 43(4), 755–78.

Holmlund, M. and Kock, S. (1998) 'Relationships and the Internationalisation of Finnish Small and Medium-sized companies', *International Small Business Journal*, 16(4), 46–63.

Huber, G. P. and Power, D. J. (1985) 'Retrospective Reports of Strategic-level Managers: Guidelines for Increasing their Accuracy', *Strategic Management Journal*, 6(2), 171–80.

Hymer, S. H. (1960/1976) *The International Operations of National Firms* (Cambridge, MA: MIT Press).

Jick, T. D. (1979) 'Mixing Qualitative and Quantitative Methods: Triangulation in Action', *Administrative Science Quarterly*, 24(4), 602–11.

Kogut, B. and Singh, H. (1988) 'The Effect of National Culture on the Choice of Entry Mode', *Journal of International Business Studies*, 19(3), 411–32.

Kogut, B. and Zander, U. (1993) 'Knowledge of the Firm and the Evolutionary Theory of the Multinational Corporation', *Journal of International Business Studies*, 24(4), 625–45.

Langley, A. (1999) 'Strategies for Theorizing from Process Data', *Academy of Management Review*, 24(4), 691–710.

Lincoln, Y. S. and Guba, E. G. (1985) *Naturalistic Inquiry* (Thousand Oaks: Sage).

Loane, S., McNaughton R. B. and Bell, J. (2004) 'The Internationalization of Internet-enabled Entrepreneurial firms: Evidence from Europe and North America', *Canadian Journal of Administrative Sciences*, 21(1), 79–96.

Manolova, T. S., Brush, C. G., Edelman, L. F. and Greene, P. G. (2002) 'Internationalization of Small Firms. Personal Factors Revisited', *International Small Business Journal*, 20(1), 9–31.

Moen, Ø., Gavlen, M. and Endresen, I. (2004) 'Internationalization of Small, Computer Software Firms. Entry Forms and Market Selection', *European Journal of Marketing*, 38(9/10), 1236–51.

Mullins, J. W. and Forlani, D. (2005) 'Missing the Boat or Sinking the Boat: A Study of New Venture Decision Making', *Journal of Business Venturing*, 20(1), 47–69.

Musteen, M., Datta, D. K. and Herrmann, P. (2009) 'Ownership Structure and CEO Compensation: Implications for the Choice of Foreign Market Entry Modes', *Journal of International Business Studies*, 40(2), 321–38.

Ojala, A. and Tyrväinen, P. (2006) 'Business Models and Market Entry Mode Choice of Small Software Firms', *Journal of International Entrepreneurship*, 4(2–3), 69–81.

Papadopoulos, N. (1987) 'Approaches to International Market Selection for Small- and Medium-sized Enterprises' in Rosson, P. J. and Reid, S. D. (eds) *Managing Export Entry and Expansion* (New York: Praeger Publishers), 128–58.

Pedersen, T., Petersen, B. and Benito, G. R. G. (2002) 'Change of Foreign Operation Method: Impetus and Switching Costs', *International Business Review*, 11(3), 325–45.

Petersen, B. and Welch, L. S. (2002) 'Foreign Operation Mode Combinations and Internationalization', *Journal of Business Research*, 55(2), 157–62.

Petersen, B., Welch, D. E. and Welch, L. S. (2000) 'Creating Meaningful Switching Options in International Operations', *Long Range Planning*, 33(5), 688–705.

Pettigrew, A. M. (1990) 'Longitudinal Field Research on Change: Theory and Practice', *Organizational Science*, 1(3), 267–92.

Pettigrew, A. M., Woodman, R. W. and Cameron, K. S. (2001) 'Studying Organizational Change and Development: Challenges for Future Research', *Academy of Management Journal*, 44(4), 697–713.

Piekkari, R., Welch, C. and Paavilainen, E. (2009) 'The Case Study as Disciplinary Convention', *Organizational Research Methods*, 12(3), 567–89.

Root, F. R. (1994) *Entry Strategies for International Markets* (San Francisco: Lexington Books).

Sarkar, M. and Cavusgil, S. T. (1996) 'Trends in International Business Thought and Literature:
A Review of International Market Entry Mode Research: Integration and Synthesis', *The International Executive*, 38(6), 825–47.

Schwens, C. (2010), 'The Link between Entry Learning, Growth Orientation, and Mode Choice in the Internationalization of Technology Firms', *Proceedings of the 36th EIBA Conference*, 9–11 December 2010, Porto.

Smith, N. C. (1991) 'The Case-Study: A Vital yet Misunderstood Research Method for Management' in Smith N. C. and Dainty P. (eds), *The Management Research Handbook* (London: Routledge), 145–58.

Van de Ven, A. H. (1992) 'Suggestions for Studying Strategy Process Research', *Strategic Management Journal*, 13 (Special Issue), 169–91.

Welch, L.S., Benito, G. R. G. and Petersen, B. (2007) *Foreign Operation Methods. Theory, Analysis, Strategy* (Cheltenham, UK: Edward Elgar Publishing).

Welch, C. and Paavilainen-Mäntymäki, E. (2010) 'Explaining the Internationalization Process of the Firm: A Process-based Critique', *Proceedings of the 36th EIBA Conference*, 9–11 December 2010, Porto.

Werner, S. (2002) 'Recent Developments in International Management Research: A Review of 20 Top Management Journals', *Journal of Management*, 28(3), 277–305.

Yin, R. K. (2003) *Case Study Research, Design and Methods* (Thousand Oaks, CA: Sage).

8
The International Growth of e-Commerce Ventures
Antonella Zucchella and Birgit Hagen

Introduction

At the beginning of the internet era in the 1990s, the hypothesis of a borderless world was put forward and profound changes in international business practices were imagined (for example, Quelch and Klein, 1996; Hamill, 1997). Hamill (1997, p.300) saw the internet as 'a fundamentally different environment...and new international marketing paradigms may have to be developed to explain internationalization processes'.

Reality in the following years did not fully match the so-called internet hype. Together with the downturn of the new economy, starting early in the year 2000, many internet-related e-commerce businesses either failed or underperformed. One of the reasons, according to Porter (2001), was the fact that the internet was just a surrogate for firm strategy. Again, in 2010, Etemad et al. (2010) introduced the term 'internetization' and posited the internet as the necessary condition to be successful in internationalization. However, being the necessary condition does not automatically imply that it is also a sufficient condition.

After almost two decades of substantial changes in ICT, the time has come for a reflection: most of the empirical work available was done in the early years when the internet landscape was substantially less developed and this work is mainly conceptual. With this chapter, we aim at understanding the enabling role of the internet in the continued internationalization processes of e-commerce ventures (ECV). Many scholars have pointed to this relationship but little empirical evidence has been presented and longitudinal work is largely missing.

The internet diminishes distance and 'levels the playing field between companies' (Porter, 2001). By reducing problems related to size and scale, it opens up substantial opportunities for reaching international markets early and it holds the potential to speed up SME internationalization in general.

Companies, especially small ones, were expected to take advantage of the borderless internet world in their international expansion.

Following this line of thought, it was postulated that e-commerce ventures (ECV) were international or global from inception (Kobrin, 2001; Oviatt and McDougall, 1999). However, the internationalization processes of ECVs are not necessarily deterministic or homogeneous. International pathways reflect different international strategies and decisions about market scope and timing (Loane et al., 2004) and are in no way a mere question of availability and adoption of technology.

Here, we investigate the role of the internet as ECVs emerge and develop internationally. There have been many calls for researchers to pay attention to time and process effects in analysing the internet's effect on internationalization (Petersen et al., 2002; Aspelund and Moen, 2004; Mata et al., 1995). Gabrielsson and Pelkonen (2008) call for the inclusion of at least one period of crisis to properly explain the role of the internet over time. We use the case study methodology to explore the internet's impact on internationalization patterns and dimensions in a longitudinal setting. Our overall objective is to gain deeper insight into the enabling role of the internet in a firm's internationalization strategy and to add knowledge to the internet-enabled internationalization literature from a longitudinal perspective. Secondly, we will enrich international entrepreneurship (IE) by partially responding to the call of Rialp et al. (2005) for more studies 'on the nature and processes of early internationalizing firms'.

We first identify key elements in the existing literature that relate to early and rapid internationalization and use of the internet. The literature review is followed by a presentation and discussion of the cases. The chapter ends with a conclusion that focuses on the implications of our findings as regards theory, practice and policy. Research limitations and future research opportunities are outlined.

Early and rapid internationalization and the internet

The internationalization processes of SMEs have been increasingly characterized by early and accelerated expansion. Labels such as born-globals (BG) or international new ventures (INV) have been coined for those ventures that seek to achieve international revenue from or near their inception. Extant research has widely explored the factors that have given rise to the phenomenon. A number of mutually reinforcing factors facilitate their development: macro-environmental factors; organization-related factors; and founder-related factors were suggested as the main categories (e.g. Rialp et al., 2005).

Among the macro-environmental drivers of the phenomenon, advances in ICT in general and the internet in particular are considered important because they provide firms with new ways of conducting business and open new business opportunities. Many authors contend that the internet offers small firms, especially, an invaluable resource for internationalization activities, creating an immediately global reach by means of a website. Oviatt and McDougall (1999, p.8) state that 'while the small firm may not have an explicit international expansion strategy, the Web site automatically positions the firm in the international marketplace ... with the predicted explosion in electronic commerce, the Internet may greatly increase the level of internationalization of even the smallest businesses of the 21st century'. Also Kobrin (2001, p.688) comments that 'cyberspace and e-commerce are intrinsically international'. According to conceptual work and empirical studies the potential of the internet to accelerate and broaden internationalization should exist for the following reasons

(1) *The internet presents a vast source of information.* The ability to access and use information is regarded as one of the key elements in reducing uncertainty about foreign markets (Johanson and Vahlne, 1977). With the internet, information becomes location-independent and firms, regardless of their size, are able to obtain and disseminate information on a global scale. Additionally, the vast array of global information sources allows for the cross-validation of market information and thus further reduces risk and uncertainty when a firm does not possess experiential knowledge (Yeoh, 2000). Berry and Brock (2004) emphasize that, through the internet, firms have the opportunity to accumulate market-specific knowledge that traditionally might only have been acquired through direct involvement abroad. Kotha et al. (2001) and Arenius et al. (2006) noted that the internet, when properly used, can reduce the liability of foreignness and newness. Petersen et al. (2002) advance the prediction that the internet holds the potential for reducing uncertainty about foreign markets (as perceived by a firm's decision-makers) providing fast and extensive access to relevant information. Jean (2007), in the same vein, finds that SMEs use ICT to compensate for experiential learning opportunities. The internet is thus seen to enhance learning processes leading to knowledge, which adds speed to market expansion.

(2) *ICT developments diminish distance.* The internet is said to bring states and consumers closer – physically and culturally (Levitt, 1983), thus eliminating not only geographic but also psychic and cultural distance, which has been seen as a major barrier in traditional internationalization theories (Johanson and Vahlne, 1977). Whereas most studies (Aspelund and Moen, 2004; Mostafa et al., 2006) see international orientation to be causal for internet adoption, Berry and Brock (2004) argue that exposure to internationalization stimuli through active participation can potentially reduce influential attitudinal barriers and increase the international orientation

of the firm. Both elements reduce perceptional barriers, and high international orientation speeds up and broadens international expansion.

(3) *The internet can diminish communication barriers* that often occur between geographically dispersed entities. Both internal and external communication are cheaper and often more convenient with the new technology (Hamill, 1997). Advanced ICT also allows communication of a wealth of information and makes the execution of an international marketing and sales strategy possible and convenient. The internet also offers the capability of targeting specific groups or individuals precisely and enables firms to practice mass customization and 'one to one' marketing strategies (Prasad et al., 2001). In general, improved communication leads to efficiencies across the whole value. Cost reduction in approaching international markets and segments is of particular value to small firms that in general are characterized by paucity of resources.

(4) Through its universal connectivity, the *internet provides access to potential business partners*. This is probably one of the internet's key benefits for internationalizing firms. Network theory has shown that networks are crucial to internationalization because of their potential for providing credibility, knowledge ,and resources (Coviello and Munro, 1997). In the same vein, Coltman et al. (2001) posit that the internet offers a new means of maintaining and developing relationships with clients, channel partners, suppliers and network partners. The internet might therefore reduce the need for intermediaries (Quelch and Klein, 1996) and, in general, enable the small firm to conduct international business from home.[1] By extending contacts and networks, the opportunities horizon is also extended (for example, increases in unsolicited orders from abroad, contacts from potential franchisees, learning from different sources, gaining reputation and so on), which enhances accelerated and broad internationalization.

(5) The internet is expected to *transform business's marketing functions*. A direct interface with customers, suppliers, and strategic alliance partners is established which reduces costs along the entire value chain. Removal of intermediaries, or direct contact with the customer, can not only reduce costs but also increase the speed and responsiveness of transactions. This in turn potentially strengthens relationships with customers and business partners (Prasad et al., 2001). Morgan-Thomas (2009) sees the major benefit to internationalizing SMEs in relational capabilities and in supporting customer relationships. In general, the speed, interactivity, continuity, and customization capabilities of the internet enables marketers to manage customers as strategic assets (Prasad et al., 2001). Direct access to the customer also facilitates the gathering of customer-related information, thereby supporting foreign market knowledge, and it could change the relation with customers from reactive to proactive. Finding and engaging international

customers is one of the key factors facilitating early and accelerated internationalization (Yeoh, 2000).

In sum, it is suggested that small firms are able to compensate for their lack of resources by trading direct physical market embededdness for the *strategic* use of the internet (Moini and Tesar, 2005). The internet, when properly exploited, may constitute a source of both cost and differentiation advantages: it represents an opportunity to create competitive advantages by combining the new resource – the internet – with the firm's existing resource bundle. The internet, from this perspective, becomes a strategic tool and holds the promise of a fast track option for international expansion (Sinkovics and Penz, 2005).

While many people point to the fact that the internet plays a fundamental role in making international entrepreneurship possible (e.g. Aspelund and Moen, 2004; Loane et al., 2004; Mostafa et al., 2006), there has been little research into how these firms can leverage the internet effectively (Morgan-Thomas, 2009; Prasad et al., 2001; Luo et al., 2005), or how extensively it has been used (Winklhofer et al., 2007). It is crucial to reach an understanding of how dedicated internet capabilities can be developed and integrated into a broad spectrum of marketing and business activities in internationalization.

This study explores the role of the internet in the continued internationalization of e-commerce ventures (defined as buying, selling, marketing, or servicing of products, services, and information through a variety of computer networks) by examining the interactions between the internet and other factors such as business strategy, customer orientation, and marketing competencies.

Methodology

For the purpose of our case analysis, we focus on a very specific, although very interesting and promising, type of firm: e-commerce ventures, defined as those companies whose business activities are entirely internet-based. An exploratory case study approach is an appropriate research strategy when attempting to examine a 'how' or 'why' question in a contemporary set of events and a real life context (Yin, 1981, p.59; 1994, p.9). Further, longitudinal research is recommended as it permits the identification and observation of processes (Kimberly, 1976). Longitudinal studies put research into the temporal and contextual frames of reference. This involves conducting a retrospective case history to understand the context and events leading up to the present strategy, with a subsequent focus on real-time observations of the events and activities while they occur in time.

The empirical investigation of this chapter, therefore, was carried out as an exploratory, longitudinal case study of two companies: *blacksocks.com* and *YOOX.com*, which were selected (Yin, 2003) on their internet-based business model, industry, comparable value propositions and coinciding time frame.

ECVs in this research context seem to be a suitable unit of analysis for a variety of reasons. First, as Luo et al. (2005) suggest, ECVs are in a position to exploit almost all the advantages offered by the internet. Secondly, an ECV allows a better identification of the 'pure' internet impact than hybrid online exporters. Thirdly, 'pure' ECVs show how the unique internet capabilities and functions may be leveraged for early, accelerated, and broad internationalization. The distinction between internet-based and hybrid organizations has significant implications in understanding the internet's interaction with other elements of the business. For example, adopting internet operations as a market channel may require the start-up to rethink established channels of distribution, sustain short-term losses and require different competencies and financial resources (Bengtsson et al., 2007). In a similar vein, by deliberately choosing our e-businesses from mature industries, we also exclude general ICT developments from our investigation, and we add an important and growing new sector to International Entrepreneurship research (Reuber and Fischer, 2009).

We collected the available secondary information, including press releases, financial reports, press articles and corporate websites. During the survey period, the founder and key people were interviewed many times and numerous e-mails were exchanged. Interviews have been loosely structured, lasting between 60 and 100 minutes. The case informants also include customers. The internationalization process of the case companies is described over a 10 year period from their establishment up to their current state. The time frame nicely coincides for both companies. Both companies are active in a fashion industry environment, and both are characterized by innovative business ideas for mature markets and for a traditional industry. They were set up when e-commerce was in its initial stage and both use the web exclusively as their business platform towards a predominant B2C target.

In order to capture the continued internationalization of our two companies, we employ the dimensions which have been used to characterize the initial phase of BG internationalization behaviour. We thus track speed, scope and intensity, and respective growth rates over time. The modelling over time allows for the inclusion of growth rates, and thus dynamic measures that refer to changes in scope and intensity over a certain period of time.

The internationalization pattern is made up of the firm's spatial expansion, the pace by which the firms internationalize the operation modes in foreign markets, building on Jones and Coviello (2005).

Blacksocks, initially selling black socks on subscription, was co-founded by two Swiss friends in 2000. Liechti, managing director from inception, claims that the business idea came about during a Japanese tea ceremony with business partners. He had to take off his shoes and realized that his black socks did not match and, even worse, his big toe was poking out. The team now comprises eight people, focusing on core activities such as marketing, quality assurance and purchasing, as well as finance. Liechti has developed his 'structure'

Table 8.1 Key facts and figures – *blacksocks.com* and *YOOX.com*

Company name	Foundation	Industry	Markets	Employees	Turnover total Em /% foreign
blacksocks.com	1999, CH	Apparel; initially sells black socks on subscription over the internet	72, main markets CH; D, F, US	9 (8 in CH, 1 in US)	2.86 27 %
YOOX.com	2000, I	Apparel; initially sells substantially discounted designer labels over the internet	65, I, Europe (ex-Italy), US	280 (260 in I, 20 abroad)	211.9 76 %

Note: Balcksocks.com
8 employees in China; 1 in the United States

YOOX.com
260 employees in India; 20 employees in other countries

organically with an analyst programmer/IT expert joining Blacksocks in 2003, and a marketing manager for Europe in late 2005. Finance and purchasing were in the hands of the co-founder (who went back to teaching in 2005) but were taken over by Liechti. Lori Rosen, founder of a New York-based public relations firm, serves as managing partner for US operations. The business idea, unique when the business was founded, was 'socks on subscription', operating in the business-to-consumer market. Over the years, Blacksocks also became active in the business-to-business market (for example, Blacksock subscription in company incentive schemes) but emphasis was always put on the B2C segment, which requires a much higher level of resources. Blacksocks is working a global niche, targeting a customer segment of internet buyers of a similar age, sex, occupation, and salary, who are supposed to be consistent internationally. This core target is male, an office worker in a high position, more at home in a cultured environment, and aged between 30 and 50. This definition nicely fits with the characteristics of a important global internet consumer segment described as relatively young, well educated, of mid to upper economic status, male, and in professions associated with technology. Blacksocks allows each customer to select his subscription formula according to the number of shipments per year, price, and the quality of products to fit his needs and preferences. Blacksocks have also launched underwear and white T-shirts, 'anything a man does not like to shop for can become part of what we offer', and thus keeps on extending the, perhaps, narrow product niche of black socks. The range of socks is also becoming more differentiated, now offering grey, red and navy socks as well as sports socks.

The day-to-day organization itself, and the organization of the fulfilment process, are extremely quick and customer-oriented. For example, standards are defined by Oeschger, the distribution partner for inward and outward activities. The first shipment is to be delivered within 2 working days, all other shipments are guaranteed within a maximum of 8 days. This challenging objective is achieved in 99 per cent of shipments, which provides proof of best practice in e-commerce. Internally, customer requests are answered within one working day, except at weekends. This goal, too, is reached in more than 90 per cent of cases. 'All our activities that touch the customer have to be extremely quick and add value for our customer. We always use an emotional approach, aiming at making him laugh, adding a surprise etc.'

There is no adaptation of product, service, and marketing to foreign markets, and the competitive advantage is seen to be based on higher quality and service. The only adaptation is in terms of language, running the site in German, English and French and providing after-sales-service in the corresponding customer language. 'We cannot ensure a high-quality after-sales service in too many languages', says Liechti.

One of the key instruments used was communication, leveraging (mainly free) publicity. Given the novelty of the business idea, many magazines have been very co-operative in featuring press releases or conducting interviews. Success in winning awards related to the business idea, innovative design, and customer approach has also been exploited widely, as well as the use of positive testimonials such as that the Swiss president and half of the federal governing council of Switzerland wear 'Blacksocks'. This publicity provided, and still provides, exposure that would otherwise be impossible for such a small company. Customer feedback and information is also given and shared with existing or potential new customers, again enhancing reputation. Visibility and – implicitly – reputation was obtained thereby, therefore creating one of the most valuable intangible assets that a small infant firm requires.

Customer orientation, together with reputation building success, leads to retention rates of over 70 per cent and a word-of-mouth standing that brings in a substantial 20 per cent of all new customers, much greater than the percentage gained through search engines, 'even though these work excellently' according to Liechti.

The internationalization process started *from inception.* In 2000, the venture became a 'listed' company and launched its new website, including an English version. The two years after the 'big bubble' of internet hype burst proved very hard. 'After the great enthusiasm regarding internet and e-commerce these two years were characterized by panicking suppliers and suspicious clients' (Liechti).

As regards *scope,* Blacksocks started by engaging nearby German-speaking markets with marketing activities and focusing on creating sales revenues. A US franchise went online in September 2001 but was, after only a few days of operation, completely destroyed by the September 11 terrorism attack. Blacksocks currently ships to 75 countries, a number that was almost reached in the very first years of activity. *Foreign sales and subscriptions* as indicators for intensity have never really taken off. The percentage stagnated at about 20 per cent until 2005, when Blacksocks reported considerable growth in major export markets for the first time. From 2009 onwards, international sales show a continuing growth trend. Country diversity, in terms of cultural diversity and mode diversity as a proxy for innovativeness are low, since the main export markets were culturally close and direct export was the only entry mode, except for the US franchisee.

Time intensity in Blacksocks's internationalization process was initially high. However, from 2001, no new market was actively selected or entered. Expansion was left to the word-of-mouth of existing clients, leveraging its high customer satisfaction and loyalty when introducing new products, and the spill-over effect of activities in the main countries.

We preferred to invest our marketing budget in already existing markets in order to strengthen our position and just took on opportunities when presenting. blacksocks began to actively scan new markets only after 2005 and to invest in countries like Sweden, the US and Great Britain, 'markets with high potential, high computer density, internet use, broadband diffusion and a relatively low price sensitivity'. Blacksocks recently re-entered the American market. When interviewed on the most important factors for growth, Liechti mentions the increase in overall internet use from about 10 per cent in 1999 to 80 per cent in 2006 and an extreme attention to 'over-satisfying' customers.

In the following Table 8.2, a summary of key measures and of findings related to the three dimensions under investigation is given.

Federico Marchetti co-founded YOOX in 2000 with friends from a Milan-based design group. He builds a 'place of interaction' where both men and women can buy end-of-season clothing and accessories from leading designers

Table 8.2 Blacksocks: key measures and findings as regards speed, scope and intensity

- **Speed** to first export market = 2 weeks: overall time intensity initially very high
- **Scope** of internationalization almost stable over a 10 year period: 75 countries;
- **Intensity/extent** of internationalization

	1999	2002	2003	2004	2005	2006	2009	2010 3rd quarter estimate
Sales (mio $)	na	na	na	1	1.5	1.8	3	3.9
% of international sales	10	12	13	13	20	20	25	27
Growth of international sales (%)					+ 130	+ 19	na	+ 40
Subscriptions	na	na	12,000	18,000	25,000	32000	40,000	50,000

with discounts of up to 50 per cent off retail prices. 'The objective was to bridge the fashion world and the world of Internet, two realities at that time rather distant. I imagined the bright future of fashion on the Internet, the two realities just needed a carrier to bring them closer.' Two years after foundation, the company employed about 40 people and now has a team of around 280 persons (260 in Italy and 20 abroad).

Today, YOOX manages online fashion retail under three formats. The first business line is the multi-brand store *YOOX.com* which offers savvy collections of end-of-season clothing at accessible prices. When it was founded, the company's revolutionary idea went hand in hand with a trend called mass customization. At the same time, it allowed luxury brands to offload their last year's merchandise without undermining their brands, or cannibalizing sales at their existing stores, or losing control over distribution or reducing the value of their brand. YOOX is a 'never-ending shop' as Marchetti suggests. Distinct websites are built for the various countries and regions in which YOOX distributes: each one can be adapted for its communication, product assortment, pricing strategy, currency, and payment system. The second business line is *thecorner.com*, a department store of in-season collections, where every brand has its shop-in-shop. Over the years, YOOX has positioned itself as a full service provider on a global scale in order to benefit from the shift in online luxury retailing. It launched, based on the skills acquired and the relationships established (and the success achieved), the monobrand stores for some of the most important fashion brands in the world, such as Armani and Diesel.

With these three business lines, YOOX covers all customer segments (brand lovers, the fashion savvy, bargain hunters), the entire product life cycle (in-season, off-season, clearance) and all the corresponding price segments. Common to all the business lines is a minute attention to customer and fulfilment issues. YOOX provides 24/7 customer assistance in the respective customer language, manages shipment within 2–3 days of 95 per cent of all orders and practices an extremely generous returns policy. 'Internet is the communication channel that allows you to be as close as possible to your customers but logistics and distribution to the final customers, which were aspects that were neglected during the dot.com boom, are extremely important to us. In fact, our most challenging problem was to decide on a logistics structure for stocking the goods, re-packing them and sending them to the customers'.

YOOX was established as a venture-backed privately-owned company with less than 15 million Euro as starting capital. Marchetti says 'I was lucky with timing. We started in 2000 just before the internet bubble burst – if I'd been looking for money six months after that, I wouldn't have found it'.

The *internationalization* process started right from the beginning. As regards *scope*, YOOX started approaching the international market gradually with a few European markets and, over the survey period, developed the venture into a truly global company. The first areas, and still the most important foreign market areas, are Europe (excluding Italy) and the US, followed by Japan and other countries. In total, YOOX is active in 67 countries. *Foreign sales* accounted for 76 per cent of total sales in 2010 but, already in the second year, a rate of 65 per cent was reported (please see Table 8.2). Both overall sales and foreign sales show an impressive growth trend. *Country diversity*, in terms of cultural diversity and mode diversity, is extremely high, including the main international markets, such as Japan and China, that are culturally distant. The same holds true for *mode diversity*: YOOX entered both close and distant markets with independent subsidiaries, logistic platforms, and monobrand stores, thus allocating considerable financial resources to these markets. In 2009, almost all of the 15 monobrand stores were in Europe, the US and Japan, and the first – Armani – is now ready to be an early entrant into China.

Interestingly, YOOXs' *time intensity* in internationalization – although high – was initially lower than it has been in recent years and it still seems to be accelerating. With the launch of the monobrand line, YOOX increased market presence in almost all major market areas simultaneously.

Discussion

The cases show clear similarities and differences. Both businesses started with an innovative business idea for niche markets and developed an e-commerce business model. The founders matched 'economic opportunities with new technology' (Zahra and George, 2002). Both firms extended their business over time: YOOX developed two additional business lines and Blacksocks continuously

Table 8.3   YOOX.com: key measures and findings as regards speed, scope and intensity

- **Speed** of internationalization: time to first foreign market = immediately: overall speed very high throughout survey period
- **Scope** of internationalization over 10 year period: gradual start with a few European countries, in ten years development to global scale; 67 countries; subsidiaries and logistic platforms in major areas such as Europe, US, Japan, China
- **Intensity/extent** of internationalization

(Em)	2000	2002	2004	2006	2007	2008	2009	2010
sales	1	12	34	49.4	69.0	101.4	152.2	211.9
% of foreign sales	na	65	na*	70	70	71	74	76
int sales total	na	na	na	34.7	48.3	72.4	112.4	162.1
EU (ex-Italy)	na	na	na	21.8	31.7	49.5	74.4	102.8
North America	na	na	na	8.5	11.1	16.4	25.7	41.3
Japan	na	na	na	2.6	3.1	4.6	8.8	12.7
Other countries	na	na	na	0.18	2.3	0.5	0.9	2.1
Other	na	na	na	1.6	2.03	1.4	2.6	3.2
Italy	na	na	na	14.7	20.7	29	39.8	49.8

*sales fairly even split between UK, US, Germany, Italy

broadens its product portfolio. In their start-up phases, which coincided with the internet's all-time high, the founders managed to get finance to create and implement a very costly structure. But, with the crash of the new economy they were faced with scepticism from market partners and an extremely thin financial resource base. Consequently, marketing budgets – important to create visibility, reputation and website traffic – were limited in the case of YOOX and almost non-existent for Blacksocks. *The internet made the niche more attractive because of its potential to act on a global segment, enabling a new way of doing business.*

Marketing strategies focused on customer-centred emotional and high-quality approaches, together with an extreme attention to fulfilment and reputation building activities. YOOX sets up local websites with country-specific content in terms of collections, prices and payment methods, on so on, and ensures there is customer assistance in the customer's language in order to meet local customer needs. For Blacksocks, the website and 'after sales service' is in only three different languages because they feel they cannot guarantee a high standard in too many languages, indicating that the firm cannot handle too great a 'cultural', that is, language, diversity. Communication and reputation building is mainly based on (free) publicity and word-of-mouth. *The internet enables mass customization, offers a rich and convenient communication channel and, due to its connectivity, acts as a multiplier of marketing activities. Moreover, the internet-based business rests in both cases on the development of dedicated capabilities, especially in terms of customer management.*

The integrated purchasing, inventory and distribution systems allow an extremely efficient fulfilment process. Considerable cost reduction is achieved across different business lines in the case of YOOX. They also support direct and constant communication across markets and link IT functions with selling platforms, distribution centres, and suppliers in different markets. The systems not only link different functions within the firm but also enable inter-firm linking. For YOOX these intra-firm linkages and related technology competences have helped to generate strategic alliances and build new business with major fashion houses that were initially very reluctant to engage in online shopping.

Both firms exhibit strong managerial capabilities when it comes to customer orientation. E-commerce definitely permits both businesses to obtain, absorb and transmit information more quickly to external and internal business partners. Routines are extremely efficient and reaction times extremely short. Rapid response, optimum fulfilment and problem solving also lead to better relationships and enhance customer satisfaction and loyalty.

Multi-directional information enabled by the internet facilitates exchanges and organizational learning, allowing partners in different locations to be involved and the business to learn from local sources. Both firms leverage knowledge and resources gained from partners and customers into new products and business line development. *The internet's network contribution, interactivity and connectivity are therefore confirmed.*

In both cases, the internet demonstrates its role in *transforming business practice.* This is especially evident in YOOX where luxury companies, at the beginning, were strongly sceptical about e-commerce, believing this channel would be unable to deliver the level of purchasing experience they considered necessary to protect brand equity. The appealing aspect of the business idea was to open an alternative sales channel that attracted the industry and its partners because it allowed them to offload last season's merchandise in a 'non-cannibalizing' way. Over the years, the successful introduction of flagship stores underlines the growing importance of the virtual market place and the change in customer behaviour. For both firms, e-commerce enabled a *profitable* niche *strategy – it diminishes distance but only at an initial stage.*

Both companies started internationalization immediately and on a broad scale. Although they concentrated initially on the domestic and on a few European markets, they achieved a quasi-automatic expansion in terms of number and type of foreign markets. Scope is comparable over the survey period, both companies being active in about 70 markets but speed and degree or intensity of internationalization is not. Whereas Blacksocks displayed a long period of stasis and de-internationalized from one major market, YOOX expanded at a constant pace which now seems to grow ever faster. Over the years, YOOX developed into a true global player, whereas Blacksocks's foreign sales never really took off. YOOX varied entry modes and increased its commitment in major markets, such as the US, Japan and China, where independent subsidiaries and logistic platforms were built. Therefore, *e-commerce seems to overcome barriers associated with physical presence at an initial stage. It supports a naturally international orientation but its fulfilment depends on which capabilities and resources are developed.* In particular, complex and strategic markets (Zucchella, 2010) seem to require physical and local commitment.

Conclusions

Case evidence on these two e-commerce ventures in mature industries was screened over a 10 year period. Firms were analysed regarding their internationalization processes, with a focus on the influence of the internet and how this was leveraged in international expansion.

More precisely, we investigated how an internet-based business model interacts with other factors such as the niche business strategy, international vision, customer orientation, marketing competencies and on so on, which all influence internationalization. This leads to the broader question of whether internet-enablement can be the source of sustained competitive advantage to a firm in its internationalization process. To answer this question, a longitudinal view gives a more complete idea of whether e-commerce or internet-enablement may generate a more sustained, better performance in international markets (Mata et al., 1995).

Our case evidence shows that innovation – differentiation, reputation, and customer orientation related capabilities – are the major sources of a sustained competitive advantage that can be leveraged internationally through the use of the internet. They are valuable to e-commerce start ups when leveraged to reduce uncertainty, differentiate products and services, and to gain website traffic (Prasad et al., 2001; Iyer et al., 2002; Luo et al., 2005), and they remain of key importance throughout the venture's development. In the virtual internet marketplace, reputation building is the key element in the early phase because of its uncertainty-reducing effect both for customers (Reuber and Fischer, 2009) and other business partners. The market scope and the pace of our ECVs was initially high, as the internet, almost by chance, opened up markets that, due to their cultural or geographical distance, would not have been taken into consideration otherwise. However, with increased market diversification, different consumer needs and habits require product and service adaptation, and innovation and differentiation activities were crucial to increase foreign sales and market penetration. Customer orientation also relates to customer involvement: here it provided valuable information from foreign markets and led to the identification of new business opportunities. These capabilities built the basis for both increased market penetration and an extension of the niche; and they protected these firms from imitation.

Our case evidence also indicates that even ECVs find it difficult to operate internationally without establishing local or physical facilities at a later stage. Traditional and local communication channels, such as word-of-mouth, exposure in local newspapers and magazines and so on, were necessary to build reputation in the virtual internet marketplace (Reuber and Fischer, 2009). Supplementary modes of operation are necessary in important and complex markets. This might be due to fulfilment issues related to physical products but we also find evidence that, for successful market penetration, firms are confronted with a range of demands and a need for knowledge that goes beyond offering a local or a foreign language website (Kotha et al., 2001).

Our cases therefore illustrate that the rate at which internationalization continues is not simply tied to the 'internetability' (Iyer et al., 2002) of markets; it is a function of the companies' entrepreneurial, innovative and marketing capabilities. Our findings empirically confirm the arguments advanced by strategy researchers in the IT field (Mata et al., 1995): sustainable growth lies in the ability to conceive, develop and exploit IT applications to support other business functions, both internal and external to the firm. They are also in line with IE research that views 'born-global' firms as possessing entrepreneurial competencies, and innovation and marketing capabilities (Zahra and George, 2002; Knight and Kim, 2009; Aspelund, Madsen and Moen, 2007) that are difficult to imitate and substitute.

Our findings are important to managers in that they underline the importance of both technology and managerial skills that effectively leverage the internet and their integration into the firm's international strategy. We also advise managers to explore, and make use of, the internet in enabling new ways of doing business in order to be effective and gain a competitive advantage. Policy makers should raise awareness and promote the benefits of using the technology. They should motivate SMEs to invest in appropriate internet infrastructure and applications, and seek to improve the ICT skill bases of such firms. The importance of the internet will grow even more dramatically as ever more customers and businesses adopt it.

In conclusion, our study contributes to the knowledge of how early, fast and broad internationalization processes of young and small ventures evolve and it provides two specific examples of the internet's potential as an internationalization enabler. It shows that even for pure e-commerce firms the virtual marketplace has to be complemented with physical marketplace interactions in order to achieve continued growth in foreign markets. However, it also shows that, for our firms, the internet is much more than just an internationalization enabler: without this strategic tool, these firms would not be in existence.

Note

1. The internet has been seen as a potentially effective channel to both domestic and international markets. Most of the extant research has concentrated on channel conflict or on the development of a hybrid approach to distribution channels. Concentrating on 'pure' e-commerce, this topic is beyond the focus of our work. Please see a discussion of these issues in, for example, Gabrielsson and Gabrielsson, 2011.

References

Arenius, P., Sasi, V. and Gabrielsson, M. (2006) 'Rapid Internationalisation Enabled by the Internet: The Case of a Knowledge Intensive Company', *Journal of International Entrepreneurship*, 3(4), 279 –90.

Aspelund, A., Madsen, T. and Moen, Ø. (2007) 'A Review of the Foundation, International Marketing Strategies, and Performances of New Ventures', *European Journal of Marketing*, 41(11/12), 1423–48.

Aspelund, A. and Moen, Ø. (2004) 'Internationalization of Small High-Tech Firms: The Role of Information Technology', *Journal of Euromarketing*, 13(2), 85–105.

Bengtsson, M., Boter, H. and Vanyushyn, V. (2007) 'Integrating the Internet and Marketing Operations – A Study of Antecedents in Firms of Different Size', *International Small Business Journal*, 25(1), 27–48.

Berry, M. M. J. and Brock, J. K. U. (2004) 'Marketspace and the Internationalisation Process of the Small Firm', *Journal of International Entrepreneurship*, 2, 187–216.

Coltman, T., Devinnery, T., Latukefu, A. and Midgely, D. (2001) 'E-business: Revolution, Evolution, or Hype?', *Californian Management Review*, 44(1), 57–86.

Coviello, N. and Munro, H. (1997) 'Network Relationships and the Internationalization Process of Small Software Firms', *International Business Review*, 6, 361–86.

EMarketer (1999) *The eGlobal Report* (July), *http://www.emarketer.com*.

Etemad, H., Wilkinson, I. and Dana, L. P. (2010) 'Internetization as the Necessary Condition for Internationalization in the Newly Emerging Economy', *Journal of International Entrepreneurship*, 8(4): 319–42.

Gabrielsson, M. and Gabrielsson, P. (2011) 'Internet-based Sales Channel Strategies of Born Global Firms', *International Business Review*, 20, 88–99.

Gabrielsson, M. and Pelkonen T. (2008) 'Born Internationals: Market Expansion and Business Operation Mode Strategies in the Digital Media Field', *Journal of International Entrepreneurship*, 6, 49–71.

Gregory, G., Karavdic, M. and Zou S. (2007) 'The Effects of E-commerce Drivers on Export Marketing Strategy', *Journal of International Marketing*, 15(2), 30–57.

Hamill J. (1997) 'The Internet and International Marketing, *International Marketing Review*, 14(5), 300–23, *http://www.blacksocks.com*, *http://www.YOOX.com*.

Iyer, L. S., Taube, L., and Raquet, J. (2002) 'Global E-commerce: Rationale, Digital Divide, and Strategies to Bridge the Divide', *Journal of Global Information Technology Management*, 5(1), 43–60.

Jean, R. (2007) 'The Ambiguous Relationship of ICT and Organizational Performance: A Literature Review, *Critical Perspectives on International Business*, 3(4), 306–21.

Johanson, J. and Vahlne, J. E. (1977) 'The Internationalization process of the Firm. A Model of Knowledge Development and Increasing Foreign Market Commitment', *Journal of International Business Studies*, 8, 23–32.

Jones, M. V. and Coviello, N. E. (2005) 'Internationalisation: Conceptualising an Entrepreneurial Process of Behaviour in Time', *Journal of International Business Studies*, 36, 284–303.

Kimberly, J. R. (1976) 'Organizational Size and the Structuralist Perspective: A Review, Critique, and Proposal', *Administrative Science Quarterly*, 21(4), 571–97.

Knight, G. A., and Kim, D. (2009) 'International Business Competence and the Contemporary Firm', *Journal of International Business Studies*, 4(2), 255–73.

Kobrin, S. J. (2001) 'Terrioritality and the Governance of Cyberspace', *Journal of International Business Studies*, 32(4), 687–704.

Kotha, S., Rindova, V. P. and Rothaermel, F. T. (2001) 'Assets and Actions: Firms-Specific Factors in the Internationalization of U.S. Internet Firms', *Journal of International Business Studies*, 32(4), 769–91.

Levitt, T. (1983) 'Globalization of Markets', *Harvard Business Review*, 61(May/June): 92–102.

Loane, S., McNaughton R. and Bell J. (2004) 'The Internationalization of Internet-Enabled Entrepreneurial Firms: Evidence from Europe and North America', *Canadian Journal of Administrative Science*, 21(1), 79–96.

Luo, Y., Zhao, J. and Du, J. (2005) 'The Internationalization Speed of E-commerce Companies: A Empirical Analysis', *International Marketing Review*, 22(6), 693–709.

Mata, F. J., Fuerst, W. L. and Barney, J. B. (1995) 'Information Technology and Sustained Competitive Advantage: A Resource-Based Analysis,' *MIS Quarterly*, 19(4), 487–505.

Moini, H. and Tesar, G. (2005) 'The Internet and Internationalisation of Smaller Manufacturing Enterprises', *Journal of Global Marketing*, 18(3), 79–94.

Morgan-Thomas, A. (2009) 'Online Activities and Export Performance of the Smaller Firm: A Capability Perspective?', *European Journal of International Management*, 3(3), 266–85.

Mostafa, R., Wheeler, C. and Jones M. (2006) 'Entrepreneurial Orientation, Commitment to the Internet and Export Performance in Small and Medium Sized Exporting Firms', *Journal of International Entrepreneurship*, 3, 291–302.

Oviatt, B. M. and McDougall, P. P. (1999) 'A Framework for Understanding Accelerated International Entrepreneurship' in Rugman, A. M. and Wright, R. W. (eds), *Research in Global Strategic Management: International Entrepreneurship* (Stanford, CT: JAI Press), 23–40.

Petersen, B., Welch, L. S. and Liesch, P. (2002) 'The Internet and Foreign Market Expansion by Firms: Theoretical Questions and Three Predictions', *Management International Review*, 42(2), 207–21.

Porter, M. E. (2001) 'Strategy and the Internet', *Harvard Business Review*, March, 63–78.

Prasad, V. K., Ramamurthy, K. and Naidu, G. M. (2001) 'The Influence of Internet-Marketing Integration on Marketing Competencies and Export Performance', *Journal of International Marketing*, 9(4), 82–110.

Quelch, J. A. and Klein, L. R. (1996) 'The Internet and International Marketing', *Sloan Management Review*, 37(3), 60–75.

Reuber, A. R. and Fischer, E. (2009) 'Signalling Reputation in International Online Markets', *Strategic Entrepreneurship Journal*, 3(4), 369–86.

Rialp, A., Rialp, J. and Knight, G. A. (2005) 'The Phenomenon of early Internationalizing Firms: What do we Know after a Decade (1993–2003) of Scientific Inquiry?', *International Business Review*, 14, 147–66.

Sinkovics, R. and Penz E. (2005) 'Empowerment of SME Websites: Development of a Web-Empowerment Scale and Preliminary Evidence', *Journal of International Entrepreneurship*, 3(4), 303–15.

Winklhofer, H., Houghton, K. and Chesney, T. (2007) 'How Advanced are Websites of SME Exporters? An Investigation into Drivers and Inhibitors', *Advances in International Marketing*, 17, 395–426.

Yeoh, P. L. (2000) 'Information Acquisition Activities: A Study of Global Start-Up Exporting Companies', *Journal of International Marketing*, 8(3), 36–60.

Yin, R. K. (1981) 'The Case Study Crisis: Some Answers', *Administrative Science Quarterly*, 26(1), 58–65.

Yin, R. K. (2003) *Case Study Research: Design and Methods* (3rd edn, vol. 5, Thousand Oaks, CA: Sage Publications Inc).

Zahra, S. and George, G. (2002) 'The Net-enabled Business Innovation Cycle and the Evolution of Dynamic Capabilities', *Information Systems Research*, 13(2), 147–50.

Zucchella, A. (2010) 'Analysing the Moves of International Entrepreneurial Organisations: The Entry of SMEs to Complex Markets' in Nummela, N. (ed.), *International Growth of Small and Medium Sized Enterprises* (New York: Routledge).

9
The Type and Number of Resources and the Performance of Early Internationalizing South Korean SMEs

Frank McDonald and Taekyung Park

Introduction

The growth of research into 'born-globals' (Bell, 1995; Madsen and Servais, 1997) led to research that has expanded our knowledge of early international-izing SMEs (Jones and Nummela, 2008). The literature has investigated the major drivers of the internationalization process of SMEs and the problems associated with fast growth in international markets (Chetty and Campbell-Hunt, 2003; Sujrez-Ortega, 2003). These drivers include: the role of learning; the transmission of knowledge; the acquisition and development of tangible and intangible resources; the acquiring of competencies and routines; the importance of social and relationship capital in the development of trust-based networks; and a host of industry and country-specific issues (Chetty and Blankenburg, 2000; Loane and Bell, 2006; Ojala, 2009; Zucchella et al., 2007). Many of the major drivers of the internationalization of SMEs embrace factors that are connected to the resource-based view of the internationaliza-tion process of SMEs (Westhead and Wright, 2001). There have been many empirical studies of the effects of the key resources that are thought to drive this process on the internationalization of SMEs (Andersson et al., 2004; Chetty and Blankenburg, 2000; Coviello and Munro, 1997; Knight et al., 2004). These studies have focused on different types of resource thought to effect the rapid internationalization of SMEs. There are few studies, how-ever, based on large quantitative studies of the effect on performance of such resources. Furthermore, there have been no studies investigating both the type and the number of resources considered to drive the internationalization process. Thus, although theory and empirical evidence has been developed on the early internationalization by SMEs, there is still a lack of evidence in terms of both the type and volume of resource use. Most of the studies on the internationalization of SMEs has also focused on the USA and Europe, with few studies on Asian SMEs. Consequently, there is a lack of evidence from large quantitative studies on the impact of key factors and the importance of the effect of the number of major resources on the performance of SMEs in an Asian context. This makes it difficult to provide policy and managerial advice that is likely to help SMEs in Asian economies to prosper from their internationalization processes.

This chapter investigates the impact of some of the major resource drivers of internationalization by early internationalizing SMEs in South Korea. It also considers the impact of the number of employees and networks devoted to international business activities. The effect on performance of the number of employees devoted to R&D activities is also considered. The chapter provides evidence from tests on the effects of these factors on two measures of performance (satisfaction with foreign market growth and share of sales from international activities) and also on the competencies of firms to work in international business activities. This approach secures evidence from which to begin the process of developing a more robust set of policy and managerial issues on the topic of how to more effectively plan and manage the internationalization processes of early internationalizing SMEs. By considering the relatively neglected area of the number of resources connected to international business activities, the chapter also makes a contribution towards the theory of SME internationalization.

The chapter begins by deriving a conceptual framework for the major resource drivers of internationalizing SMEs from the foreign performance and foreign knowledge competencies of such firms. The data gathering and analysis is then outlined, followed by the results and a discussion. Finally some conclusions are drawn from the study.

Conceptual framework

The existing literature suggests that at least three major resources have an impact on performance and the competencies to engage in international business activities. These are the education level of the CEO, the international business experience of managers, and the use of network relationships. There are also three other factors connected to the number of resources that we argue affect the internationalization process of SMEs. These factors are the number of network relationships, the number of employees devoted to R&D activities, and the number of employees devoted to international business activities.

The level of education of the CEO is identified as an important resource for internationalization (Zahra et al., 2000). In general, the literature suggests that the higher the level of education of the CEO, the better performance of the firm (Acedo and Jones, 2007; Zucchella et al., 2007). The arguments rest on the view that the higher the level of education, the more likely that the firm will have a leader with the knowledge and outlook to devise robust internationalization strategies and acquire and utilize the resources necessary to implement these strategies effectively.

The benefits from the international business experience of managers arise from enhanced competencies to search for useful information (Eriksson et al., 1997) and to compensate for the limited international business experience of the firms for which they work (Shrader et al., 2000). Managers with this experience can also find sources of information about foreign markets quickly (Autio et al., 2000; Zucchella et al., 2007). Importantly, they are more likely to have a global orientation that boosts the capacity of firms to operate effectively in foreign markets (Leonidou et al., 1998). The effectiveness of international knowledge transfer management can be enhanced by the development of the capabilities and routines necessary for international business activities (Loane and Bell, 2006), and also in the development of the human and non-human resources required to succeed in foreign markets (Acedo and Jones, 2007).

Obtaining value from networks via acquisition, and the development of information, human and non-human assets, capabilities and routines is strongly highlighted in the literature (Elango and Pattniak, 2007; Mudambi and Zahra, 2007; Zucchella et al., 2007). Network relationships are also useful for gaining knowledge about technology to meet the demands of foreign markets and for market intelligence and product development to enable effective operations in international markets (Chetty and Campbell-Hunt, 2003). Networks that provide valuable assets and knowledge are likely to be expanded in number as firms internationalize (Andersson et al., 2004; Belso-Martinez, 2006). Most of this literature focuses on deepening network relationships by using social capital to build trust to extract more value from networks, and thereby boost performance (Loan and Bell, 2006; Ojala, 2009). Firms will however need to expand the number, as well as the intensity of use, of network relationships in order to obtain sufficient assets to gain access to, and to develop, supply channels, and to manage regulatory systems in foreign markets (Bell et al., 2004; Sujrez-Ortega, 2003). As more foreign markets are penetrated and existing foreign markets are developed, it is likely that more network relationships will be required. Thus while developing deeper network relationships is likely to be connected to obtaining value from existing networks, a larger number of networks is needed as the number of countries and the depth of penetration of foreign markets develops. Network relationships therefore have both a type (or quality or value) component and a number component. The existing literature tends to conflate these two attributes of network relationships.

The R&D intensity of firms is considered to have important implications for internationalizing by SMEs (Autio et al., 2000; Bell et al., 2004; Lu and Beamish, 2006). The ability to adjust products and production and distribution systems to the demands of foreign markets is enhanced by the extent to which firms engage in R&D activities (Zahra et al., 2000). Thus the number of workers devoted to R&D actvities will be an important factor in sucessful internationalization strategies.

All of the resources mentioned above have at least some literature that explores the relationship between these factors and the internationalization processes of SMEs. There is however little on the number of networks or the intensity of R&D. In the case of the number of employees devoted to international business operations, no literature could be found by the authors. Neverthless, SMEs that engage in significant international business activities, which is common among many early internationalizing SMEs, are likely to require a large number of employees that spend most of their time on international business activities.

The literature in the case of all of these resources, except the number of employees devoted to international business activities, predicts that performance and competencies for engaging with foreign markets is likely to be a positive relationship. It would seem to be logical that the number of employees devoted to international business activities would also be positively related to these outcomes. However, it is also possible that the relationship between the number of networks and the number of employees devoted to international business relationships is not linear. An inverted U-shaped relationship between these resources and performance and foreign knowledge competencies would indicate the possibility of over-use of these resources. In principle, it is also conceivable that R&D expenditures for enagaging successfully in international business activities could be over extended. However, it was not possible to obtain data on those R&D expenditures that were explicitly related to international business activities, whereas the data for the other two volume measures are directly related to such activities. Therefore the chapter only checks for an inverted U-shaped relationship for number of network relationships and for number of employees devoted to international business activities.

In the case of the major controls, four major factors emerge from the literature – firm age, industry technology, firm size, and government support. Experiential learning is likely to grow with age (Autio et al., 2000) and firms with a long tenure in international business are also likely to have a positive effect on international performance because they gain resources and skills (Jantunen et al., 2005; Zahra et al., 2000). The extent of industry technology intensity affects the international activities and performance of firms due to the absorptive capacity for technology and innovation that is prevalent in the industry (Ang, 2008). Firm size is taken into account because larger SMEs have more resources, which helps them to compete effectively in foreign markets (Jantunen et al., 2005). Government support is influential for a firm's engagement in international activities, given that nearly all international entrepreneurial firms are small in size and resource-constrained and therefore benefit from help from government agencies (Fischer and Reuber, 2003).

The conceptual model is illustrated in Figure 9.1

Sample and data collection

'Early internationalizing firms', defined using the South Korean definition of SMEs, embraces firms employing less than 300 employees that have entered foreign markets within six years of establishment. As there is no national database of such firms in South Korea, following Nummela et al. (2004), a number of sources were used to identify the population of firms. Four main

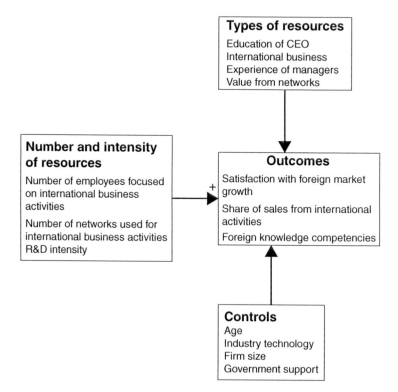

Figure 9.1   Types and number of resources and performance outcomes

sources were used: a survey conducted by the Small and Medium Business Administration in 2006; the membership lists of INNO-BIZ firms (*www.inno-biz.net*); the Bio Venture Association (*www.kobioven.or.kr*); and the database of the Korea Venture Industry Association (*www.venture.or.kr*). A list of 1,625 firms resulted, all of which were surveyed to obtain a large number of responses.

The construction of the questionnaire was informed by consideration of questionnaires used in similar types of studies (Acedo and Jones, 2007; Elango and Pattnaik, 2007; Ellis, 2007; Knight et al., 2004). The questionnaire, written in English and translated into Korean, was then reviewed by two English speaking Korean academics, who were experienced in conducting surveys. The academics checked for inappropriate translations and they identified questions that were likely to be misunderstood. Revision of the questionnaire, following advice from the Korean academics, led to the piloting of the questionnaire in ten firms. The pilot tests led to further modifications to some of the questions. The sample was reduced to 1,463 because of incorrect addresses. A total of 323 responses were returned, of which 52 were eliminated because they did not meet the requirements of the study. The response rate of 18.5 per cent is similar to other studies in this field (e.g. Wu et al., 2007).

Consideration of the major characterizitics of the sample reveals, as shown in Table 9.1, that approximately 50 per cent of the firms are centred in two industries (radio, TV and communications equipment, and chemicals and chemical products), and 37 per cent are involved in the production of various types of electronic, electrical and mechanical machinery and equipment. Nearly all the firms are located in the manufacturing sector. Most of the firms (78 per cent) employ 50 or fewer employees and just over a third have been established since 2001. Slightly more than 50 per cent began international business activities before the end of the second year of their establishment. The modal number of countries supplied is three: the main first entry mode was exporting (62 per cent) but 28 per cent of first entry modes involved licensing, international joint ventures, foreign production plants and the opening of sales offices overseas. Inspection of the revenue from foreign activities reveals that international business activities are an important source of income, and that the dominant source of these revenues is from exporting. The proportion of total revenue accounted for by foreign sales is high (a mean of 45 per cent). A high share of revenue from foreign sales has been found in other studies of early internationalizing South Korean firms (Kim and Jung, 2007; Lee and Bae, 2003).

The picture that emerges from the sample reveals a group of young, mainly small, firms that are engaged in international business activities that involve a number of entry modes, but the primary method is exporting. These firms supply three countries on average and receive a significant share of their revenue from international activities. The majority of the firms are fast internationalizers that entered foreign markets within the first two years of their existence.

Table 9.1　Sample characteristics (*N* = 271)

Characteristic	%	Characteristic	%
Year of establishment		**Number of foreign markets**	
Before 1990	6.4	1–3	56.9
1991–1995	8.8	4–6	33.2
1996–2000	49.6	7–9	5.1
After 2001	35.2	9–12	3.3
		Mode = 3 markets (33.9%)	
Industry (ISIC 2 digit)		**Speed of internationalization**	
Radio, TV and comm equip and		Year 1	35.1
apparatus (32)	30.3	Year 2	17.3
Chemicals and chemical		Year 3	12.5
products (24)	19.2	Year 4	10.7
Machinery and equipment (29)	11.8	Year 5	11.1
Electrical machinery and		Year 6	13.3
apparatus (31)	11.4		
Medical, precision and			
optical inst (33)	9.2		
Basic metals (27)	7.0		
Office, accounting and comp			
machinery (30)	4.4		
Others (15, 18, 20, 21, 22, 26, 28,			
34, 36 and 92)	6.7		
Number of employees		**First foreign market entry mode**	
10 or less	10.7	Exporting	62.0
11–20	25.1	Licensing	12.2
21–50	42.1	Opening offices overseas	8.4
51–100	13.7	Overseas production and JVs	7.4
101–150	4.8	Contracts from exhibitions	5.9
151–200	2.9	Importing for resale	1.1
201–300	0.7	Other	3.0
Foreign revenue		**Foreign revenue source**	
(as % of total sales)		**(% of total sales)**	
1–20	33.9	Export sales (mean 37.7, SD	
21–40	20.7	32.81). No. of firms = 254.	
41–60	14.8	Resale of imports (mean 3.68, SD	
61–80	14.0	12.16). No. of firms = 60.	
81–100	16.6	Sales licensing and royalties	
Mean = 45%		(mean 2.18, SD 8.76). No. of	
		firms = 28. Other (mean 4.79,	
		SD 14.53). No. of firms = 70.	

To test for non-reponse bias, extrapolation methods were used (Armstrong and Overton, 1997). The *t*-tests revealed no signficant differences between early and late responders, indicating that non-response bias is unlikely to be a serious problem. Since most of the data for the constructs were obtained from respondents, common method variance (CBV) could occur. To check for this problem, the Harman's single factor test revealed no significant problems were likely (Podsakoff and Organ, 1986). Furthermore, as the study only assesses the significance of the explanatory variables, and does not assess the importance of the variables on the dependent variables by using the size of the coefficients, any problems of CBV are unlikely to affect the validity of the results (Doty and Glick, 1998).

Variable constructs and testing techniques

The dependent variables are foreign knowledge competencies, satisfaction with foreign market growth, and share of sales from international activities. Using Aspelund and Moen (2005) and Knight and Cavusgil (2004) to guide possible measure of foreign knowledge competencies, three measures amenable to South Korean conditions emerged from the advice of the South Korean experts. These are international customer satisfaction, development of technology for international activities, and knowledge acquisition about international markets. The two measures for international performance were satisfaction with foreign market growth and share of sales from international activities. These measures for performance used the type of approach of Knight and Cavusgil (2004) as a starting point to determine measures, which were subsequently refined through the advice from the Korean academics and the results of the pilot tests. The measures of foreign knowledge competencies and of satisfaction about foreign market growth were based on assessments by managers of their views on knowledge competences required to operate in foreign markets, and of satisfaction with their foreign market growth, relative to their major competitors, over a period of three years (See Table 9.2). This method of measuring avoids requiring managers to disclose confidential information. Furthermore, it does not require managers to retrieve and process detailed financial and other data to assess their competences and performance. The three year period for the comparsions with major competitors also enables managers to provide an assessment that miminizes the effects of short run effects that may arise from temporary factors. Approaches similar to this of comparing foreign performance capacity and performance measures with major competitors has been established in other studies in this area (e.g. Knight et al., 2004). The other measure of performance (share of sales from international activities) was based on data reported on share of sales over the last three years.

The explanatory variables are the international business experience of managers, value and number of network relationships, education of CEO, R&D intensity, and number of employees mainly involved with international business actvities (IBA).

Three factors have commonly been used to measure the international business experience of managers: experience of international business activities

(Mudambi and Zahra, 2007; Nummela et al., 2004); experience of foreign travel (Leonidou et al., 1998; Ruzzier et al., 2007); and foreign language ability (Acedo and Jones, 2007; Zucchella et al., 2007). These measures were therefore used to construct the variable for the international business experience of managers. Measuring network relationships often involves complex interactions between various factors. However, the importance of obtaining value from networks is commonly highlighted in the literature and this is often seen to require a number of network connections (Belso-Martinez, 2006; Lane and Lubatkin, 1998). Using an approach similar to Andersson et al. (2004), the constructed variables for the the value and number of networks was based on four areas – product development for foreign markets; development of foreign market supply channels; development of foreign market intelligence; and R&D for foreign market development. Large firms will have more network partners than smaller firms but a larger number of network partners does not necessarily mean that a large firm has more partners relative to its size than smaller firms. By using a five-point Likert scale to measure the number of networks, rather than asking for a metric measure of the number of networks, this potential problem was avoided. Measurement of the CEO's level of education required indication by respondents of the level of education attained from five possibilities: secondary school (1); technical training qualification less than degree level (2); first degree (3); masters degree (4); and a PhD (5). The ratio of R&D employees to the total number of employees provided an estimate of the R&D intensity of firms. The number of employees involved in international business activities is measured by the percentage of employees that spend most of their time (over 50 per cent) on international business activities.

Control variables included age (Autio et al., 2000), firm size (Zahra et al., 2000), industry technology (Ang, 2008) and government support (Fischer and Reuber, 2003). To measure the age of the firm, consideration was given to the length of international business experience, as this is thought to have an effect on international performance (Jantunen et al., 2005; Zahra et al., 2000). However, as the sample firms all engaged in international activities within six years of establishment, the variable is highly correlated with the age of the firm ($r = 0.78$). In order, therefore, to avoid problems of multi-collinearity, only the length of international experience was used as a control for age. Firm size was measured through the total number of employees. Industry technology intensity was based on the OECD's classification of industries into high, medium-high, medium-low, and low technology intensities. Government support was captured by asking respondents a question using a five-point Likert-type scale, ranging from 1 (very low) to 5 (very high): 'Governmental agencies provide good advice and support to help with the financial requirements of the industry my firm is in'.

Confirmatory factor analysis was performed to test the reliability of the constructed variables. The result of this analysis along with the Cronbach's alpha values of the constructed variables is shown in Table 9.2. Discriminant validity was tested using χ^2 difference test, represented in Table 9.3. These results indicated that convergent and discriminant validity was secured. Tests for outliers, skewness and kurtosis were used to identify any possible problems with the multivariate normality of the variables. Quadratic regression analysis was used to permit estimation of the square of the number of employees mainly involved with IBA squared and the square of the number of networks. Six models were tested, three for each of the dependent variables and three for these variables with the square of IBA and number of networks.

Results and discussion

The results (see Table 9.4) provide strong support for the significance of the number of employees mainly involved with international business activities, number of networks, and the international business experience of managers. These resources significantly relate to the dependent variables in nearly all cases, including the more objective performance measure of the share of sales from international activities. These results confirm the importance of the international business experience of managers found in the literature (Leonidou et al., 1998; Nummela et al., 2004; Reuber and Fischer, 1997). The support for the number of networks provides evidence for that literature that hints that this might be an important factor for the internationalization process (Belso-Martinez, 2006). The clear evidence from the findings that the number of employees mainly involved with international business is important confirms that this is a significant factor, although it is currently absent from the literature.

There is only support for the value of networks in the case of foreign knowledge competencies. It is possible that this resource mainly influences performance through the enhancement of foreign knowledge competencies. In other words, the value of networks boosts the competencies of firms to operate effectively in foreign markets, which then affect performance in these markets. The study provides no evidence for the impact of the education of CEOs, or for proportion of employees engaged in R&D. The latter result may connect to the small size of most SMEs, which precludes the ability of most firms to devote employees to R&D activities.

The results show that number of employees mainly employed in international business activities is an inverted U-shaped relationship. This indicates that some firms may be over-using labour in their international activities. There is however no indication that such an inverted u-shaped relationship exists for the number of networks. The significance of the change in R^2 for

Table 9.2   Measurement of constructs

Constructs and indicators	Standardized factor loading	t-value
Number of networks [NN] (α = 0.855)		
Approximately how many network relationships does your firm have to help in the following activities? 1= low, 3 = moderate, 5 = high		
Product development for foreign markets	0.670	11.325
Developing foreign market supply channels	0.788	13.371
Developing foreign market intelligence	0.887	14.464
R&D for foreign market development	0.732	–
Foreign knowledge competency [FKC] (α = 0.705)		
How would you rate your firm's competencies in comparison with your major market competitors over the past three years? 1 = low, 3 = moderate, 5 = high		
International customer satisfaction	0.717	7.379
Development of technology for international activities	0.570	8.620
Knowledge acquisition of international markets	0.502	–
Satisfaction from foreign market growth [SFMG] (α = 0.818)		
How would you rate your firm's performance in comparison with your major market competitors over the past three years? 1 = low, 3 = moderate, 5 = high.		
International sales growth rate	0.771	12.436
International market share	0.904	–
International business experience of managers [IBE] (α = 0.782)		
Indicate your degree of agreement with the following statements 1 = strongly disagree, 3 = moderately agree, 5 = strongly agree		
Our top management possesses a great deal of international business experience	0.707	9.908
Our top management has extensive experience of foreign travel	0.752	10.177
Our top management is experienced in foreign languages	0.775	–
Value of networks [VN] (α = 0.868)		
What is your assessment of the value of your network relationships in helping with the following network relationships? 1 = low, 3 = moderate, 5 = high		
Product development for foreign markets	0.722	12.700
Developing foreign market supply channels	0.823	14.630
Developing foreign market intelligence	0.867	15.242
R&D for foreign market development	0.758	–

Notes: One loading among paths from a construct to indicators was fixed to 1 in all constructs as a reference item.
Model fit: χ^2/df = 153.350 (df = 89, p = 0.000), χ^2/df = 1.790, GFI = 0.932, AGFI = 0.896, RMR = 0.051, RMSEA = 0.054, NFI = 0.931, TLI = 0.957, CFI = 0.96.

the models with the squared items suggests that the addition of these items improves the goodness of fit of the model.

The results for the controls reveal that only length of international business experience and industry technology is significantly related to share of sales

Table 9.3 Discriminant validity results

Pair		Free	Constrained	Chi-square difference (Δdf = 1)
IBE	NN	51.2	129.4	78.2
	VN	25.8	110.5	84.7
	FKC	15.0	97.3	82.3
	SFMG	15.2	64.9	49.7
NN	VN	63.2	125.2	62.0
	FKC	56.2	131.3	75.1
	SFMG	42.2	105.3	62.8
VN	FKC	39.7	132.4	92.7
	SFMG	21.9	113.5	91.6
FKC	SFMG	2.2	25.9	23.7

Notes: In all cases, the χ^2 value of the unconstrained model was significantly less than that of the constrained model, which provides evidence of discriminant validity for all of our constructs, with $\Delta\chi^2$s falling within the range 23.7 to 92.7.

Table 9.4 Regression results

Independent variables	Model 1	Model 2	Model 3	Model 4	Model 5	Model 6
Explanatory Variables						
Number of employees mainly involved in IBA	.210***	.578***	.218***	.503***	.105*	.397***
Number of networks	.246***	.542*	.195***	−.028	.260***	.074
Number of employees mainly involved in IBA^2	–	−.394***	–	−.307**	–	−.315**
Number of networks^2	–	−.331	–	.218	–	.179
CEO's educational level	−.004	−.018	−.018*	−.017	.044	.044
International business experience of managers	.158**	.152**	.153**	.147**	.103*	.097
Value of networks	.015	.005	−.110	−.120	.191**	.183**
R&D intensity	−.081	−.073	.022	.023	.046	.048
Control Variables						
Firm size	.083	.098	.031	.048	−.013	.004
Length of international business	.056	.050	.121**	.115*	.076	.070
Industry technology intensity	.019	.016	.137**	.136**	−.050	−.052
Government support	−.078	−.078	.009	.009	.027	.033
R^2	.196	.224	.158	.174	.242	.258
Change in R^2	–	.0.28**	–	.016*	–	.016*
Adj R^2	.165	.187	.126	.135	.212	.223
F-value	6.241***	6.110***	4.818***	4.460***	8.171***	7.358***

Notes: Standardized coefficients are reported.
*< .10, **< .05, ***< .01.
VIF values range from 1.047 to 1.634.
Models 1 and 2 dependent variable – Satisfaction with foreign market growth.
Models 3 and 4 dependent variable – Share of sales from international activities.
Models 5 and 6 dependent variable – Foreign knowledge competencies.

from international activities. The other controls reveal no significant relationships to the dependent variables. Hence, at least for early internationalizing South Korean firms, it seems that most of these factors are not significant related to the performance outcomes tested in this chapter.

In terms of the call to develop a theory of SME internationalization (Jones and Nummela, 2008), these results indicate that the international business experience of managers, the number of networks, and the number of employees devoted to international business should be at the core of any theory. The role of the international business experience of managers already figures in most theories on SME internationalization but the other two factors are rarely prominent in current theories. The role of the value of networks for international performance and the links between the number of networks and the value of networks perhaps needs more exploration in theory and also to be subjected to rigorous testing in a variety of different countries. The significance of the education level of CEOs and number of employees engaged in R&D perhaps needs to be reconsidered, at least in the case of early internationalizing Korean SMEs.

The implications of the results for strategy and management centre on placing greater emphasis on the significance of the number of employees devoted to international business activities and the number of networks. These issues have not been prominent in previous work, whereas factors not consistently found to be significant to performance in this study, such as education level of the CEO, government support, and the R&D intensity of firms, are often to the forefront of strategic and management issues. It appears that these neglected factors of the number of networks and number of employees devoted to international business activities may be more important for performance that some factors which have to date attracted more attention. The results suggest that firms may devote too many of their employees to international business activities, implying a need to bring optimal labour allocation polices to bear in the search for high performance.

Conclusion

The results provide support for the view, at least for early internationalizing SMEs in South Korea, that the international business experience of managers, the number of networks and number of employees devoted to international business activities are important factors for the international performance and the foreign knowledge competencies of SMEs. The first of these factors has already been supported by the literature but the latter two have not thus far been directly examined in most studies. The support for the importance of these factors suggests that strategies of internationalization should pay more attention to them in the assessment of the necessary resources for successful internationalization of SMEs. Moreover, the finding that the relationship between the number of employees devoted to international business activities and performance outcomes is an inverted U-shape implies that over-use of employees devoted to international business activities may be occuring. The inverted U-shaped relationship implies that careful management of employees devoted to international business activities is necessary.

The difference in the signficance of the results on number of networks compared to value of networks suggests that more investigation of these network concepts is needed. The linkages from the value of networks to outcomes may come by developing competencies to engage in international business activities, whereas the number of networks seems to be more directly related to performance outcomes. The results show that firms do not appear to be overusing the number of networks, because there is no evidence of an inverted U-shaped relationship for this factor. The focus of the current literature is connected to obtaining value from networks by developing trust and deepening relationships within existing networks. This may be important for enhancing competencies to engage in international business activities, but a focus on the number of networks also seems to be an important factor for performance.

Further work is required to develop a deeper understanding of the factors that underpin the international performance of SMEs. Such work could provide a sound basis for theory and policy development in these areas. Tests of the model in other countries, particularly economies with a longer period of developed status, and with SMEs from a wider range of industries, are necessary to check for country and industry specific factors. Models with more, and differently measured, dependent and independent variables are required to ensure that the factors identified in this study do have a measurable and significant impact on performance and foreign knowledge competencies. Another important area for future work is exploration of the number of networks and their relationship to the value of network.

References

Acedo, F. and Jones, M. V. (2007) 'Speed of Internationalization and Entrepreneurial Cognition: Insights and a Comparison between International New Ventures, Exporters and Domestic Firms', *Journal of World Business*, 42(2), 236–52.

Andersson, S., Gabrielsson, J. and Wictor, I. (2004) 'International Activities in Small Firms: Examining Factors Influencing the Internationalization and Export Growth of Small Firms', *Canadian Journal of Administrative Sciences*, 21(1), 22–34.

Ang, S. H. (2008) 'Competitive Intensity and Collaboration: Impact on Firm Growth across Technological Environments', *Strategic Management Journal*, 29(10), 1057–75.

Armstrong, J. and Overton, T. (1977) 'Estimating Nonresponse Bias in Mail Surveys', *Journal of Marketing Research*, 14(3), 396–402.

Aspelund, A. and Moen, Ø. (2005) 'Small International Firms: Typology, Performance and Implications', *Management International Review*, 45(3), 37–57.

Autio, E., Sapienza, H. J. and Almeida, J. G. (2000) 'Effects of Age at Entry, Knowledge Intensity, and Irritability on International Growth', *Academy of Management Journal*, 43, 909–24.

Bell, J. (1995) 'The Internationalization of Small Computer Software Firms: A Further Challenge to Stage Theories', *European Journal of Marketing*, 29(8), 60–75.

Bell, J., Crick, D. and Young, S. (2004) 'Small Firm Internationalization and Business Strategy: An Exploratory Study of 'Knowledge-Intensive' and 'Traditional' Manufacturing Firms in the UK', *International Small Business Journal*, 22(1), 23–56.

Belso-Martinez, J. (2006) 'Why Are Some Spanish Manufacturing Firms Internationalising Rapidly? The Role of Business and Institutional International Network', *Entrepreneurship and Regional Development*, 18(2), 207–26.

Chetty, S. and Blankenburg, D. (2000) 'Internationalization of Small to Medium-Sized Manufacturing Firms: A Network Approach', *International Business Review*, 9(1), 77–93.

Chetty, S. and Campbell-Hunt, C. (2003) 'Explosive International Growth and Problems of Success amongst Small to Medium-Sized Firms', *International Small Business Journal*, 21(1), 5–27.

Coviello, N. E. and Munro, H. J. (1997) 'Network Relationships and the Internationalization Process of Small Software Firms', *International Business Review*, 6(4), 361–86.

Doty, D. H. and Glick, W. H. (1998) 'Common Methods Bias: Does Common Methods Variance Really Bias Results', *Organizational Research Methods*, 9(4), 374–406.

Elango, B. and Pattnaik, C. (2007) 'Building Capabilities for International Operations through Networks: A Study of Indian Firms', *Journal of International Business Studies*, 38(4), 541–55.

Ellis, P. D. (2007) 'Paths to Foreign Markets: Does Distance to Market Affect Firm Internationalisation?', *International Business Review*, 16(5), 573–93.

Eriksson, K., Johanson, J., Majgard, A. and Sharma, D. (1997) 'Experiential Knowledge and Cost in the Internationalization Process', *Journal of International Business Studies*, 28(2), 337–60.

Fischer, E. and Reuber, A. R. (2003) 'Targeting Export Support to SMEs: Owners' International Experience as a Segmentation Basis', *Small Business Economics*, 20(1), 69–82.

Hair, J., Black, W., Babin, B., Andersen. R. and Tatham, R. (2006) *Multivariate Data Analysis* (6th edn, New Jersey: Prentice Hall).

Jantunen, A., Puumalainen, K., Saarenketo, S. and Kylaheiko, K. (2005) 'Entrepreneurial Orientation, Dynamic Capabilities and International Performance', *Journal of International Entrepreneurship*, 3(3), 223–43.

Jones, M. V. and Nummela, N. (2008) 'International Entrepreneurship: Expanding the Domain and Extending Our Research Questions: Editorial', *European Management Journal*, 26, 350–53.

Kim, H. and Jung, D. (2007) 'A Study on the Born Global Venture Corporation's Characteristics and Performance', *Journal of Korean Academy of Marketing Science*, 17(3), 39–59.

Knight, G. and Cavusgil, T. (2004) 'Innovation, Organizational Capabilities and the Born-Global Firm', *Journal of International Business Studies*, 35(2), 124–41.

Knight, G., Madsen, T. and Servais, P. (2004) 'An Inquiry into Born-Global Firms in Europe and the USA', *International Marketing Review*, 21(6), 645–65.

Lane, P. J. and Lubatkin, M. (1998) 'Relative Absorptive Capacity and Interorganizational Learning', *Strategic Management Journal*, 19, 461–77.

Lee, J. and Bae, L. (2003) 'A Study on the International Marketing Strategy of Venture Firms: Focus on Foreign Market Entry Strategy', *Journal of Strategic Management*, 6(2), 131–51.

Leonidou, L., Katsikeas, C. and Piercy, N. (1998) 'Identifying Managerial Influences on Exporting: Past Research and Future Directions', *Journal of International Marketing*, 6(2), 74–102.

Loane, S. and Bell, J. (2006) 'Rapid Internationalization among Entrepreneurial Firms in Australia, Canada, Ireland and New Zealand: An Extension to the Network Approach', *International Marketing Review*, 23(5), 467–85.

Lu, J. W. and Beamish, P. W. (2006) 'SME Internationalization and Performance: Growth vs. Profitability', *Journal of International Entrepreneurship*, 4(1), 27–48.

Madsen, T. and Servais, P. (1997) 'The Internationalization of Born Globals: An Evolutionary Process?', *International Business Review*, 6(6), 561–83.

Mudambi, R. and Zahra, S. (2007) 'The Survival of International New Ventures', *Journal of International Business Studies*, 38(2), 333–52.

Nummela, N., Saarenketo, S. and Puumalainen, K. (2004) 'A Global Mindset: A Prerequisite for Successful Internationalization?', *Canadian Journal of Administrative Science*, 21(1), 51–64.

Ojala, A. (2009) 'Internationalization of Knowledge-Intensive SMEs: The Role of Network Relationships in the Entry to a Psychically Distant Market', *International Business Review*, 18(1), 50–9.

Podsakoff, P. M. and Organ, D. (1986) 'Reports in Organizational Research: Problems and Prospects', *Journal of Management*, 12(4), 531–45.

Reuber, A. and Fischer, E. (1997) 'The Role of Management's International Experience in the Internationalization of Smaller Firms', *Journal of International Business Studies*, 28(4), 807–25.

Ruzzier, M., Antoncic, B., Hisrich, R. and Konecnic, M. (2007) 'Human Capital and SME Internationalization: A Structural Equation Modeling Study', *Canadian Journal of Administrative Sciences*, 24(1), 15–29.

Shrader, R. C., Oviatt, B. M. and McDougall, P. P. (2000) 'How New Ventures Exploit Trade-Offs Among International Risk Factors: Lessons for the Accelerated Internationalization of the 21st Century', *Academy of Management Journal*, 43(6), 1127–247.

Sujrez-Ortega, S. (2003) 'Export Barriers: Insights from Small and Medium-Sized Firms', *International Small Business Journal*, 21(4), 403–19.

Westhead, P. and Wright, M. (2001) 'The Internationalization of New and Small Firms: A Resource-Based View', *Journal of Business Venturing*, 16(4), 333–59.

Wu, F., Sinkovics, R., Cavusgil, T. and Roath, A. (2007) 'Overcoming Export Manufacturers' Dilemma in International Expansion', *Journal of International Business Studies*, 38(2), 283–303.

Zahra S. A., Ireland, R. and Hitt, M. (2000) 'International Expansion by New Venture Firms: International Diversity, Mode of Market Entry, Technological Learning, and Performance', *Academy of Management Journal*, 43(5), 925–50.

Zucchella, A., Danicolia, S. and Palamara, G. (2007) 'The Drivers of the Early Internationalization of the Firm', *Journal of World Business*, 42(3), 268–80.

10
Cyberspace: A Paradigm Shift for International Entrepreneurs' Relationships?

Thor Sigfusson and Simon Harris

Ever since Bott (1955) first presented the concept of social networks as a systematic way of understanding relationships in London families, social network researchers have observed and developed the idea of close-knit and loose-knit networks of relationships. This dichotomy has since become a well developed line of enquiry in both entrepreneurship and international entrepreneurship research. Network relationships between firms and individuals have a powerful influence on the internationalization of small high tech firms (Coviello, 2006; Moen et al., 2004; Oviatt and McDougall, 2005). Entrepreneurs' social or interpersonal relationships make them aware of foreign market opportunities (Loane and Bell, 2006).

Studies of the history of commercialization and industrialization suggest that when entrepreneurs in related lines of activity work well together, the speed of 'take off' is higher (Grassby, 1995), so entrepreneurs work better as a co-operative network than as a collection of competitive individualists (Casson, 1997). As the internationalization of small firms can be both sudden and destabilizing, internationalization through business networks is the only feasible way (Chetty and Campbell-Hunt, 2003), which makes relationship-creating skills key resources for international entrepreneurial growth (Ellis, 2000; Harris and Wheeler, 2005). The qualities of international entrepreneurs' relationships have therefore attracted research interest (Coviello, 2006; Komulainen et al., 2006; Oviatt and McDougall, 2005; Sharma and Blomstermo, 2003).

These studies, however, have given conflicting indications regarding the value of strong or weak relationships for embryonic international firms. We have indications, however, that the context within which these relationships form can make a difference. The strength of relationships in internationalization might be affected by national cultural aspects (Zhou et al., 2007), by the structure of the industry concerned (Fernhaber et al., 2007), and the extent of both social and non-social linkages (Coviello, 2006; Ellis, 2011).

One dramatic context shift in recent years has been the explosion in the role of electronic communication through computer networks, in which online communication takes place, which we will here call 'cyberspace' or 'cyber'. As technology changes, and the potential of new cyber technology affecting business relationships develops, cyberspace becomes of greater potential importance for international business ventures. Researchers have long recognized the potential role for cyberspace in stimulating bridging social capital (Lin, 1999), and it has, after a short stall at the beginning of this century, begun to enable new collaborative forms of organization (Loane, 2006).

Cyberspace now plays a vital part in bridging emotionally and geographically distant people (Kavanaugh et al., 2005; Wellman, 2001), especially in the internationalization of small firms (Loane, 2006). As cyberspace is 'intrinsically international' (Kobrin, 2001, p.688), Pitt, van der Merve and Berthon (2006) note that it 'has become a pervasive mechanism for conducting international trade, and this is particularly true in industrial markets' (p.607).

As it is becoming such an important mechanism for the formation of relationships, it is likely to be having some influence on the types of relationships that international entrepreneurs develop and use for the development of their relationships. Indeed, since cyberspace changes the way in which people communicate with one another, it has the potential to generate a fundamental shift in the way that business relationships and networks develop, and how those relationships can influence the development of the international firm. This field, however, remains under-researched (Lewis et al., 2008).

This chapter presents some key questions that international business researchers can address in the area, and combines social network theory with previous international entrepreneurship research to help develop some useful research propositions in relation to the role of cyberspace for international entrepreneurial embeddedness. These propositions together suggest that cyberspace may lead to a paradigm shift in the relationship formation of international entrepreneurs and the use of weak and strong relationships by entrepreneurs. It is hoped that the chapter may form a practical basis for future empirical studies in the field of the relationship formation of international entrepreneurs, and the chapter concludes with some suggestions for future research avenues in the relationships of international entrepreneurs.

The role of trust in international business

Trust between parties is a fundamental for the development of the agreement between people that is needed in all international business, because all international business requires co-operation between people at one stage or another (Buckley and Casson, 1985; Williamson, 1985). It lies at the heart of the relationships that are fundamental for entrepreneurial internationalization (Johanson and Vahlne, 2003) by offering the necessary linkages to networks in other countries (Welch and Luostarinen, 1993).

The development of trusting co-operative relationships between businesses has long been recognized as an essential element of international business, whether this is through joint ventures, alliances, contracts, informal understandings, or network arrangements (Axelsson and Easton, 1992; Blankenburg and Johanson, 1992; Child et al., 1997; Johanson and Mattsson, 1997). It is these linkages that provide the foundation for the search for opportunities abroad (Ellis, 2011).

Investment in a relationship through commitment enhances parties' credibility at the beginning of the relationship, improves trust, and reduces uncertainty and the risk of opportunism (Wuyts and Geyskens, 2005). For two parties to co-operate, however, *both* must be prepared to co-operate, and *both* must sufficiently trust the other party (Harris and Dibben, 1999). Being embedded in a network of relationships therefore helps people to co-operate with one another because there can be a context of trust between known partners or people who can be endorsed by known others (Uzzi, 1997). Trust promotes commitment to a relationship, and this commitment, when expressed in co-operation, builds trust in turn (Uzzi, 1997).

How trust develops in relationships, and the extent to which it needs to do so for the necessary co-operation to take place, is subject, however, to the context: we can expect different levels of trust within different contexts (Grossetti, 2005). Internationalization increases the distance from markets and relationships and requires a broader focus towards other and new networks (Fletcher, 2001). New international entrepreneurs' relationships need not be permanent alliances but need to provide market knowledge and opportunities, which may require less commitment between the parties involved. These relationships may therefore be valued for knowledge and market access rather than for permanent commitment (Hadjikhani and Sharma, 1999; Hite, 2003).

The benefits of strong relationships

Relationships can be strong or weak, and strength has therefore been seen in terms of trust and commitment; indeed, the primary conceptualization of the relationship marketing model sees relationships in these terms (Morgan and Hunt, 1994). Granovetter (1973) presents the strength of a relationship as a 'combination of the amount of time, the emotional intensity, the intimacy and the reciprocal services that characterize the tie' (p.1361).

Strong relationships have high levels of social relationship or personal interaction with high frequency (Granovetter, 1982), which motivates the individuals involved to protect and assist one another when required (Hite and Hesterly, 2001). Weak relationships are not as heavily based on personal interaction but may nevertheless provide access to, for example, resources or markets (Granovetter, 1973).

Most entrepreneurship studies have focused on the role of strong relationships. The trust inherent in strong relationships can be very important for young firms. Domestic advice networks also provide strong mechanisms which include criticism or disapproval, which can lower transaction costs (Mesquita and Lazzarini, 2008). This advice-giving between entrepreneurs depends on trust between entrepreneurs, often based on shared past experiences and repeated interactions (McGrath et al., 2003). The idea that the relational trust that smaller firms can develop helps them also with their globalization by building useful long-term international relationships has been supported by Svejenova (2006) and by Sasi and Arenius (2008). The internationalization of the venture relies heavily on intangible assets such as the relationship networks of the entrepreneur (Keupp and Gassmann, 2009; McDougall et al., 1994). Indeed, Harris and Wheeler (2005) present strong domestic relationships to be the most important assets that young internationalizing firms can have: they can open the doors to new foreign market opportunities and build further market knowledge.

The importance of weak relationships for international entrepreneurs

Ellis (2011) proposes that when looking at the relationships of international entrepreneurs seeking opportunities in the global market, 'the sum total of the entrepreneur's relationships with others' needs to be examined (Ellis, 2011, p.102). This sum total includes not only a few strong relationships, but a possibly large number of weak relationships as well. For new ventures accessing a global market, most relationships are relatively new (Morse et al., 2007), and because trust may not have had time to develop, so they will be weak. McDougall and Oviatt (2005) therefore suggest that when entrepreneurial ventures have an international aspect, weak relationships are very important. Oviatt and McDougall (2005) note: 'Because of their small number and the investment required, we believe strong ties are not the most important type for internationalization. Weak ties are. They are relationships with customers, suppliers, and others that are friendly and business-like. Weak ties are far more numerous than strong ties because they require less investment. Their number can grow relatively quickly, and they are important because they are often vital sources of information and know-how' (Oviatt and McDougall, 2005, p.545).

International entrepreneurship focuses on the 'discovery, enactment, evaluation, and exploitation of opportunities' (Oviatt and McDougall, 2007, p.7) and recognizes how opportunities are recognized by individuals (Aldrich and Zimmer, 1986). For all new ventures, scarcity of resources requires relatively more use of relationships than other resources in comparison with more established firms (Harris and Wheeler, 2005). International entrepreneurs' relationships are very important (Keupp and Gassmann, 2009; McDougall et al., 1994), but their differing context places different demands on them. The geographical or locational demands involved in opportunity seeking are considerably greater for international than for domestic entrepreneurs since the ties tend to be long, connecting socially distant locations (Centola and Macy, 2007). Weak ties, that research often overlooks, play an important role in the ventures of the international entrepreneur in the INV, as they provide opportunities and bridge these gaps (Komulainen et al., 2006; Sharma and Blomstermo, 2003).

Oviatt and McDougall (2005) have therefore argued that the international aspect of the venture may involve a completely different set of relationships, where the weak relationships are very important, and a growing body of research has been linking the early internationalization of the firm to the use of weak relationships (Duque et al., 2009; Komulainen et al., 2006; Presutti et al., 2007; Sharma and Blomstermo, 2003). We still do not have, however, a clear picture of the role of weak relationships in the internationalization of small ventures.

From a strong/weak dichotomy to evolving relationship portfolios

Jones, Coviello and Tang (2011) suggest that network research in international entrepreneurship is becoming more sophisticated and that we should abandon the notion of just 'strong' or 'weak' in relationships. Relationships do different things, combined and singly. Introducing the notion of 'virtual embeddedness', Morse, Fowler and Lawrence (2007) present the idea that strength can be seen in very different ways. Separately, Ozcan and Eisenhardt (2009) have proposed that rather than regarding relationships 'as simply strong or weak' (p.246), we should be regarding relationships and alliances in 'portfolios'. These portfolios develop and evolve according to the different resource and strategic needs of the firms concerned, and can be managed in a strategic way.

In their classic model of network development, Larson and Starr (1993) suggest that, over time, network relationships are transformed from simple dyadic exchanges to a dense set of multi-dimensional and multi-layered organizational relationships. They propose that, in the emerging stage, the ties shift from reliance on dyadic ties with family and friends or previous contacts to a stage which clarifies more mutual business interests, causes social and economic relationships to overlap and the number of economic ties to increase. Developing from this, Hite and Hesterly (2001) argue that an entrepreneur's personal network evolves from strong ties, towards an intentionally managed one rich in weak ties. Jenssen and Koenig (2002) have supported this view, arguing that the entrepreneur's personal friendships are crucial for the initial venture creation, making strong relationships more important in the start-up and early growth stage than in later stages (Starr and MacMillan, 1990). So we have a dynamic picture of emerging enterprises relying on strong relationships who will provide resources, later expanding their networks to include weaker relationships that will help to provide information on new business leads.

Greve and Salaff (2003) and Steier and Greenwood (2000) argue that the mix of strong and weak relationships develops very differently. They observed more weak relationships in the emergence phase, seeing this as enhancing the search for new information that helps the development of an entrepreneur's business plan. Elfring and Hulsink (2007) propose some reconciliation of these conflicting ideas by suggesting that different patterns of relationship portfolio evolution will result from different initial founding conditions and different post-founding entrepreneurial processes. This debate about the value of relationships at the emerging stage of entrepreneurship has not, however, included an international dimension.

The dynamic aspects of relationship portfolio evolution are critical for young internnational firms, and have been subject to much research (Oviatt and McDougall, 2005; Coviello, 2006; Komulainen et al., 2006; Sharma and Blomstermo, 2003), but it remains far from conclusive (Kiss and Danis, 2008). Notwithstanding the conflicting research evidence, a pattern can be drawn from what we have, as suggested in Figure 10.1, which helps us to induct a conceptual framework. With this framework we can consider the evolution of

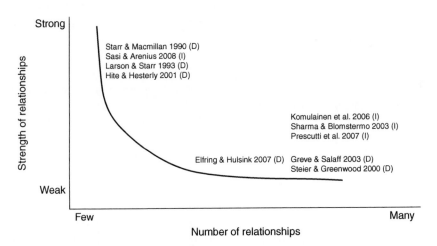

Figure 10.1 Studies on relationship strength for entrepreneurial firm foundation in domestic (D) and international (I) firms

relationship portfolios of entrepreneurs in domestic (D) and international (I) contexts.

The framework proposes that relationship networks of entrepreneurs will be a mix of weak and strong relationships at the initial development of the venture. We can see that most domestic entrepreneurship studies have emphasized the role of strong relationships at the early stages, while more studies in international new ventures are emphasizing a greater role for weak relationships. We can now use this conceptual model to examine how the developing use of cyberspace might affect these initial relationship portfolios.

Cyberspace can make it easier to form and manage international relationships

Cyberspace provides new tools for relationship building that open further the opportunities for individuals to have relationships, strong and, particularly, weak ties, with a large group of people. Researchers have also recognized how cyberspace plays a vital part in bridging emotionally distant and geographically diverse actors (Kavanaugh et al., 2005; Wellman, 2001). The formation of networks on Facebook, LinkedIn, and Twitter, for example, has transformed the 'community' within which people develop their social capital and has made it less dependent on physical space (Wellman, 2001). We see these networking tools easily extending across borders. It is already evident that many international entrepreneurs are actively using cyberspace for their relationship building in international ventures (Sigfusson and Chetty, 2011). These entrepreneurs have large social networks in cyberspace, and these networks seem to particularly affect the formation and development of international new ventures. It appears to be leading to new trends in the relationship formation of international entrepreneurs.

First, we see that international entrepreneurs using cyberspace 'know' many more people, albeit not deeply. But these people are useful. By finding new relationships within cyberspace, many international entrepreneurs establish contact with people who are also connected to other members of their relationship networks. International entrepreneurs seek opportunities through the large number of weak relationships that they hold in cyberspace, in the anticipation that a few of these will lead them to competent relationship partners.

Secondly, there is a profound change in the way that these portfolios, the social capital of the firms, are managed. There have always been methods of organizing relationships, from the exchange and stacking of business cards to e-mails. Cyberspace has opened new ways of managing and organizing a large set of weak relationships. Cyber-based networking services allow individuals to (1) construct a public or semi-public profile within a bounded system, (2) articulate a list of other users with whom they share a connection, and (3) view and traverse their list of connections and those made by others within the system (Boyd and Ellison, 2007). This allows the cyberspace-using international entrepreneur to manage large numbers of relationships in an active way, as is illustrated in Figure 10.2.

As the relationship networks of international entrepreneurs in the cyberspace become larger and more complexed, there is more urgency to organize these networks. Entrepreneurs with the largest numbers of weak relationships appear to perceive them and manage them as portfolios within Linkedin or Facebook, which share some geographical or professional characteristics. (Sigfusson and Chetty, 2011). Relations are therefore kept in different portfolios, such as a portfolio of relations in a particular country, which will be activated if the firm decides to expand to that territory and a portfolio of expertise, which is activated if the firm's agenda becomes more focused on that specific field of specialization.

The networking tools allow the international entrepreneurs to archive several hundreds of often 'sleeping ties' within useful categories, which can be drawn on or re-approached as need be. These tools help them to visualize their portfolios in the context of an entire network, not as a series of single relationships, in the way that Ozcan and Eisenhardt (2009) found practiced by executives in firms with high-performing network portfolios. Cyberspace tools help relationships to be formed 'in the context of building portfolios' (p.246). This leads us to our first proposition:

Proposition 1 International entrepreneurs who actively use cyberspace will have more relationships in managed relationship portfolios.

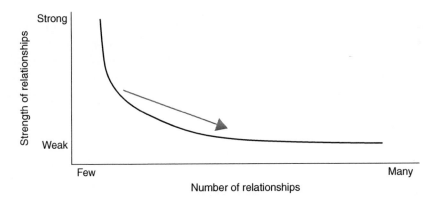

Figure 10.2   Cyberspace may result in more relationships

Cyberspace makes it easier to form the trust necessary for opportunity seeking

Relational exchange theory emphasizes trust to be critical for fostering and maintaining value-enhancing relational exchanges. (Lewicki and Bunker, 1996; Uzzi, 1997). Barney and Hansen (1994) distinguish weak trust, when partners have no significant vulnerabilities to exploit, semi-strong trust, when partners have contractual safeguards to protect them from opportunistic behaviour, and strong trust, when formal safeguards are unnecessary because the parties are confident that their vulnerabilities will not be exploited (Currall and Inkpen, 2002; Dyer and Chuh, 2000). So, relationships based only on a calculation of value are of a lower quality than those that have a social aspect within which trust is developed (Hite and Hesterley, 2001). Trust 'alleviates the fear of opportunistic behaviour and enhances the stability of the relationship' (Steensma et al., 2000, p.593).

Research suggests, however, that the nature of trust in business is changing. Trust, historically, has been identified as being based on incremental investments, associated with the development of knowledge of each partner, and a commitment on each side (Barney and Hanson, 1994; Lewicki and Bunker, 1996; Morgan and Hunt, 1994). Now, especially with high-tech firms in information technology, we are seeing swift or fast trust, where actors have neither a shared history nor a shadow of the future (Jarvenpaa et al., 1998; Blomqvist, 2005). There are two powerful roots to this trend of cyberspace to enhance the speed with which trusted relations are formed.

First, cyberspace tools present an effective virtual system that lowers co-ordination costs and helps timely responses to take place, itself developing an effective instrumental social system of exchange (Lee, 2009). This enables international entrepreneurs to trust people they make contact with in cyberspace; people who are, in every other respect, strangers. In a study of computer networks, Constant, Sproull and Kiesler (1996) use the term 'kindness of strangers' to show how individuals access mainly technical advice from strangers through a global computer manufacturer's computer network. They collected survey and observational data from a group of employees that they split into information seekers and information providers. They found that, although information seekers were strangers to the information providers, they gave useful advice to solve technical problems.

Using Granovetter's (1973) 'strength of weak ties' concept, Constant et al. (1996) argue that the information seekers are obtaining information that is unavailable from their friends and colleagues, as it is easier to provide information to strangers through cyberspace than through face-to-face interaction. The motivation to contribute can be a personal benefit, such as emotions, values and self identities (Bandura, 1986; Schlenker, 1985). But cyber networks also involves large numbers of people in observing others contributing information in response to requests, which encourages norms of contribution within a computer network community. There is a community sanction against inappropriate or malicious information.

Secondly, we have the powerful force of virtual embeddedness. Fowler, Lawrence, and Morse (2004) introduce the emergence of virtually embedded ties which are 'interorganizational linkages that are initiated and maintained through electronic technologies and that provide distinctive solutions to the same problems with exchange relationships that are addressed by socially embedded ties' (p.648). Cyberspace opens the opportunity for virtually embedded relationships to develop within a cyber community and this, in turn, allows a form of fast trust to be developed very quickly. As Constant et al. (1996) conclude: it is not the number of weak ties that is useful but the ability of these weak ties to bridge relationships – as Granovetter (1982) had originally proposed.

Being developed through cyberspace, the international entrepreneur's new relationships are also connected to other members of their relationship networks, within a virtual community. Though new relationships, they are strong enough to do the job of bridging people across countries with sufficient trust to protect the entrepreneurs from opportunism (Uzzi, 1997). This allows them to expand a 'sufficiently trusted' portfolio of relationships network much faster than traditional methods would allow (Morse et al., 2007), in the way represented in Figure 10.3.

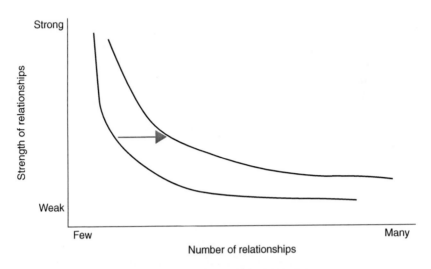

Figure 10.3   Cyberspace may result in more trusted relationships

We see here the role of the virtual community, within which these entrepreneurs and their relationships are embedded without generating strong trust, but based on confidence in the other party that comes from a history of personal experience with the other party (Barney and Hansen, 1994). Nor even is it Barney and Hansen's semi-strong trust based on contractual agreements.

Rather, this virtual embeddedness considerably reduces the level of opportunism often associated with new ventures (Uzzi, 1997), and by decreasing the liability of newness associated with new ventures' lack of strong trust relationships. We have a semi-strong form of trust developed fast within the virtually embedded community, that is entirely sufficient for the co-operative behaviour that the entrepreneurs seek, but which is based on an 'important alternative form of inter-organizational connection' (Uzzi, 1997, p.140). This leads us to our second proposition:

Proposition 2 International entrepreneurs who actively use cyberspace will have more semi-strong relationships in their relationship portfolios.

Cyberspace offers new approaches to relationship portfolios

The advent of cyberspace is not a direct force for change; rather, it is a facility that may or may not be adopted by international entrepreneurs. Those who do adopt it may well adopt it in different ways.

Notwithstanding the shifts noted earlier, many international entrepreneurs using cyberspace may have relatively few relationships These entrepreneurs may well be implicitly adopting the pattern advocated by Larson and Starr (1993), and use the new network now made available in a similar way to the way that they used their old networks. The network may well be much larger, but little of it will actually comprise relationships to be used in the way considered in this chapter.

Instead, cyberspace is used for screening opportunities and as a way of identifying and contacting the 'right contacts' with the 'right resources' (Larson and Starr, 1993). At different stages of firm evolution and growth, these resources will change. In Shirky's (2008) observation of writers on weblogs, a 'power-law distribution' is noted, whereby most writers have few readers, and they can all pay similar attention to one another, forming tight conversational clusters. This mirrors behaviour outside cyberspace, so that cyberspace is used to enact behaviour previously seen outside it, and cyberspace is just used to make it easier. We might especially expect this pattern among international entrepreneurs whose relationship behaviour developed before the use of cyberspace became more established. In short, the older international entrepreneurs may well have smaller relationship networks.

If the establishment of the firms and the creation of ideas has mainly been based on relationships in cyberspace, however, the pattern may well be very different. Many of the younger high-tech entrepreneurs have been living and thriving in cyberspace for the larger part of their lives. The world in which they have developed their ventures, from the initial start-up, to the development of ideas and to the formation of groups is increasingly shaped by their experience of using cyberspace, and is very different from more traditional methods of conducting business ventures (Sigfusson and Chetty, 2011). The international entrepreneurs with the largest relationship networks seem to begin with a large number of contacts, in effect, a large crowd. They may broadcasting their ideas to crowds in cyberspace and only later begin to create concrete links, depending on the reactions received.

This use of crowds in cyberspace to come up with the best, most clever, solutions, this letting cyberspace vote on your ideas, and this gaining of trust through cyberspace by promoting your ideas among crowds to whom you have displayed network strength, is a completely different approach. It is problematic to see this new pattern in the same way as we have understood network relationships hitherto. For example, it is difficult to define these crowds either as portfolios of relationships (Ozcan and Eisenhardt, 2009), as weak ties (Hite and Hesterly, 2001) or as 'social or business ties' (Coviello, 2006).

Perhaps we can better see these crowds as a wide global community of international entrepreneurs (Roberts, 2010), as a 'sea of informal ties' (Powell et al., 1996) within which ideas can be broadcast, and within which there is a certain basic level of virtual embeddedness, that will come into play only when a response is provoked. The new international entrepreneurs in cyberspace seem to rely on these anonymous crowd communities out there (Roberts, 2010), but use them as large portfolios of weak relationships (Ozcan & Eisenhardt, 2009) to obtain ideas and create business plans in their ventures. In a similar way to that observed by Shirky (2008), some have thousands of 'readers' from whom a response may be elicited.

Figure 10.4 shows these two extremes in our conceptual framework. We can expect international entrepreneurs in new ventures to work at each end of this spectrum: those with a relatively small relationship network in cyberspace and those with a large network, while a small portion of the population has a large relationship network. At the same time as these patterns become more evident, we may also find international entrepreneurial firms working at both ends of the spectrum. One 35 year old international entrepreneur based in Edinburgh, Scotland, having followed the Larson and Starr approach very successfully, has recently recruited a 22 year old as a marketing manager to pursue the next stage of his internationalization through crowd-sourcing. This evolving diversity of patterns of relationships strategy leads us to our third proposition:

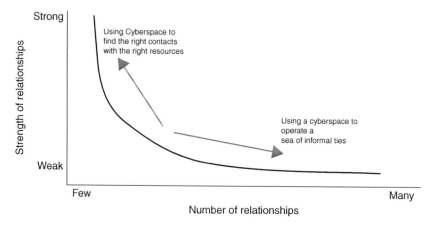

Figure 10.4   Cyberspace leading to greater diversity in relationship portfolios

Proposition 3 International entrepreneurs who actively use cyberspace will show much greater diversity in their use of weak and strong relationships for their internationalization.

Conclusion

This chapter has presented three propositions that all argue, in a concrete way, that the advent and use of cyberspace is international. Entrepreneurship may be leading to paradigm shifts concerning the role of relationships in the internationalization of the firm, an issue that lies at the heart of much international entrepreneurship research. Just as new communication methods are changing society, so will they change the conduct of businesses and trust building. As existing international entrepreneurs become increasingly involved in social networking in cyberspace, and as new international entrepreneurs increasingly come from a generation where cyberspace social networking is the norm, this issue will become more important.

Much of the work reviewed here presents weak relationships that can be more quickly developed into fuller business relationships than previously suggested (Morse et al., 2007). But the world of relationships in cyberspace means that we will need a new language to examine the relationships involved: 'weak' and 'strong' will no longer do (Jones et al., 2011). Work being done in social networks may well point the way: Opsahl, Agneessens and Skvoretz (2010) value relationships according to, for example, their length, position and significance.

The use of cyberspace networks by international entrepreneurs offers new questions concerning the relationship networks of international entrepreneurs:

how they are changing over time; and whether the new kinds of relationships are leading to different organizational forms and patterns of internationalization. Observing new young international entrepreneurs might give us some pointers. This presents a challenging arena for future research but one in which the cyberspace networking systems themselves carry with them tools that could help our research. For example, research has been conducted on Facebook, using the Facebook programmes, into individuals' social capital (Ellison, Steinfield and Lampe, 2007) and taste sharing (Lewis, Kaufman, Gonzalez, Wimmer and Christakis, 2008). If international entrepreneurship researchers can gain access to entrepreneur contact lists on, for example, Facebook, Linkedin, or Twitter, we could gain a more complete picture of their larger networks than by examining only those we find in the transcripts of our interviews, which will inevitably only describe their most used or memorable, and not neccessarily their most useful relationships.

References

Aldrich, H. and Zimmer, C. (1986) 'Entrepreneurship Through Social Networks' in Sexton, D. L. and Smilor R. W. (eds), *The Art and Science of Entrepreneurship*, 3–23.

Axelsson, B. and Easton, G. (1992) *Industrial Networks: A New View of Reality* (London: Routledge).

Bandura, A. (1986). *Social Foundations of Thought and Action: A Social Cognitive Theory* (Englewood Cliffs, NJ: Prentice-Hall).

Barney, J. B. and Hansen, M. H. (1994) 'Trustworthiness: Can it be a Source of Competitive Advantage?', *Strategic Management Journal*, 15(2), 175–203.

Bijlsma-Frankema, K. (eds), *Trust under Pressure, Investigations of Trust and Trust Building in Uncertain Circumstances* (Cheltenham: Edward Elgar Publishing, Inc.), 127–47.

Blankenburg, D. and Johanson, J. (1992) 'Managing Network Connections in International Business', *Scandinavian International Business Review*, 1(1), 5–19.

Blomqvist, K. (2005) 'Trust in a Dynamic Environment – Fast Trust as a Threshold Condition for Asymmetric Technology Partnership Formation in the ICT Sector' in KleinWoolthuis, R. and Bott, E. (1955) 'Urban Families: Conjugal Roles and Social Networks', *Human Relations*, 8(8), 345–85.

Boyd, D. M. and Ellison, N. B. (2007) 'Social Network Sites: Definition, History, and Scholarship', *Journal of Computer-Mediated Communication*, 13(1), 210–30.

Bratkovic, T., Antoncic, B. and Ruzzier, M. (2009) 'The Personal Network of the Owner-Manager of a Small Family Firm: The Crucial Role of the Spouse', *Managing Global Transitions*, 7(2), 171–90.

Buckley, P. J. and Casson, M. (1985) *The Economic Theory of the Multinational Enterprise* (London: Macmillan).

Casson, M. (1997) 'Entrepreneurial Networks in International Business', *Business and Economic History*, 26(2), 811–23.

Centola, D. and Macy, M. (2007) 'Complex Contagion and the Weakness of Long Ties', *American Journal of Sociology*, 113, 702–34.

Chetty, S. and Campbell-Hunt, C. (2003) 'Explosive International Growth and Problems of Success amongst Small to Medium-Sized Firms', *International Small Business Journal*, 21(5), 5–27.

Child, Yau, Y. and Lu, (1997) 'Ownership and Control in Sino-Foreign Joint Ventures', in P. W. Beamish and J. P. Killing (eds) *Co-operative Strategies* (San Francisco: Lexington), pp. 181–225.

Constant, D., Sproull, L. and Kiesler, S. (1996) 'The Kindness of Strangers: The Usefulness of Electronic Weak Ties for Technical Advice', *Organization Science*, 7(2), 119–35.

Coviello, N. E. (2006) 'The Network Dynamics of International New Ventures', *Journal of International Business Studies*, 37, 713–31.

Currall, S. C. and Inkpen, A. C. (2002) 'A Multilevel Approach to Trust in Joint Ventures', *Journal of International Business Studies*, 33(3), 479–95.

Dimitratos, P. and Jones, M. (2005) 'Future Directions for International Entrepreneurship Research', *International Business Review*, 14(2), 119–28.

Duque, R. R., Shrum,W. M., Barriga, O. JR. and Henriquez, G. (2009) 'Internet Practice and Professional Networks in Chilean Science: Dependency or Progress?', *Scientometrics*, 81(1), 239–63.

Dyer, J. H. and Chuh, W. (2000) 'The Determinants of Trust in Supplier-Auto-Maker Relationships in the US, Japan, and Korea', *Journal of International Business Studies*, 31(2), 259–85.

Elfring, T. and Hulsink, W. (2007) 'Networking by Entrepreneurs: Patterns of Tie-Formation in Emerging Organizations', *Organisation Studies*, 28(12), 1849–72.

Ellis, P. (2000) 'Social Ties and Foreign Market Entry', *Journal of International Business Studies*, 31(3), 443–69.

Ellis, P. (2011) 'Social Ties and International Entrepreneurship: Opportunities and Constraints Affecting Firm Internationalization', *Journal of International Business Studies*, 42(1), 99–127.

Ellison, N. B., Steinfield, C. and Lampe, C. (2007) 'The Benefits of Facebook "Friends": Social Capital and College Students' Use of Online Social Network Sites', *Journal of Computer-Mediated Communication*, 12(4), 1143–68.

Fernhaber, S. A., McDougall, P. P. and Oviatt, B. M. (2007) 'Exploring the Role of Industry Structure in New Venture Internationalization', *Entrepreneurship,Theory and Practice*, 31(4), 517–42.

Fletcher, R. (2011) 'Internationalisation Strategies for SMEs in the Decade Ahead: Are Our Theories Relevant?', *International Journal of Entrepreneurship and Innovation Management*, 13(3–4): 246–262.

Fowler, S. F., Lawrence, T. B. and Morse, E. A. (2004) 'Virtually Embedded Ties', *Journal of Management*, 30, 647–66.

Granovetter, M. (1973) 'The Strength of Weak Ties', *American Journal of Sociology*, 78(6), 1360–80.

Granovetter, M. (1982) 'The Strength of Weak Ties: A Network Theory Revisited' in Marsden, P. V. and Lin, N. (eds), *Social Structure and Network Analysis* (Beverly Hills, CA: Sage), 105–30.

Granovetter, M. (1985) 'Economic Actions and Social Structure: The Problem of Embeddedness', *American Journal of Sociology*, 91(3), 481–510.

Grassby, R. (1995) *The Business Community of Seventeenth-century England* (Cambridge: Cambridge University Press).

Greve, A. and Salaff, J. W. (2003) 'Social Networks and Entrepreneurship', *Entrepreneurship Theory and Practice*, 28(1), 1–22.

Grossetti, M. (2005) 'Where do Social Relations Come From? A Study of Personal Networks in the Toulouse Area of France', *Social Networks*, 27(4), 289–300.

Hadjikhani, A. and Sharma, D. D. (1999) 'A View on Political and Business Actors', in Ghauri, P. N. (ed.), *Advances in International Marketing*, Vol. 9 (Stamford, CT: JAI Press), pp. 243–257.

Harris, S. and Dibben, M. (1999) 'Trust and Co-operation in Business Relationship Development: Exploring the Influence of National Values', *Journal of Marketing Management*, 15(4), 463–83.

Harris, S. and Sigfusson, T. (2011) 'Developing Relationship Portfolios for Initial Internationalization: A Resource-based Perspective', paper presented at the EIBA conference in Porto, Portugal, December 2010.

Harris, S. and Wheeler, C. (2005) 'Export Market Development Activity: Entrepreneur Relationships As Exchange Opportunities', *International Business Review*, 14(3), 187–207.

Hite, J. M. (2003) 'Patterns of Multidimensionality among Embedded Network Ties: A Typology of Relational Embeddedness in Emerging Entrepreneurial Firms', *Strategic Organization*, 1(1), 9–49.

Hite, J. M. and Hesterly, W. S. (2001) 'The Evolution of Firm Networks: from Emergence to Early Growth of the Firm', *Strategic Management Journal*, 22(3), 275–86.

Jarvenpaa, S. L., Knoll, K. and Leidner, D. E. (1998) 'Is Anybody Out There? Antecedents of Trust in Global Virtual Teams', *Journal of Management Information Systems*, 14(4), 29–64.

Jenssen, J. I. and Koenig, H. F. (2002) 'The Effect of Social Networks on Resource Access and Business Start-Ups', *European Planning Studies*, 10(8): 1039–1046.

Johanson, J. and Mattsson, L. G. (1997) 'Internationalization in Industrial Systems – A Network Approach' in Ford, D. (ed.) *Understanding Business Markets* (London: Dryden), 194–213.

Johanson, J. and Vahlne, J. E. (1977) 'The Internationalization Process of the Firm – A Model of Knowledge Development and Increasing Market Commitments', *Journal of International Business Studies*, 8(1), 23–32.

Jones, M. V., Coviello, N. and Tang, Y. K. (2011) 'International Entrepreneurship Research (1989–2009): A Domain Ontology and Thematic Analysis', *Journal of Business Venturing*, doi:10.1016/j.jbusvent.2011.04.001.

Kavanaugh, A. L., Reese, D. D., Carroll, J. M. and Rosson, M. B. (2005) 'Weak Ties in Communities', *Information Society*, 21(2), 119–31.

Keupp, M.M. and Gassmann, O. (2009) 'The Past and Future of International Entrepreneurship: A Review and Suggestions for Developing the Field', *Journal of Management*, 35(3), 600–33.

Kiss, A. N. and Danis, W. M. (2008) 'Country Institutional Context, Social Networks, and New Venture Internationalization Speed', *European Management Journal*, 26(6), 388–99.

Kobrin, S.J. (2001) 'Territoriality and the Governance of Cyberspace', *Journal of International Business Studies*, 32(4), 687–704.

Komulainen, H., Mainela, T. and Tahtinen, J. (2006) 'Social Networks in the Initiation of a High-tech Firm's Internationalization', *International Journal of Entrepreneurship and Innovation Management*, 6(6), 526–41.

Krackhardt, D. (1992) 'The Strength of Strong Ties: The Importance of Philos in Organizations' in Nitin, N. and Eccles, R. G. (eds), *Networks and Organizations: Structure, Form, and Action* (Boston, MA: Harvard Business School Press).

Kraus, S. (2011) 'State-of-the-art Current Research in International Entrepreneurship: A Citation Analysis', *African Journal of Business Management*, 5(3), 1020–38.

Larson A. (1992) 'Network Dyads in Entrepreneurial Settings: a Study of the Governance of Exchange Relationships', *Administrative Science Quarterly*, 37, 76–104.

Larson, A. and Starr, J. A. (1993) 'A Network Model of Organization Formation', *Entrepreneurship Theory and Practice*, 17(2), 5–15.

Lee, R. (2009) 'Social Capital and Business and Management: Setting a Research Agenda', *International Journal of Management Reviews*, 11(3), 247–73.

Lewicki, R. J. and Bunker, B. B. (1996) 'Developing and Maintaining Trust in Working Relationships' in Kramer, R. M. and Tyler, T. R. (eds), *Trust in Organizations: Frontiers of Theory and Research* (Thousand Oaks, CA: Sage), 114–39.

Lewicki, R. J., McAllister D. J. and Bies, R. J. (1998) 'Trust and Distrust: New Relationships and Realities', *Academy of Management Review*, 23(5), 438–58.

Lewis, K., Kaufman, J., Gonzalez, M., Wimmer, A. and Christakis, N. (2008) 'Tastes, Ties, and Time: A New Social Network Dataset Using Facebook', *Social Networks*, 30(4), 330–42.

Lin, N. (1999) 'Building a Network Theory of Social Capital', *Connections*, 22(1), 28–51.

Loane, S. (2006) 'The Role of the Internet in the Internationalization of Small and Medium Sized Companies', *Journal of International Entrepreneurship*, 3, 263–77.

Loane, S. and Bell, J. (2006) 'Rapid Internationalization among Entrepreneurial Firms in Australia, Canada, Ireland and New Zealand: An Extension to the Network Approach', *International Marketing Review*, 25(5), 467–85.

McDougall, P. P., Shane, S. and Oviatt, B. M. (1994) 'Explaining the Formation of International New Ventures: The Limits of Theories from International Business Research', *Journal of Business Venturing*, 9, 469–87.

McGrath, C. A., Vance, C. M. and Gray, E. R. (2003) 'With a Little Help from their Friends: Exploring the Advice Networks of Software Entrepreneurs', *Creativity and Innovation Management*, 12(1), 1–10.

Mesquita, L. F. and Lazzarini, S. G. (2008) 'Horizontal and Vertical Relationships in Developing Economies: Implications for SMEs' Access to Global Markets', *Academy of Management Journal*, 51(2), 359–80.

Moen, Ø., Gavlen, M. and Endresen, I. (2004) 'Internationalization of Small, Computer Software Firms: Entry Forms and Market Selection', *European Journal of Marketing*, 38(9–10), 1236–51.

Morgan, R. M. and Hunt, S. D. (1994) 'The Commitment-Trust Theory of Relationship Marketing', *Journal of Marketing*, 58(3), 20–38.

Morse, E. A., Fowler, S. A. and Lawrence, T. B. (2007) 'The Impact of Virtual Embeddedness on New Venture Survival: Overcoming the Liabilities of Newness', *Entrepreneurship Theory and Practice*, 31(2), 139–59.

Opsahl, T., Agneessens, F. and Skvoretz, J. (2010) 'Node Centrality in Weighted Networks: Generalizing Degree and Shortest Paths', *Social Networks*, 32(3), 245–51.

Oviatt, B. M. and McDougall, P. P. (2005) 'Defining International Entrepreneurship and Modeling the Speed of Internationalization', *Entrepreneurship: Theory and Practice*, 29(3), 537–54.

Ozcan, P. and Eisenhardt, K. M. (2009) 'Origin of Alliance Portfolios: Entrepreneurs, Network Strategies, and Firm Performance', *Academy of Management Journal*, 52(2), 246–79.

Pitt, L., van der Merve, R. and Berthon, P. A. (2006) 'Global Alliance Networks: A Comparison of Biotech SMEs in Sweden and Australia', *Industrial Marketing Management*, 35, 600–10.

Powell, T. C. (2003) 'Research Notes and Commentaries. Strategy without Ontology', *Strategic Management Journal*, 24, 285–291.

Powell, W., Kogut, K. and Smith-Doerr, L. (1996) 'International Collaboration and the Focus of Innovation: Networks of Learning in Biotechnology', *Administrative Science Quarterly*, 41: 116–145.

Presutti, M., Boan, C. and Fratocchi, L. (2007) 'Knowledge Acquisition and the Foreign Development of High-Tech Start-ups: a Social Capital Approach', *International Business Review*, 16(1), 23–46.

Ring, P. S. and van de Ven, A. H. (1994) 'Developmental Processes of Co-operative Interorganizational Relationships', *Academy of Management Review*, 19, 90–118.

Roberts, J. (2010) 'Community and International Business Futures: Insights from Software Production', *Futures*, 42(9), 926–36.

Sasi, V. and Arenius, P. (2008) 'International New Ventures and Social Networks: Advantage or Liability?', *European Management Journal*, 26(6), 400–11.

Schlenker, B. R. (1985) 'Identity and Self-identification' in Schlenker, B. R. (ed.), *The Self and Social Life* (New York: McGraw-Hill).

Sharma, D. D. and Blomstermo, A. (2003) 'The Internationalization Process of Born Globals: A Network View', *International Business Review*, 12(6), 739–53.

Shirky, C. (2008) *Here comes Everybody. How Change Happens when People Come Together* (London: Penguin Books).

Sigfusson, T. and Chetty, S. (2011) 'Building International Entrepreneurial Virtual Networks in Cyberspace', paper presented at the AIB annual Conference in Japan, June 2011.

Starr, J. S. and MacMillan, I. C. (1990) 'Resource Cooptation via Social Contracting: Resource Acquisition Strategies for New Resources', *Strategic Management Journal*, 11(1): 79–92.

Steensma, H. K., Marino, L. and Weaver, K. N. (2000) 'Attitudes towards Cooperative Strategies: A Cross-cultural Analysis of Entrepreneurs', *Journal of International Business Studies*, 31(4), 591–609.

Steier, L. and Greenwood, R. (2000) 'Entrepreneurship and the Evolution of Angel Financial Networks', *Organization Studies*, 21(1), 163–92.

Svejenova, S. (2006) 'How Much does Trust Really Matter? Some Reflections on the Significance and Implications of Madhoc's Trust-based Approach', *Journal of International Business Studies*, 37, 12–20.

Uzzi, B. (1997) 'Social Structure and Competition in Interfirm Networks: The Paradox of Embeddedness', *Administrative Science Quarterly*, 42(1), 35–67.

Welch, L. and Luostarinen, R. (1993) 'Inward–Outward Connections in Internationalization', *Journal of International Marketing*, 1(1), 44–57.

Wellman, B. (2001) 'Physical Place and Cyber Place: The Rise of Personalized Networking', *International Journal of Urban and Regional Research*, 25, 227–52.

Williamson, O. E. (1985) *The Economic Institutions of Capitalism: Firms, Markets, Relational Contracting* (New York, NY: The Free Press).

Wuyts, S. and Geyskens, I. (2005) 'The Formation of Buyer–Supplier Relationships: Detailed Contract Drafting and Close Partner Selection', *Journal of Marketing*, 69(4), 103–17.

Zhou, L., Wu, W. P. and Luo, X. (2007) 'Internationalization and the Performance of Born-global SMEs: The Mediating Role of Social Networks', *Journal of International Business Studies*, 38(4), 673–69.

Part IV
The New Practices of International Businesses

Simon Harris

In Chapter 11, Tamer Cavusgil interviews three managers experienced in managing complex cross-border collaborative (CCBC) projects. In a session chaired by Volker Mahnke, he discusses these issues with Hillary Sillitto of the Thales group, Hermine Schnetler of the UK Astronomy Technology Centre, and Paul Holbourn, from the Selex Galileo group. Discussion topics explored some of the most salient problems managers face, and pinpointed rewarding research avenues in tackling the challenges in organizing multinational projects such as CCBCs. They include: the risks involved in complex cross-border collaborative projects; the motivation for doing them; the meaning of success and failure; how to manage for success in them; the role of the contract; dealing with conflicts; competing whilst collaborating within them; the management of complexity and the loss of control; moral hazard; timescales; the political dimension; and doing business in the BRIC countries.

In Chapter 12, Pervez Ghauri interviews four managers experienced in managing the process of internationalization. In a session chaired by Simon Harris, he discusses this issue with Carla Mahieu of Aegon and formerly of Philips, Ian Stevens, of Mpathy and formerly of Optos, Paul D'Arcy, from Raytheon, and Arten Moussavi whose new INV BioFood Nutrition follows his previous international entrepreneurial experience. Discussion topics include: the process of deciding where and how to internationalize; the partnerships involved in international business; dealing with uncertainty and change in overseas territories; the opportunities and challenges of internationalizing to emerging markets; the risks of counterfeit goods and the problems of intellectual property protection; learning in the internationalization process; and the issue of ethical behaviour in international business.

In Chapter 13, Yong Kyu Lew and Rudolf Sinkovics usefully show how focal firms in alliances generate innovation from within those alliances by gaining access to overseas complementary resources, by internalizing these, by developing new products, and by commercializing them. They draw on the findings of previous international business research which indicates that global technology alliances can be useful ways for firms to acquire complementary resources, to develop new business models, and to help them penetrate new markets. To investigate the interrelationships between complementary resources, global technology alliances, and innovation capabilities in a high-tech market context, they then study a global technology alliance between a South Korean personal computer software firm and its global hardware and software technology partners, which involved them in undertaking interviews with senior managers and drawing on secondary sources of information. This study contributes not just by showing that the alliance is useful but by showing how it is.

11

Managing Complex Cross-Border Collaborative Projects: Tamer Cavusgil Interviews Four Managers Experienced in Doing It

Tamer Cavusgil and Volker Mahnke

Introduction

Managing complex cross-border collaborative projects (CCBC) is an important emerging research field relevant to both the theory and practice of international business (IB). Yet, as compared to the growing need for professionals in firms involved in such high stake multi-party projects, meagre attention has been given in IB education and literature to the associated managerial challenges involved in such new forms of organization. More specifically, given scant empirically corroborated insights, what are the key problems IB scholars and practitioners could address in developing a research agenda on CCBCs that is both managerially relevant and theoretically rigorous? This conversation is one between researchers with experience of working with practitioners, and some practitioners very experienced in managing CCBCs. In a public conference session chaired by *Volker Mahnke,* with an audience of practitioners and researchers, *Tamer Cavusgil* and Volker explored some of the salient problems managers face, and pinpointed rewarding research avenues for tackling the challenges in organizing multinational projects such as CCBCs. This is a lightly edited transcript of that interview.

The international management of complex cross-border projects matters within a wide variety of settings and contexts. An obvious case in point is the design of military aircraft which involves several political stakeholders from different nations. Here complexity is increased, for example, because the same players initiate, fund, and intervene in the project, whilst acting simultaneously both as the main customer and as political lobbyists protecting national industrial interests and jobs. Managerial challenges are no less present in civil airplane construction, where project complexity can be further increased by cultural and geographic distance. The design and construction of the Airbus 380 segments involves several European locations, from which inputs are shipped via Bordeaux to Toulouse, the impressive final assembly facility. Optimizing such internationally complex and geographically distributed projects requires novel socio-technical capabilities that IB research is only slowly beginning to recognize. The absence of capabilities concerning the best governance of such CCBSs offers a fertile ground for research on the failure of the new organizational forms involved.

While managers involved in CCBC face challenges of additional complexity, these projects also come with distinct advantages. For one, many CCBCs exhibit sustained survival despite adversity, since a survival advantage results from the stakeholders in CCBSs being organized in a web of interlocking interests. For example, while almost all cash strapped European governments would have liked to pull back commitments to the Eurofighter, none of them could escape the lock-in of mutual contractual obligation and organized interest. Additionally, while human resources from different locations and cultural backgrounds complicate coordination and incentive alignment in CCBSs, joint design and learning in design communities enables the generation of technological capabilities that would erode if the underlying CCBCs governance structure were disssolved.

Taken together, judging project failure and success in CCBCs is a complicated matter worthy of future investigation. What are the features that distinguish successful from failing CCBS? When does a CCBC project failure (in terms of time and budget overrun) result in a successful outcome, but one that is delayed? How do contractual provisions and partnering behaviour within CCBCs interact and adapt over the lifetime of the project? Addressing these and other salient research issues will stimulate better conversation, in future, between theory and practice in international business.

Introducing the participants and our interviewer's interest

Volker Mahnke – I would like to welcome you to this session on Managing Complex Cross-Border Collaborative Projects. The idea of the session is to discover new problems of interest to IB research, and such big problems usually derive from practice. Let me introduce you to the panel here.

- Tamer Cavusgil, Georgia State University, is an esteemed and famous IB scholar, who doesn't really need an introduction: just read one of the hundreds of papers he has written in our field to appreciate his profound insights.

- Hillary Sillitto, from the Thales group, is now the UK director of system engineering. He started with optical systems, and then became interested in defence and aerospace applications. He is also the holder of several patents and a visiting professor at the University of Bristol.
- Hermine Schnetler is the head of system engineering at the UK Astronomy Technology Centre, and she is very much interested in managing large international complex projects.
- Paul Holbourn, from the Selex Galileo group, is chief technology officer for the radar and advanced targeting group. He has several diverse degrees, including a PhD in solid state physics and he is a member of the Royal Academy of Engineering.

Tamer Cavusgil – It's not every day that we get to cover this subject area well in our research or the classroom. Even though these projects are very important, and financially they mean a lot to their respective economies, and there is a very large cadre of companies engaged in these projects, whether it is construction, defence, high technology, infrastructure and so on, the topic of managing megaprojects deserves much greater scholarly attention. My own experience in international collaborative projects – project-based collaborations, megaprojects, high-stakes games – is limited but, recently, I have been involved with the so-called Joint Strike Fighter (JSF) F-35 military aircraft project, sponsored by the US and an alliance of eight other countries. Lockheed Martin Aero is acting as a major contractor in a global supply network of over 1,000 companies in these countries. When the Pentagon decided to sponsor this project –perhaps, the most expensive project it has ever undertaken – it wanted to do it with a number of allies, so there are eight other partner countries. Collaboration includes design, production, and sustainment. Scheduled to be available in 2014, the aircraft is expected have a lifetime of forty years. It will be purchased by the same eight other countries and perhaps others.

The risks involved in complex cross-border collaborative projects

Tamer Cavusgil – The first question I'm going to ask the panellists is what are the risks, and the unique challenges that one experiences as a player in these highly risky collaborative projects? Let me give you just a bit of background on the Lockheed Martin Aero (and its prime partners, Northrop Grumman and BAE). The sponsor nations participated in the design, and they are participating in the manufacturing assembly of the project, plus they will also be customers. So it's interesting how they were pulled into the project for mostly political reasons, and these folks will elaborate on the multiple motivations behind a multinational project like that. The project has not been without wrinkles. Cost overruns, project delays, feuds among the suppliers are some of the challenges. Recall the experience of Boeing with its 787 commercial aircraft project – the Dreamliner. If you recall, Boeing started this a number of years ago, and what they also did that was different, just like in the case of the F-35 project, was that they engaged suppliers from something like 15 different countries. Managing a global supplier network certainly adds to the risks. Just like in the case of the F-35, there are two other major partners like NG, Northrop Grumman, and BAE. In fact, there's something like 1000 plus suppliers engaged in the production of components that will go into the final aircraft. So that in itself really adds complexity to the project and if you can think about the difficulty of understanding your supply chain, beyond tier 1, there are tier 2, tier 3 suppliers, scattered all around the world, many of whom are new to contractors like Lockheed Martin and have not been tested before. In addition, they have divergent expectations from the project and their interests do not align perfectly.

Consider, for example, what these suppliers can expect in the way of a steady stream of contracted work – the so-called work share. Often these expectations are not fulfilled, causing misalignment and half-hearted commitment to the project. In addition, these global suppliers do not want to be seen as subcontractors, they want to be seen as long-term partners. In other words, they want to be able to keep working on the project, receive increasingly larger pieces of the pie, and so on.

Hillary Sillitto – The biggest risk in this sort of thing is socio-technical interoperability, which means: am I going to be able to get social organizations and technical systems to work together effectively across national, organizational and cultural boundaries? Thales is a multinational electronics company. The thing that characterizes everything we do is high integrity: the market we sell into is not a consumer market, it's a highly regulated market. A lot of it is safety critical, a lot of it is politically sensitive. So these projects don't obey normal market rules. In the Eurofighter project, we, Thales, partner Selex Galileo in supplying some of the equipment in that aircraft. The programme started about 1980 and it'll probably go out of service in 2050 or later, so it's a 70 year international enterprise, delivering support and operating that aircraft. It took 20 to 25 years from initial commitment to go into service.

For the Airbus A380, a collaborative European project, led by Airbus, which is part of EADS, we supplied the avionics. That took seven years from commitment to first commercial flight. So why do airliners get into service much more quickly than military aircraft? For the dockland light railway, we provided the automatic control system that allows the driverless train operation, using equipment from within our company but also from Canada, Portugal, Germany, as well as the UK.

Major segments of the A380 aircraft are built in several different European countries, taken by boat to Bordeaux, loaded on barges, then sailed up the Garonne river, and taken by lorry for 100 kilometres through little French villages with all sorts of hydraulic rams to move the parts around so they don't knock down bridges or houses. And eventually, they're put together in a very impressive final assembly facility in Toulouse. Organizational complexity dominates these projects, and this means it is not perhaps economically efficient, but it is robust because having so many stakeholders committed to the project means that the project is much more likely to go ahead and come to fruition.

Tamer Cavusgil – Well, this last comment is very interesting. In a sense, you're looking for optimization; you're not necessarily optimizing efficiency in these complex, large projects. What is it that you're really optimizing, Hillary?

Hillary Sillitto – From the point of view of a lot of procurers, it's a long-term project. Because they are constrained by cash flow rather than the total amount of money, governments have a nasty habit of cancelling projects that will not give a short term return, if they are short of money. So for example, the British military had a lot of key programmes cancelled in the 1960s, and they discovered that an international collaborative project ties these stakeholders into an interdependent web, and this means that no one stakeholder can kill the project. For example, every government has wanted to pull out of the Eurofighter at some point, but none of them have been able to. So although the project has probably taken longer and cost more than originally intended, the air forces now have their aeroplane. If it had been a national programme, the probability of it being cancelled would have been much higher.

Tamer Cavusgil – So are you certain they have a longer term view when it comes to validating the performance of the project? You are looking really at the robustness and survival in a sense of all of the partners. You need everybody who is on board to stay on board, committed, and participating in a positive way.

But why are these projects high-risk? Due to their scale? Because of the number of parties that are involved? Or because the projects themselves outlast the technologies that you start with – technologies are always evolving because they're dynamic. So you need to revisit the technology continuously and make appropriate changes to the design. Is it the organizational complexities, the process and people issues, the human touch issues involved, and so on?

Hermine Schnetler – I do not think the big risk from the human side is different from any big development project. For the project to work, for the team to gel, you still have the same issues that you would have internally, even if you are working with people from various nationalities. People need to work together with one another, and for that you have to establish a team spirit, establish relationships. Once people are interacting in a social way with one another, they tend to understand one another better. Once you can actually put names and faces together and you start knowing more about people, you're building those relationships. In my world of technology, we build telescopes and instrumentation for the UK and European astronomers. We work with people who are highly intelligent. Everybody has got their own specialist areas and you have to understand where they are coming from; you have to put in that effort. Complexity is added when you involve labs with specialist interests. For example, one in France is into variable control mirrors, so they think every system should have a variable control mirror in it, whether it is needed or not. The UK ATC specializes in cryogenic systems, so all our instruments need to be in a cryostat, and that means every system we involve needs to be cold. So I think it's those things, and it's the amount of effort you put into relationships that makes projects work or fail. I don't believe in contractual stuff. I believe in buying personal goodwill and if you've got that you can actually get things for free as well.

Tamer Cavusgil – In a sense you're saying that technology is easier to manage than people. I mean, getting the people management, people in traction in the first place is really the beginning.

Paul Holbourn – I would tend to support that. My experience derives from international programmes like the PANAVIA NATO and Eurofighter Typhoon project. Generally, the technology is the easy bit. The most difficult challenge is to create a business arrangement, a management structure where the very disparate collaborative partners are brought together with a clear focus and a clear motivation to work together. One of the lessons we've learned is that each of the participants will have their own individual specialities and very clearly identified work share. Collectively, the consortium owns the development result of the systems undertaking, and although there might be a lead systems contractor, all the participants participate in the system design and own the system design. The business arrangements, the commercial arrangements, the customer, are such that the milestones mean that we all get paid together, on delivering the system milestone, or none of us get paid. We all sink or swim together. If one partner gets paid and the other ones don't get paid, it is not going to work. If we're all in a situation where we sink or swim together, we are motivated to help each other and work together. The other key thing is money, sufficiency of money. Most international projects are under-budgeted from the outset. There may even be a conspiracy for the project to be underbid by the participants to ensure that it happens, or there is irrational exuberance by the bidders in the bid phase. If there's insufficient money, you'll not get the necessary give and take at the working level between the consortium members to make a complex undertaking work. Everyone will revert to their statements of work and their specifications in their contract and do what they're obligated to do in their own particular domain, but not work together to deliver the project holistically. So the right budget is necessary and very important.

These are also long-term projects where businesses and the people will have to work together for many decades. It requires commitment at a senior level between the collaborative partners to put it all together. One useful mechanism that we have found to date is that we effectively create a board of directors for an international project. The senior directors from each of the participating collaborative companies meet, perhaps quarterly, to receive a report from the international project team, and if there are problems and real big issues which cannot be resolved within the project, they act as a court of appeal. The board of directors are empowered by their businesses to make decisions and make financial commitments to resolve these things. It's a sign of weakness, though, if a project has to report anything but success to the BOD.

The motivation for these cross-border collaborations

Tamer Cavusgil – Earlier, my colleagues also commented that, if anyone is studying failures in international business, this industry, these types of projects, are rife with examples. This raises an interesting issue which, in this field, people refer to as the megaprojects paradox. We know that they are high-risk, high-failure cases. The failure rate is probably among the highest, maybe 50–60 per cent, according to some observers. Yet, these projects are not abandoned and we keep on doing more and more of them. So why do we get into more of these highly complex, collaborative, global projects, even though the failure rate is so high? What are the expectations that compel us to get into collaborative projects of this nature?

Paul Holbourn – I think the biggest motivation for the customer is reduction in cost. Developing and building military aircraft is a very expensive undertaking. The US is probably the last country that can afford one by itself. In Europe, we've now developed these things collaboratively and there's a hope by the participating governments that the costs would be less than doing it by themselves. But there are other challenges and it's not as efficient as they would like to think.

Tamer Cavusgil – Is the the value that one gets out of these just economic value?

Hillary Sillitto – There are a whole lot of strategic political, industrial, and military factors. With the Joint Strikefighter for example, the US is trying to pull its allies into the programme to keep them on side, to stop them developing competing aircraft, to make sure that they are able to form alliances quickly and have partners if they want to operate militarily anywhere in the world. The partner countries can't afford to develop the aircraft on their own. They get support in their high technology industry. It is much more difficult to have an international programme cancelled on you than a national one. So there are are all sorts of strategic benefits that you get by being more interdependent. It also gives you resilience problems. There will be one logistics base for the joint Strikefighter somewhere in America. So some guy is going to know where every aircraft is in the world and pretty much where it's flying at any given time. That's quite interesting if you want to be able to operate independently. There are incentives to participate; there are incentives to firewall yourselves a bit, to keep separate. I'm not sure that these megaprojects necessarily have a 50 per cent failure rate because the momentum keeps them going when other projects have failed. I'm not sure.

Success and failure: what it means and what drives it

Tamer Cavusgil – In general, megaprojects are defined as projects costing one billion dollars or more, typically involving ten or more years, and many of them are outside defence and high technology, in dam construction, airport construction, and so on. What makes one a failure, another a success?

Hillary Sillitto – The nature of these projects is that they have risk in them and I think there's a public perception issue as to what actually constitutes failure. Failure is not getting to service, delivering value. Stumbling may or may not be a failure depending on whether you're managing the risk properly. So I would challenge the understanding of what constitutes failure. Spending a little bit more on the twenty year high risk, complex technology programme when there may have been political reasons for declaring a budget that is not the real one – from the point of view of the project participants, that's not a failure.

Tamer Cavusgil – With the Dreamliner, they fell behind their predetermined or set delivery date by at least three years, they experienced at least six billion dollar overruns, and so on. They embarrassed themselves, disappointed their stakeholders, and their shareholders. They lost the confidence of some of their partners and suppliers. There were a lot of orders that were cancelled. So when you look at these, so far it's a failure, but what could they have done differently perhaps, is the question?

Hillary Sillitto – Well the thing you have to ask is – If they had been honest about the schedule earlier would they have lost orders to Airbus? There's probably a game between Airbus and Boeing to try to maintain the pretence of everything being OK, to secure orders and customer commitment. So the engineers probably knew perfectly well what was going to happen long before it became apparent to the public. There are a very complex set of incentives concerning what failure is, and what a difficulty is. This is not about making bricks or little bits of steel. There is inherent risk, as Paul said. There are two ways you can reduce the bid for these jobs. One is to be the best and to have mastered all the risks. The other is to fail to appreciate them. And in a thousand company supply chain, somebody who has taken on a contract they're not competent to deliver stops the whole job until it's sorted out. That, I would suggest, is normal. With these megaprojects, there will be failures, but the outcome will still be good if the project is set up to be robust to the failures, to have the momentum to carry on through. If, in thirty years' time, there are 2000 Dreamliners flying, giving faultless passenger service, then in retrospect that will be a success.

Tamer Cavusgil – It's all about one's perspective.

Hillary Sillitto – Yes, and whether you are looking at project success or system success. Project success is cost, time, performance to delivery. System success is thirty years of successful service.

Paul Holbourn – You need to distinguish between project failure, total abject failure, and delayed success. And many of these so-called failures are delayed success.

Hermine Schnetler – How many big projects can you say we had in the world where we start out with a huge big idea, and never ever got that system or that item or that product to be in service? I can't think of any of those. The Titanic was bold and it was supposed to last forever, so maybe that can be considered as a failure because it went into an iceberg. But it was still a success as a product development. We need really to think carefully when we declare something as a failure.

Paul Holbourn – I think we should define failure quite carefully because Eurofighter Typhoon has had a lot of bad press about schedule delays, cost overruns. But, in many ways, it's very successful. It really is a great aircraft. But it was conceived initially in the cold war, to keep the Russians at bay, and now times have changed. The military environment of that aircraft is now very different, so the operational requirement is as well. And much of the extra cost, much of the schedule delay has been to adapt that aircraft to the new world in which it is now operating. And it is a success that the original system design was sufficiently flexible to allow this change of role.

Managing for success in complex collaborative projects

Tamer Cavusgil – Let's turn to the positive side a little bit. What contributes to the success of these complex projects? We know that gaining the cooperation and commitment of the parties is absolutely essential. And we know that we're not operating in these projects in a 'command-and-control' type of environment. So it's not one integrated organization, but a loosely aligned network. It's really partners that you're trying to get on board, incentivize them, and keep their interest at a high level. You want them to be stakeholders. What are some best practices in this regard? How do you build relationships? How do you gain the commitment and ongoing participation – committed participation – of these partners?

Hillary Sillitto – Terminal 5 was a project success. It was a £4½bn programme which opened on the day it was planned to open, ten years later, within budget. This illustrates both a very successful approach and what goes wrong. The commercial construct that was put together to build Terminal 5 was a gain-sharing, risk-sharing arrangement, so all the partners, all the contractors were paid for the work they did. A risk budget was retained. If a problem happened, whoever could deal with it most quickly, most cheaply, dealt with it. If there was any money left at the end, this was shared out as profit. And that held the consortium together to deliver on time on the day.

When they delivered, all of a sudden it moved from consortia collaboration to a transactional handover and, at the same time, the complexity ratcheted up two notches from an engineering system to a socio-technical system. And it was the failure to keep the collaborative approach running through the transition to operation that caused the problems on the opening day, which was branded as a disaster, though within three weeks it was operating perfectly normally, which was a tribute to the good basic design of the system.

On a very much smaller scale, we at Thales at the moment are doing the new communications system for the new aircraft carrier in Britain. We have a French project team delivering to a British project team, which is in turn delivering to the carrier alliance. I was called in when there was a lot of transactional behaviour between the programme managers in France and the programme managers in Britain. So we set up a series of very carefully structured technical review teams, with joint French/British chairmanship meeting alternately in France and Britain. We also got the technical teams talking to each other, and they found they could quite easily resolve difficulties that the programme guys couldn't see how to deal with. If you have to appeal to the contract, you've failed.

Paul Holbourn – I would tend to agree. One thing we have tried is to create within the consortium what we term a single equivalent business, and within that, a single management structure. We have done this quite successfully on some big developments internationally, for example, Radar and Electronic Warfare systems. The commercial arrangements are that we sink or swim together, so there is senior level interest from the participating companies, and it is visible across the participants that we're getting a roughly similar 'risk to reward' type ratio, and no one partner is getting far richer at the expense of the others. And there is sufficiency of money, because insufficiency of money means you all look at your contracts.

Tamer Cavusgil – What do you mean by the 'single equivalent business.' and how do you build it?

Paul Holbourn – That really describes effectively the teaming arrangements, the collaborative arrangements, statements of work that we have, business arrangements that we have that motivate us to work effectively together, so we are tied together, so we succeed together or we don't succeed together.

Tamer Cavusgil – So, in a sense, this is an informal organization that you have created.

Paul Holbourn – Correct. We avoided creating things like joint venture companies formally, and so on. This is effectively a teaming arrangement independent of the commercial arrangements.

Tamer Cavusgil – Getting people to think that they are now part of a new mission, a new organization.

Paul Holbourn – Correct, because we're dealing with extremely complex systems. There is a man millennium of software development going into the Radar and EW system, which means you cannot specify exactly the responsibilities of each partner in their statements of work. You need to create an environment where there's motivation for give and take across contractual boundaries. Where you don't look for payment if you go beyond your statement of work but we keep a rough balance throughout the twenty year to thirty year life cycle.

Volker Mahnke – Would you say that contracts do not matter for that reason?

Paul Holbourn – Contracts do matter when things go badly, but when things are going well, they remain in the drawer.

Hillary Sillitto – If the contract drives the incentives, and that is different from the way you need to succeed, then you have a problem. It is really important that the contract provides a framework within which you can have effective collaboration. I was seconded to the British Ministry of Defence for a while and we were running a quite small but very complex collaboration with industry. It was incredibly important that the contract was set up in such a way that the desired behaviours were not disincentivized, and that they were incentivized to the extent you could define it in the contract. There is a contractual axis and there is a behavioural axis, and the two can be going in different directions. If the two are fighting, then the contractual axis will end up winning. So you've got to make sure the contract does not prevent the behaviours you want, but you cannot contract for behaviour. That means that you've got to manage behaviours separately from the contract, but in a way that the contract enables and preferably supports.

The role of the contract

Tamer Cavusgil – Does it make a difference with different types of players or partners though? Whether your partners are at the same level as you are, or whether they are SMEs, or lower level tier 2, tier 3 suppliers, who really need a contract and very precise specifications?

Paul Holbourn – Very much so. We're looking at the collaborative partners, the principal participants in the contract who'll be together for 40 or 50 years for some of these major undertakings. They will have to make it work and will have to live with each other for a long time. It's like marriage, it's not like pillage and rape.

Tamer Cavusgil – So for them, the contract really doesn't matter. It's the relationship that you're counting on. Whereas with the smaller, lower-tier suppliers, you need to be very helpful and also very timely too, because you don't want them to be bankrupt.

Paul Holbourn – No, there's no merit pushing an SME into bankruptcy if they make a small widget upon which a multi-million pound aircraft depends. You work with them to help them succeed. With their success will be your success.

Hillary Sillitto – On the other hand, if the contract has requirements which people ignore, then you get problems that are just as great. If people say never mind the contract, let's work together, and if there isn't trust and interdependent good behaviour, then it very quickly breaks down. This is a real risk because it only needs a personnel change in the commercial department of one of the parties for the partner to insist on reverting to the contract. So you've got to make sure that the contract is either completely decoupled from the behavioural issues or is structured in such a way that it is complementary to it, the contract is coherent with the behaviours that you want. You can't ignore it: if the contract says something different from what you want to do, you've got to change it. If it doesn't say all of what you have got to do, then you can work to generate the behaviours that you want as well.

Tamer Cavusgil – Hermine, you have a very interesting background. This includes various fields and disciplines including systems engineering. Part of the complexity of these projects is that you have the need for expertise in so many different disciplines in engineering, science, and so on. Systems engineering has a different contribution to the success of these projects: you take that big-picture view, integrating view, in managing these projects. What's the role of the systems engineer and what is the role of the project manager?

Hermine Schnetler – We actually start off with a science case. A group of astronomers in Europe, in the UK, want a capacity to do certain experiments. You then need to work together in the team and provide them with a structure, with an integrated approach to achieving their goals, because we are at the forefront of technology. One example is the European extremely large telescope or the thirty metre telescope. (Astronomers aren't very innovative with the naming of their products!) If you are building a 42 metre telescope, and these telescopes are normally on the top of a very high mountain, you not only have to deal with the highly technical part but somebody actually needs to go and cut the top of the mountain off to present a flat piece of land. Here you need civil engineering, because you need to create a new town there, where people will need to work, and to live, with residential capacity. You need to bring your own water, your own power, and the people need to be able to work at high altitude. You need a small hospital there because some people will go there fully fit and suddenly suffer from high altitude sickness. So it's very complex.

Dealing with conflicts

Tamer Cavusgil – Conflicts, disputes arise in the course of this interaction – a dynamic interaction among the partners.

Hermine Schnetler – You work with scientists who know how to do things best. But not everybody thinks of the bigger picture, and if you're a systems engineer, you really need to have the ability to understand all the disciplines. This can include optical engineering, electrical, software, and mechanical structures. You have to understand the big picture, but you also need to make sure in the end that, when things are being brought from bottom up, they get through the system. So you need to have the ability to move between the layers. You also have to have the ability to tell people off in the nicest possible way, so if you're a good systems engineer, you might sometimes think that everybody hates you, but in the end when it comes to party time and everybody speaks to you, you know you have done a good job.

When working through various cultures, it's different, because expectations are different. In my view of the world if you go to a meeting in France, they want to make decisions. If you go to a meeting in Britain, they just want to brag. So you have to learn, why are we going to meetings, what do we want to achieve in the meetings? So, it depends, and if you really want to be successful in a multinational environment, you have to be sensitive to those things.

Tamer Cavusgil – Who has the ultimate responsibility to come in and make a final resolution of the conflict? Is it the role of the project manager or the systems engineer?

Hermine Schnetler – Well, it depends. If it's a technical issue, I think the systems engineer will be sort of the mediator of the whole thing. In most of my projects we don't have those disputes. In one, two

French guys didn't agree on the specifications and they exploded in the room, really very emotional. But the principle investigator, also a Frenchman, was really apologetic about the misbehaviour of his countrymen. In the end, we solved the problem because nobody was wrong. When you use logic – if you've got 50 people, there are 50 people each with a different logic – one is no better or worse than another. I think in the world it's the personal thing that counts for success or failure.

Volker Mahnke – As a follow up, when they have all these different languages and cultures and perspectives, does system engineering present a language which they can all relate to?

Paul Holbourn – I think it really is the glue that holds a complex multinational project together. The systems engineering, the system design, expresses the objective of the project, from the customer requirements right down to the subsystems specifications. It's the soul of the project, and if the all participants own it and help create it, it holds the project together.

Volker Mahnke – Would you go even further and say that a technical language – I mean you're all engineers, PhDs in physics – overrides or can cancel out cultural differences?

Paul Holbourn – Partially.

Tamer Cavusgil – Partially.

Hermine Schnetler – Or, introduce new ones!

Hillary Sillitto – I think the diversity is also good, because you get new thoughts, different thoughts.

Paul Holbourn – I think the international dimension can be very, very strong. But there is also a danger in international projects that the consensus process can sometimes lead to decision-making by lowest common denominator. If this happens you get a more disappointing outcome than one you can achieve with a single nation, single company project.

Hillary Sillitto – I have had an example of that. A very long time ago, when I worked for a different company, we were talking to an Italian firm that is now part of Selex Galileo, at that time it was not. We were trying to develop some options for an optical system design. I was suggesting that we should look at something that I called a Delta Prism, which is a particular kind of optical device for rotating an image. We had a long conversation. They said, 'No, no, we don't want to do that'. I got the feeling that there was almost a deliberate misunderstanding of language. Suddenly, one of the Italians declared, 'Ah! Is "Astori" prism It was invented by an Italian. Yes, we will use it!'

One got the feeling that, when you agreed, the response was 'Yes, I understand you perfectly now,' and when you disagreed, it was, 'I'm sorry my English is not good enough to understand the subtlety of your position'. That happens and that's part of life. I'm a Fellow of the International Council on Systems Engineering and I'm involved in an international project to create a systems engineering body of knowledge (*www.sebok.org*) that we're deliberately trying to make a multinational, multi-perspective domain. We see the different behavioural styles of different nations in meetings. There's the sort of behaviour you get with Americans and Europeans, and that's quite a difficult environment for people from the Far East to work in. And we know that we're not pulling in Far Eastern guys that have got a huge amount to offer. Singapore is, I think, one of the most systems-aware nations in the world. They do a brilliant job of treating Singapore as a whole system. But engaging people from Japan, Korea and so on, it's proving to be very difficult. Behavioural style has to be watched.

International collaboration and international competition

Tamer Cavusgil – These global companies, with a global footprint, and with groups and divisions within your organizations, competing for projects. How do you manage the collaboration and the competitions simultaneously?

Paul Holbourn – I work for Selex Galileo, a subsidiary of Finmeccanica, the Italian aerospace and defence company, with a significant UK, Italian and US footprint. Thales are one of our biggest competitors, but there are many programmes on which we collaborate. What we discover is that on the successful international collaborations, the engineers and the project managers participating in the collaborations tend to go native. They align themselves with the project and not with the companies. That is a good thing, and we can be reasonably successful at, not firewalling, but isolating those international projects on which we are collaborating from the areas where we are going to compete, and compete very fiercely.

Hillary Sillitto – Within the companies, I think there are also different styles for mediating internal competition. Generally, in a multinational you want to do several things. You want to spend R&D money where you'll get the most benefit from it. And benefit includes both the ability to convert it into marketable product, and the ability to leverage government investment. So you find that when we're discussing where to place internal R&D projects – if they can be done in several different places – there are considerations such as 'I want to do it to build my business because my local customer wants a product' and 'I want to do it because I'll get tax advantages spending it here' that need to be reconciled. All sorts of internal politics are camouflaged by what appear to be rational arguments.

Some parts of Thales collaborate very effectively across nations. The rail division is sourcing critical components from several different countries, to put systems together. The electro-optics unit, based in Glasgow and Basingstoke, has almost parallel development in Britain and France. The UK is very strong in land systems; the French guys are very strong in airborne systems. The French guys collaborate with the British Selex Galileo on airborne systems; we collaborate with them on land systems. So it's a very, very complex set of decisions, driven by market conditions, capabilities, investments, tax breaks, restrictions on transferring information across borders depending on who has paid for it, whether there are national security issues, whether you're tied into a supply chain, such as with Airbus or Boeing where you've got to be careful not to compromise the interest of either customer.

Tamer Cavusgil – The nature of the sponsor makes a big difference. Hermine, you work for a public, government-funded organization. How is it different in your world, because you have worked in both private and public sectors?

Hermine Schnetler – I'm working for the Science and Technology Facilities Council and they also give grants to the universities. So, there is a lot of competition between the UK ATC and Oxford, Durham, and Cambridge Universities for the funds. At the same time, we also work together on projects. Traditionally there are more universities involved in the science aspects but, when it comes to building telescopes and instrumentation, the names I mentioned are the ones competing. In many cases we compete against one another but sometimes we're together in the same consortium. For example, in the Gemini consortium, Durham University was in together with Australia and us, the UK ATC. We were working more with people from the USA. They had two teams doing the same design study and, luckily, we won the whole competition. In the end it was all useless because it wasn't funded. Today, the observatories are getting very large and the facilities we need have become so expensive that people end up all working on the same project. You first fight it out, and then, whoever gets the bone, invites the other back in. So it's being a family!

Paul Holbourn – There is always internal competition for resources inside any big business. Inside Finmeccanica, there's a strong US presence, there's a strong UK presence, there's a strong Italian presence. Ultimately, there's the strategy of the business to which no investment decisions are being compared, which involves where we are trying to take the business in terms of market and so forth. There are also the business cases of the respective claimants for investment money, arguing which will provide the best return for the shareholder. There are also other things which need to be considered in a pragmatic world. Where the skills are, where the competences are, where work is needed. In particular, there are elements of social programmes as well.

Management in complexity and the loss of control

Tamer Cavusgil – Coming back to the complexity of megaprojects, we talked about the many dimensions of complexity. I think part of the complexity is the inherent uncertainty of the environment. Uncertainty in the technological world, uncertainty in the performance of your partners, uncertainty in funding – there's a lot of uncertainty. In my reading of the literature, I came across this terminology – 'illusion of control' – or over-optimism, overconfidence in the future. This apparently plagues some of the decision-makers in this business. By illusion of control, these writers refer to project leaders mistakenly believing that one has the ability to influence outcomes when the outcomes are obviously determined by chance. Do you think this is a serious ailment on the part of project leaders? Do we always have such over-optimism and overconfidence in the future?

Paul Holbourn – I think that it's being driven out of the business, even on these major projects. The project managers and project leaders normally have a very good handle on the inherent risks – what they're doing, where they're going, and what can be achieved. There are very rarely technology risks on these megaprojects because technology development is usually decoupled from major development programmes. I think most of the problems arise from the management of complexity, and the underestimation of the difficulty of managing complexity. This is both systems integration complexity and organizational complexity with international management, which depends on human frailty.

For Typhoon, the radar system had over 1000 man years, a man millennium of software effort, and that will continue as we go forward with upgrades and evolution because of the level of systems complexity.

But when we started 15 or 20 years ago, the tools for managing this complexity were very immature. The tools for managing complexity and the procedures, the processes and disciplines have advanced many times in that period. I think we're far more capable now of handling and managing such complexity, if we do it in a systematic and organized manner.

Hermine Schnetler – A man millennium...what if you had made use of a woman?

Hillary Sillitto – We need more female engineers, different perspectives. There's a number of things. First of all the laws of physics are invariant across the planet. Fifteen years ago, there was a lot of macho project behaviour that said that if you shout at everybody loud enough, they'll do what you want. You can shout at people and you may change their behaviour, but shouting won't change the laws of physics. It is an illusion that we can deal with the laws of physics. We know a lot more now about the limits to our ability to predict. We can control the telescope so it adapts to the way the atmosphere is behaving, and that is a huge step forward, but as Hermine was saying, we can't predict what the atmosphere is going to do above the telescope.

You have to do the same thing with the really complex projects. Different cultures have different expectations of how people will react to interactions. You can't predict behaviour, but you have to monitor and control and align incentives so that individual decisions by individual people with their own motivations add up to the product result. If you employ six or seven thousand people, you can't tell them all what to do every morning. You can give them a general direction, a general intent, you can employ intelligent people. If you give them the right motivation, the right guidance, they will be far more dedicated, focused and successful, if they are given the information to make their decisions, than they ever will be if you tell them what to do.

Volker Mahnke – This is the idea of how to manage when you don't have control, right? So you bet on complex adaptive systems, but this type of idea depends on individual parts being disposable. We're able to lose the sick parts of the system.

Hillary Sillitto – I'm a great believer in using our understanding of complex adaptive systems, the complex systems of the organizational domain we work in. You have to be very careful not to take analogies too far, but obviously there is an evolutionary element. One of the evolutionary mechanisms tends to be companies buying each other. If we need a Turkish company or a Dutch company or a

Spanish company in a consortium, even if it is not able to perform, what happens is that one of the other partners in another country may buy them out. We've seen this in the Eurofighter programme, where the same people are working in the same factory, but with a lot fewer different organizational business cards now than at the beginning. So there's a kind of supportive evolution rather than destructive evolution.

Volker Mahnke – This would require a pool of common understanding which is based on the clannishness of this global defence industry. Basically, you can dispose of parts, but the parts you dispose are legal shells while people stay in the system.

Hillary Sillitto – And of course, people retire, so you've got natural replenishment through demographics. The Scottish lighthouse is a kind of international, large-scale complex system around our coast. They decided they were going to automate it forty years ago, so they stopped recruiting lighthouse keepers. So the rate of automation has matched the rate of retirement. That was an international system because we used 18th century French optical technology from the Fresnel brothers, so that's a two century system that has been running continually since about 1800.

Moral hazard

Tamer Cavusgil – What about moral hazard? Is moral hazard one of the risks that you encounter in managing complex mega projects? Do you get into circumstances where the firm that you hire is not fully mobilizing its resources. It's not serving the best interest of the project, but it is serving its own interests, or perhaps the interest of some other client. Does this occur frequently?

Paul Holbourn – Sometimes, some of our subcontractors may not be performing as we would wish but generally in aerospace and defence, part of normal risk mitigation is to second source or have alternatives for the more critical built elements of technology or subsystem. And you would dispose of such a miscreant as quickly as possible. With a frontline partner, that very rarely happens, because they are their national champion, their government will be unhappy if they fail to perform and, so long as the right contractual arrangements and business arrangements are in place, they will generally perform to the best of their ability. They may not have the ability that you may wish, but they will perform to the best of their ability.

Tamer Cavusgil – Are there things that you can do upfront to minimize the chances of running into this challenge?

Paul Holbourn – Absolutely. Usually there is a very long and protracted lead-in time. For example, on the Radar programme for Typhoon, there were three years of intense competition. So by the time the contract is awarded, I would say that the ground rules are well established, the understanding between the partners is well established. You'll not go with these major megaprojects with an unknown partner from the outset. The aerospace and defence business is a large business but there are only a few major participants and everyone knows everyone else. We're all in it for the long term; these projects are for forty, fifty years. So I think moral hazard is not really a problem we face; we don't very often face major partners who don't want to be there. We sometimes face major partners who don't have the skill set to do what we would wish them to do, then we have to work together to acquire or to help them acquire the skill set we think they need.

Hillary Sillitto – There are some cases, as people move to set up collaborations with countries they're not familiar with, when dealing with assumptions, ground rules, local issues, local politics. For example, if you are collaborating with a country that suddenly finds a war or a crisis on its hands, then resources will be diverted to the national emergency. But, if a company has unwittingly taken on board projects that it can't actually resource, then there will be resource contention. If you don't understand the partner, you're at much more risk. If you do understand the partner and have seen how they operate over several years, you can understand what's going on and plan to take that kind of behaviour into account, and plan to try to influence its behaviour by making sure that everyone has a common interest, common purpose, common timescale of return.

Tamer Cavusgil – Timescale, that's a good cue. We need to talk about it, because many of these international large projects take longer than expected. This seems to be the nature of these projects because it is uncertain in the beginning, so it's hard to find the end point. Earlier, you said that you want to optimize its robustness, not efficiency, so nobody seems to be terribly in a hurry. Neither the politicians who founded the project nor the industry that was behind the project. So do you see a moral hazard problem in international projects?

Hermine Schnetler – I don't think it's actually true that we're not in a hurry: we are not aiming at profits but we are trying to define the laws of physics that Hillary wants to move in more precisely. The laws of physics are changing because there are still a lot of things we don't know. There is hurry, we want to get there, but the thing that keeps us back is money. The more money you've got the more you can do. But I don't think in terms of a schedule, in this sense we're not in a hurry.

Paul Holbourn – Schedule is the variable, annual money is generally not a variable. Governments have fixed cash flow and if the project is going to cost more, it will take longer as well. Another thing, I think, is often underestimated in complex international projects: the decision making, on the customer side, can be very long and protracted and slow, particularly when the requirements are changing during the course of the programme. The operational requirement for the Typhoon aircraft, for example, has changed over the years since the Cold War era. But getting a new consensus between the four participating nations has been a very time- consuming process. One nation takes its time making up its mind, four nations take four times as long. Getting four nations to say 'yes' at the same time is very difficult. Four nations will say 'yes' at different times, but there will always be one or two dissenters.

Tamer Cavusgil – In fact, in the context of the US/ Pentagon relationship with defence contractors, even if the defence contractor gets a project for a foreseeable period, they get reviewed annually. They receive budget allocations annually. So there is an incentive for them to speed up the process and not fall behind and not run into cost overruns.

The timescales involved in military projects

Hillary Sillitto – There's a lot of quite complex issues here. Defence programmes tend to take about twice as long as equivalent civil ones. The Airbus took seven years and an equivalent military one would take about 14 years. In a military one, half the total cycle time is decision time, with a pause for decision. So if you take the decision time out, you can develop defence stuff as fast as you can civil. We all think that things were much quicker in the old days before the Second World War. The Spitfire took about eight or nine years to develop. Now that's bringing in new technology, but the Spitfire took as long to develop as the A380. The other thing is that for any given project there is a most efficient time, or there is a cheapest schedule. You only know the cheapest schedule in retrospect because if you don't understand the risks at the beginning you don't get the plan schedule right. So if you can't run that most efficient schedule, either because the decision has been delayed for so long that everyone's in a desperate hurry and wants it now, or there's an annual spend rate that says you cannot spend at the optimum rate, then it will certainly cost more, and it's more likely to run into trouble.

There's been a lot of improvement over the last 15 years in the concepts called capability maturity models, which are a way of improving predictability about the outturn of fairly complex, fairly risky projects, so an organization with a higher capability maturity should have more predictable performance. If the political imperative is to involve other countries, with less mature industries in learning, then, again, you're adding in a risk. And, though moral hazard is not a concept we're familiar with, I think that moral hazard is involved almost by definition, because you are then engaging people who are learning as well as people who are competent.

Paul Holbourn – I think that is quite an important point because for a major military programme, the work share will not be optimum for efficiency. For example on the Typhoon programme, the work share was determined by the aircraft uplift by the nations, so 31–32 per cent each for UK and Germany, 21 and 12 per cent for Italy and Spain. These are the national champions. These companies will get the work, irrespective of their competence or skill or ability to contribute. Which amounts to some unplanned adventures on the way.

Tamer Cavusgil – I think a lesson to draw from this is that the success rate, and the performance of government-funded projects and privately funded projects is very, very different. They are different cases. Hillary you mentioned that it takes twice as long to complete government-funded projects.

Paul Holbourn – Airbus 380 was a very interesting example. It was effectively paid for by Airbus. They knew what they wanted, they went ahead and built it. They did not have to refer to their national governments as to specification changes as they went along. And they had probably the most demanding customer in the world, Singapore Airlines, as a large customer to encourage them.

Tamer Cavusgil – What about this dynamic? Hillary, you made a reference to the larger, growing portfolio of countries that are involved in these projects. Twenty years ago, it was just European, American, maybe Japanese companies. Now you have the companies from emerging markets. You have the Turks, you have the Indonesians, you have the Chinese, and you have the Brazilians, and so on. What kind of complexity does that add? Certainly there are different types of economies, different types of political regimes, and many new partners to contend with. What are your thoughts on that?

Hillary Sillitto – Well, certainly, there's the issue of expectations, different people need different things in the contracts, and despite the best efforts of lawyers, different cultures have different risk attitudes when bidding for work. Different cultures have different expectations of being able to re-negotiate once they've got on the team. Some cultures are terrified of saying no or having an open argument, others are extremely rude and impolite and will do things that are socially unacceptable. So again, there's this mixture. As soon as you say you have Turkish and Indonesian partners for necessary reasons, most European or American engineers' hearts will sink. We can learn an awful lot from these countries but to do that we've got to take things in their world, not in ours. I spent two weeks in Indonesia two years ago; it's fascinating, a completely different perspective. People there have a different background, they work much harder and they are motivated in quite different ways. If you can exploit that, it's very powerful. If you try to run a non-Western operation using a method that has grown up in Western cultures, if it isn't culturally adaptable, you're going to have big problems.

Paul Holbourn – I would support what Hillary has said. My experience of some of these emerging nations that are trying to grow in aerospace defence capabilities is actually quite positive. They can be very surprising, because they don't have the fifty, sixty, seventy years of history which often makes us slower at doing things, and process bound. They can be very agile and very quick sometimes, but you need to go into these collaborations with an open mind. You also need to make sufficient contingency to allow you to transfer technology or technical support to help them succeed, because if they cannot succeed there will be a loss of face, and it will be a disaster. You have to make that provision to transfer technology, or transfer some level of engineering effort to help them succeed. This is because they go into these projects, not just to get the output, but to get the learning experience developed in their industry on the way.

Tamer Cavusgil – Is it to create employment?

Paul Holbourn – Well not create employment, but to create an industry in their nation, and you have to recognize that you are effectively creating competition, potentially a competitor in the future; but this is the price of doing business. If you recognize that at the outset, and make the appropriate contingency and provision for it, these can be very successful projects. And whilst, on the one hand you can say you're creating a competitor, with the next generation of technology, you will always be one step ahead. I don't see the risk there, I see you have to approach this with an open mind. You will get some positive surprises, but you will also get some negative surprises.

Volker Mahnke – For one, there are some examples of nations who developed their own aircraft and their own defence systems.

Paul Holbourn – One nation I'm very, very impressed with because I've done work with them and have been involved in some major supply contracts work, is Sweden. Sweden is a nation of about 8 or 9 million people that has created the jet fighter called the Gripen. It's a very impressive fourth generation aircraft, and its been put into service in Sweden and a number of export customers around the world. The Swedish government, with nine million tax payers, cannot afford to create a modern advanced system but we have a collaborative programme with Eurofighter, Typhoon, with four of the richest countries in Europe making an aircraft which is only a little bit better and many times the cost. And the four nations are whining and complaining and crying about the cost. It's quite interesting. I also look at the JSF, which is an international collaborative programme now, which was originally touted as a low cost aircraft and is now rapidly becoming a high cost aircraft. So I think there are some interesting models to look at in Sweden, where a single nation, with a very clear focus, working collaboratively with its industry and without competition, can achieve great things.

Volker Mahnke – What can we learn from the Swedish model?

Paul Holbourn – Sweden just now is undergoing a bit of renaissance in its defence industry because Sweden had a capable aircraft competence, jet engine competence, submarine competence, military communications competence. I think they're now realizing they can't afford all these competences, but they will sustain their aircraft business in the future.

The political dimension

Floor Question – In international projects, particularly defence ones, but most international projects where governments are involved, politics are involved. If I became a project leader for a major project, the first person I would want to employ is a political adviser, no matter how well you've done your systems engineering, no matter how good your business skills. At the end of the day, when you're doing these projects, there's a political decision to be made.

Paul Holbourn – You're exactly right. Politicians are very fickle creatures. And I think this is one of the reasons why defence projects take longer than their civil equivalents – because they're subject to political interference, erratic funding, poor decision making, and, if five countries are involved, you get five sets of politicians, and the joint probability of agreement is very low.

Hillary Sillitto – It is apocryphally said that in the United States, every system needs fifty subsystems or service elements, one for each state, to secure the vote of every congressman. So the political element is making stuff robust. One of the reasons for multinational collaborations is actually to get people so interdependent they don't start fighting each other.

Tamer Cavusgil – Certainly politics is a major contributor to the complexity of these projects.

The role of the contract

Floor Question – I have a question about whether contracts are used or not. I would be surprised to hear that, when there are conflicts, contracts are used. My understanding is that contracts are also not used where there are conflicts , because you never go to litigation on these types of projects.

Hermine Schnetler – I think that when you have to use a contract and you have to go to litigation, the parties at dispute are both losing. It is not only that the lawyers are winning. It's always much, much better to just sit down and talk. If you had managed to build a team, you won't get to that point, because it is like going to war, and we know the consequences: there are no winners in war.

Paul Holbourn – Yes, I would agree that conflict resolution is far better. But there are two layers of contract, between the consortium and their customer and within the consortium, which effectively defines the business arrangements. And I would say that generally industry will sort itself out without reference to the contract or to lawyers for conflict resolution, but sometimes between the customer and consortium, there will ultimately be difficult and protracted legal and commercial dispute.

Doing business in the BRIC countries: the effects of buyback arrangements

Floor Question – I was interested in what effects are going to emerge from buyback arrangements, and so on, in BRIC countries, and what this means for the skills of the employees going there.

Paul Holbourn – The way that we do business with customers is changing all the time. Twenty years ago we would sell a black box, get paid for a black box, and deliver a black box. Nowadays, when we make a sale, particularly to a BRIC country, there is a lot of expectation of technology transfer and offset. We have to embrace this thinking, and that requires a different skill set in our own company. And we've got some very successful partnerships now in various countries. These partnerships are rarely temporary, and are rarely just for one particular project. We often find that companies and arrangements we made for one project will serve as our international supply base for other projects.

Tamer Cavusgil – It's my observation that buyback and offset agreements are kind of going away in favour of performance-based logistics. It's really what can you do, what can you deliver for me? – in quality, design, and so on. It is more of a free market, and it is competitive; even though the work share is decided at the top level for the countries.

Hillary Sillitto – You'll often try to design a system with elements that you are happy to subcontract into a country to generate this activity. This business is not a matter of getting on a plane to a BRIC country, having a conversation with somebody, and coming back with an order. It's not like that, because it is a long term, whole-business comprehensive discussion before you get anywhere near a major contract. You're building relationships at all levels in the industry in order to generate confidence to go ahead.

Tamer Cavusgil – I would like to thank these very experienced executives for sharing their thoughtful observations and perspectives with us. They have greatly enlightened us on the topic of managing megaprojects. Thank you!

12

Managing the Process of Internationalization: Pervez Ghauri Interviews Four Managers Experienced in Doing It

Pervez Ghauri and Simon Harris

Introduction

This conversation is one between researchers with experience of working with practitioners, and some practitioners very experienced in the process of internationalization. In a public conference session chaired by *Simon Harris,* with an audience of practitioners and researchers, *Pervez Ghauri* explored a number of issues that are of current research interest, and we found them to be of significant practitioner interest as well. Here we present a lightly edited transcript of that interview.

After introducing the participants and their businesses, the participants discuss the process they go through in deciding where and how to internationalize, including the information they use and their sources, where we find some surprising consistency between the larger and the smaller firms. The partnerships involved in international business are then discussed, what is sought in them, what is important about them, and whether and how they are necessary for internationalization. The participants, all from different business sectors, then discuss the adaptation to local market conditions that they find to be necessary.

We then discuss a number of specific issues, starting with how they deal with uncertainty and change in overseas territories within their businesses. This leads on to an extensive discussion of the opportunities and challenges of internationalizing to emerging markets, as compared to more mature markets, where we find some surprising and diverse perspectives. This leads to a consideration of one of the major risks often presented for knowledge-based businesses in emerging markets, the risks of counterfeit goods and the problems of intellectual property protection. Before opening up to questions from the floor, the responses to which are included here in full, we discussed two topics that have been the focus of other chapters in this volume, and which were a focus for special paper sessions within the conference. One is the issue of learning in the internationalization process, and what is the learning that you can accumulate from internationalizing into one market that can then be used when internationalizing to another. Finally, the issue of ethical behaviour in international business is considered, a topic that was picked up again in the question and answer session.

Introducing the participants and their businesses

Simon Harris – Welcome to this session on managing the internationalization process. I'll start by introducing our guests. Most of us are familiar with the work of Pervez Ghauri and his extensive work on the internationalization process; looking at different types of companies and the processes that they go through in internationalizing. That variety is reflected in the group we are fortunate to welcome today.

- Carla Mahieu, from Aegon, which is not the kind of company that one would normally think of approaching for their internationalizing experience, but Aegon has made dramatic progress in recent years in internationalizing in China and India. Carla also brings some different experiences from other companies, like Philips and Shell.
- Ian Stevens, from Mpathy, has had a contrasting experience. Formerly at Optos, he's now at a company whose experience has mainly been in North America.
- Paul D'Arcy, from Raytheon, is from a successful subsidiary of a large American multinational, and brings experience of taking technology products to many countries around the World.
- Arten Moussavi is now starting up a new company, Bio Food Nutrition, which will be international right from the very start. He brings experience of doing that in a previous company in a different product area.

Pervez Ghauri – Good afternoon everybody. I think we have a very exciting session ahead of us. We have a very distinguished panel from different fields of business and also different types of companies, from multinationals to very small start ups. We will give about three to five minutes to each person to tell you a little bit about themselves and their experiences so that we can place their answers in context. Then I will ask a few questions about issues on which we are in fact doing research. I believe most of us are working in one way or another on the internationalization process. We will also ask some questions about the very specific type of risks involved when going abroad. We will also talk about some contrasts between going to various emerging markets; what types of challenges are there, and whether emerging markets are a threat or an opportunity. Then of course we will talk a little bit about learning effects. Do companies really learn when they go successively from one market to the next, and do they get any help from previous experiences when they engage with new experiences?

Carla Mahieu – Good afternoon everybody. I've worked for three different companies in very different sectors over a time span of over twenty five years. I've worked in Shell, oil and gas, Philips electronics, focusing on consumer and healthcare markets, and I now work for Aegon, where I am globally responsible for human resource management. In those twenty five years in different sectors and in different businesses, I've seen the approach towards emerging markets change from an international company perspective. Many companies used to think of emerging markets for relatively cheap production opportunities. Over time, companies have come to understand that they are really emerging markets, with demanding customers with their own requirements. More and more it will also, in future, become the source of innovation and of talent. Aegon is active in twenty countries. We serve forty million customers globally, and of the thirty thousand people we employ globally, 80 per cent are in markets like the US, UK, and the Netherlands, and 20 per cent are in emerging markets. But we're building up our presence there rapidly. We moved into China a number of years ago and we have been active in India since 2008 with joint venture partners, another topic to explore later on.

Ian Stevens – The organizations that I've been working with most recently are Optos and Mpathy, both Scottish start-up life science companies. Internationalization for both was imperative – the UK healthcare market was not where Optos or Mpathy needed to go. Both those companies went from zero turnover and zero employees. Optos floated in 2006. Mpathy started in 2007, to be acquired by one of its main competitors in 2010. Optos had an invention, a scanning laser to look at the back of the eye to determine eye disease, such as retinopathy or hypertension diabetes. It was put into retail locations all over America, where eyes were checked annually and the patients' were charged. There were lots of challenges, with regards to how you run an international medical retail business from Dunfermline. Mpathy was completely different. It's a surgical business to deal with stress incontinence and pelvic floor prolapse in women. Again it needed to go to the US market to make it successful.

Paul D'Arcy – I work for Raytheon, which is predominantly a defence aero-space company. We're about eighty thousand people worldwide so we reach into to most regions. We're dealing more and more with the emerging economies and that brings more and more differ-ent challenges. We realize we can't take the same business models wherever we go, so we have different ways of dealing with differ-ent regions. My experience is Scandinavia, the Far East, The Middle East, and North America. I'm sure that what you'll hear from me is that it's all about the people you involve where you trade.

Arten Moussavi – I've got experience with small companies, very small com-panies, micro companies. I started life as a scientist in Edinburgh. I co-founded a technology business called Lux Innovate and also learned that sometimes your home market isn't necessarily the mar-ket you want to be in. This is maybe because of slow uptake, large barriers to entry, and the competition being very large and having a long history in those markets. So we decided to move into profes-sional markets after two years of being established, in the start up phase. Now, very recently, in October 2010, I have co-founded a bio food nutrition company. It's a different kind of business, more in the food market. Within a month of looking at the strategy of the business, I decided to move the focus to the emerging markets and that's what we've been doing since then and we have found that those markets are actually a great opportunity and not necessarily that expensive to get into.

The process of deciding where and how to internationalize

Pervez Ghauri – OK, very good. Now we know everybody and a little bit of background. So, maybe Paul we can start with you. You come from a very big multinational company, perhaps you can tell us how do you really do it, how do you go abroad, especially, how do you pre-pare to go? How do you decide that?

Paul D'Arcy – One of the challenges when we were moving into a region is finding out what's going on in the market. We have field offices. We use the reach of our local government representatives in those regions and we pick up intelligence before we go to those regions, and then we adopt business models that are appropriate for them.

Pervez Ghauri – So intelligence, do you have an intelligence unit, in the com-pany?

Paul D'Arcy – Like many big companies, we have large databases of central-ized intelligence. I'm not a big fan of that, personally. I believe in people on the ground, a permanent presence, networking. Customer relations databases can be the fad one day but they're not my particular interest. So, we use local governments, networks, trade associations in country, and we get to know the region.

Pervez Ghauri – So you do have different databanks in the company for different markets?

Paul D'Arcy – Yes, that's more for understanding the organizations, the buying organizations and the regions. So, we have databases of who is in what positions, what levels of authority. There are client databases of who've we've contacted. What's the strength of those relationships? Who are the power players? But for me it's all about being on the ground because that changes. Governments change, regimes are changing, databases fold, so your database can be obsolete once you've changed government.

Ian Stevens – To answer the question for both companies, we're talking about the US health market. Up to about three or four years ago, one in every twenty dollars spent worldwide was spent on the US healthcare system. So its quite a big market. We were looking at the ophthalmology and optometry market, so we employed someone to go and look at the ophthalmology and optometry markets worldwide, see the size of the markets, see where the care was provided, where was primary care, secondary care, what the price points were and who was providing it. And having done that, we decided to go to America because it was 50 per cent of the world market. I guess we could have done that straight away because anyone could have told us that but we wanted to know which other markets to go into as well. When we started Mpathy, we just went to America because the main competitors in the women's health market were all headquartered in the United States of America. But to get the market data, in order to kmow how we were going to run the business in America, in a particular small subsection of the healthcare market, you go to the major events and you can see all the products. In fact, I was asked to do that by the owners of Mpathy as part of a due-diligence exercise. That was part of the work I did before joining the company.

Pervez Ghauri – So, for China, did you have a local agent? Or did you employ a person in the company whose job was to help in China with the research.

Ian Stevens – For Optos, we employed a local person who went and did the work. They did access information for other countries. So, it was a person within the company who looked at market size, at where the procedures were being performed, and at the cost and revenue for each of those procedures. Without that I don't think we could have got enough detailed information. We had to make a decision at a certain point: Are we actually going to go on? But we knew we would find out a lot more later about how to do more business. But the early data on a macro level told us it was a suitable market.

Pervez Ghauri – And Carla, you come from a services industry, which is not perhaps something relevant for all emerging markets. If we look at cultural differences, and risk avoidance, and uncertainty indices, we think perhaps insurance is not for the markets we are talking about.

Carla Mahieu – Well it's true that insurance is often a local market, because it's regulated and influenced by local legislation. Yet, at the same time, in many of the emerging markets you see a fast growing middle class and they do show an interest in the products that we have to offer, like pensions, like life insurance, and it is therefore growing fast. I must say also, that in the other companies I have worked for, I have actually seen situations where there was the most fantastic data on the table, the most fantastic power points and reports, and yet, the business never came to the point of really doing something different in China. And I'm not just talking about Aegon. I'm talking also about other companies. It only really starts to happen when you organize for it on the ground. And once you get that commitment going with more in depth marketing information from people who are there in that market, who do understand the local requirements, who do have the contacts, then you can start really organizing for it. Until then, on the basis of yesterday data alone, it's often a paralysis by analysis.

Pervez Ghauri – You were also in Philips, a truly global company. These types of companies have intelligence units and they collect information on different aspects. Are you referring to that, or does it really not help?

Carla Mahieu – It started to help the moment we start to organize for it. So a company like Philips had all the necessary information available to make the rational decision for a long time. The moment you start organizing yourself differently, that's the moment it truly starts to happen.

Pervez Ghauri – So Arten, is it different for smaller companies? How do you do it?

Arten Moussavi – In terms of market information, market data, we don't have the resources to commission primary research. Our most expensive investment is to go travel out to the country market that we're interested in entering. We do a lot of desk research with the free sources of information that you find on the internet. We also leverage the government bodies, for example Scottish Trade International. We're in London, so we use the UK Trade offices and quite often they have local representatives in several key places within emerging markets. It is not so much about demographics and buying patterns but more who the major players are in terms of distribution channels and things like that. Some of the regulatory requirements are important because we have some products which are heavily regulated in the infant nutrition market. So that's how we try to overcome some of the expense of gathering data. We don't have a sophisticated database, we're much more focused on relationship building.

Pervez Ghauri – The bigger companies, do you mobilize your government? If you want to go to China, do you go to your government and ask for help, or ask the embassy over there?

Paul D'Arcy – In certain regions, yes, through Scottish Trade International or UK Trade and Investment, who will be in partnership with the embassies locally. They will not only give you intelligence but they will promote you and connect you in those regions. So we do use the government outposts in the regions. In defence, the market is sometimes all about the politics as well as the business. So it's essential for us to be politically connected, in any region.

Ian Stevens – Contrasting that to a small company: as I said, we do use Scottish Trade International. They are very resourceful but there are limited resources in a small company, so choosing which conversations you're going to have and who you're going to ask to help you is very important. Some people may supposedly be there to help, but they may not help move your business forward very much. Those decisions about where to spend your time, or how, are crucial.

The partnerships for international business

Pervez Ghauri – So may I ask about your criteria for partners in your business, your industry. Why Sony for example?

Carla Mahieu –When Aegon went to the emerging markets, we found strength in going for joint venture partners. In different emerging markets, we have very different joint venture partners in different sectors than ours but who were all well known in their particular country. So, for instance, in China we have a joint venture with Seanook. Seanook is a national oil and gas company. In Japan, we have a joint venture with Sony and in India with Velager. So we have found a sort of strength and representation in our entrance into these markets by working closely with our joint venture partners. One of the things we certainly look for is the company values. Apart from old business criteria that you might have in terms of financial strength, business channels, access to certain markets and so forth, we certainly look for soft things such as the sort of values the other companies stand for. Working with well-established reputable companies is an important criteria.

Pervez Ghauri – OK. So, well-established brands or companies that already have some representation in the market. So, Arten, do you go for joint ventures?

Arten Moussavi – Yes, there are two businesses I've been involved in. In the first business, one division was taking our in-house technologies and applying them to very different uses. So we applied our life science technologies to, for example, removing radioactive traces in oil fields. So we were pioneers at that and that drove us into the more mature market where ageing assets, for example in the North Sea and Mexico, really did require a better and more accurate flow of technologies. More recently, our Bio nutrition company has been able to compete with some large multinational companies in their markets because we're still in the early stages. But, they are approaching these markets as if they were mature markets and taking a lot of their own learning and cultures and trying to impose those on the market. In going into a new market, what we look for are well established players that have a lot of the right business, financial stability, and access to the right sales channels. But they do not need necessarily to be selling our products. More important is the reputation that a company has in that market. If it has a good reputation like Sony has in Japan then we can use that to our advantage.

Pervez Ghauri – So it seems a lot of companies are using joint ventures. But why joint ventures?

Paul D'Arcy – Joint ventures, collaborations, partnerships, teaming arrangements, the preference varies from region to region. Some will form joint ventures that are formal, and a lot more formal than is appropriate in some countries. When going into certain regions as part of big aerospace programmes, a part of the deal is to offset and to buy back and to put in technology, to set up factories, and to acquire companies. There are two reasons for that. One is that this is a part of the deal and, secondly, you instantly get that local knowledge as you acquire companies and get local presence. When you are working in different cultures that's the quick entry into the market. We do it for business reasons because it is a part of the negotiated contract, but it's also good business sense because with limited resources you cannot run a big market promotion campaign in every region you go to.

Ian Stevens – We did not use joint ventures at all. What Mpathy wanted to do was to choose the best market to go into, and to create from zero a reasonably substantial business which can later be bought by one of the competitors. Boston Scientific, American Medical Systems, are competing head on, so there was no option to join a venture with any of them. We wanted to create a small but excellent company that could then be purchased, both products and people. We didn't go down the distributor route, which would be the closest to a joint venture in the medical model. We put together a direct sales force and ran the business that way. A lot of companies invent products, spending millions and millions of dollars, and then give it to somebody who doesn't care about the product to sell it, a distributor. Its easy to think, especially when working overseas, that it's too difficult, and to let a foreign distributor deal with the sales. But this wasn't our objective.

Adaptation to local markets

Pervez Ghauri – Another issue which many of us are doing research on is how much adaptation we have to do when we go abroad. How much of your product or service is global and how much of it is local. How do you make the decision about how much you have to adapt to local markets?

Carla Mahieu – Insurance, by its very nature, always has to respond to local market requirements. For instance, if you look to the sort of products that we sell in India, 7 per cent of the life insurance products that we sell are pension arrangements in rural areas. So that requires you to approach your end customer in a different way. So, sometimes the innovation is about the product, sometimes the innovation is about the distribution channel that you use. One of the key challenges, especially for large companies, is that ability to enable different business models in one organization. I happen to sit in a headquarters building, and the tendency in headquarters is that they like to run the world according to headquarter guidelines, and that doesn't always work. If you allow or enable, that flexibility, then I think you can truly be successful in different markets.

Pervez Ghauri – Arten, do you adapt your product?

Arten Moussavi – Yes and no. For the infant formulas, we have regulatory guidelines we adhere to, but we also try to enhance the products as much as possible with the latest scientific medical recommendations, so they're functionalized as much as we can and we're allowed to give the products that differentiation. But, the adult nutrition side does cause a few headaches, because of the diversity of the products we've ventured in to, and quite rapidly so, and because of different tastes and requirements. In the Middle East, we have a nutritional supplement for breastfeeding, lactating mothers. They want something which is very high in vanilla content and quite sweet to taste. In the Far East, Cambodia, Vietnam, they prefer something that tastes more like cow's milk with less of the flavourings and sweeteners. For a small company that poses quite a lot of pressure on the supply chain, and variety in your products makes the prices start to go up.

Pervez Ghauri – So do you adapt your marketing for each market, country to country?

Arten Moussavi – Yes, we try wherever possible to put the production, the marketing and the promotion in the hands of local distributors. We haven't had much time to develop beyond some product literature to accompany the sales, such as for the infant formula, which goes into the medical community, and into primary care. For adult nutrition, we're in supermarkets. We have designers in Europe and Denmark who have developed a strong appetizing design history. We produce the graphics and then send it out. So there is a consistency in the brand but the way it's presented sometimes is quite surprising to us.

Coping with change and volatility

Pervez Ghauri –One last factor these days is that environments have become very volatile, things are changing rapidly over night. Countries like Egypt or Bahrain are changing totally with different groups coming to power. Paul, in your company, how do you handle these changes.

Paul D'Arcy – The traditional way in the past was for many companies to do PEST and SWOT analysis of all this sort of thing in the region, put it in the draw and assume it'll be OK for five years. The level of dynamism going on is reflected in the example recently where someone gets off a plane in a region, and the regimes had changed during the flight. You have to be thorough and rigorous with competitive intelligence, and when you go to a region you've got to think about the competition. They're not going to sit on their hands. So how are they going to react, what's your plan? Your environmental analysis has to be vigorous, thorough, and it has to be continuous. That's not second nature to many companies, many big companies, who are too busy trying to do the transactions, while the playing field is changing. It's looking at your feet and looking at the horizon at the same time which is a problem for large and for small organizations. So the winners will be the people who constantly scan, and get competitive edge by turning someone else's weakness in to an opportunity for themselves. It's having people in the country with these networks. You cannot sit back at HQ, as Carla says, doing video conferences into regions and thinking you're going to understand what's going on. You have no sense of what's going so you have to have a permanent presence there.

Pervez Ghauri – Ian, do you have some type of contingencies or plans?

Ian Stevens – I hope I never get off a plane in Boston and find that Sarah Palin's in charge overnight. I think America's less likely to be prone to a regime change.

Pervez Ghauri – But there has been a regime change in America.

Ian Stevens – President Obama has got a very different view on healthcare provision to president Bush. But a small company like Optos or Mpathy just cannot deal with changes as big as that. The Optos product was one of the reasons that we went to the United States in the first place. The product that we sold in the States was a product to detect whether the disease was present or not. That meant that it was taken out of the reimbursement system altogether and patients paid an extra sum of money for it. So whether President Obama decided he was going to reimburse eye tests it didn't matter to us: the patients paid. We made that decision early on.

The opportunities and challenges of emerging markets

Pervez Ghauri – So Arten, how come you're not selling in UK but you are in many emerging markets?

Arten Moussavi – The UK markets, sales channels, pharmacies and the supermarkets are dominated by a few players, very large companies, that charge huge fees for stacking products on the shelves and it's a similar situation across Europe and North America. You have to have quite a large start up capital to enter these mature markets. Our strategy has been to move to the emerging markets where we can form partnerships with established distributors. But sometimes not so. We're moving into China, not through a distributor but through a property group. This is a completely logical move for us because the property group is establishing a distribution network in one of the largest chains of pharmacies and supermarkets, which they helped build and put together. So their strategy is now to diversify, so we're going to try and go along with them now and really take advantage of the growth and investment they're putting in to the sales channel. So, we don't have to do that and we won't have much involvement in the marketing. We can concentrate on education, running seminars, training, putting pressure on key leverage points. Being a small organization that's easier to do than than to take a stake in titled goods in the supermarket, to pay for a logistics operation, and to pay for the marketing and the promotion. That becomes very expensive very quickly.

Pervez Ghauri – So you are saying it's easier to go to emerging markets than to go to developed markets.

Arten Moussavi – Yes, that's what I believe. I can't see our financial success, – we became profitable within three months – happening in the UK.

Pervez Ghauri – Do you agree Carla, is it easier to get into emerging markets than developed markets?

Carla Mahieu – I wouldn't say easier but if I look to the Aegon business in India, for instance, we started out in 2008 and it was a true Greenfield operation. Now there's three thousand employees, in two and a half years, but this took the recruitment of almost double that number. That is another feature of emerging markets: it is all growing so rapidly, is so buoyant, that it is sometimes very hard to retain the people. So is it easier, to grow your business, to grow with the middle class, with GDP growth, and so on? It is relatively easy to catch those growth opportunities, but to sustain that growth and to build a sustainable organization, in many ways I would say it is harder.

Pervez Ghauri – Paul, what is your opinion on that, is it easier to go to emerging markets?

Paul D'Arcy – In some ways, if you already have solutions, if you've already developed, achieved high quality, you can sell your product straight in and you don't have to make that investment. That can sometimes be easier, but there's a flip side to that as well. Our experience in America can be easier because we've tried and tested our technology platforms for there. The challenge of going in to emerging markets is that the return on investment is over a longer time frame, so the view has to be different from established markets. Typically, you'll be moving in to regions where you have a twenty year business plan for a permanent move to that region; you're not moving there for a three year transaction. It's hard to get your stakeholders and your investors to take that longer term view. There's always the conflict within companies where everyone's competing for investment. Getting into emerging markets, is a longer game and that's not always understood by investors, whether they're private investors or corporate investors.

Pervez Ghauri – Another issue I want to deal with, or discuss here, is that when we are doing business, different cultures do business differently, in some we say personal relationships are very important, in others they are not.

Ian Stevens – It's all about the business and it's not about the personal relationship and the length of time you've spent with that person. But if you are going to do business with somebody, a good business, you need to be there with them. You need to find out what other things will make them want to buy from you or make a group of customers want to buy from your company. Unless you're there, you won't find that information out. So there's a bit of both. There's a soft side to the relationship. Being friends with somebody is more or less important in some countries rather than others. But everywhere, you have to make sure that you're getting the good message across about your product otherwise you won't be successful.

Pervez Ghauri – So once you're in the market and you want to grow further, so what do you think is the most important issue there?

Ian Stevens – Well, to draw on my experience, we made a decision that we wanted to be excellent, because we knew that, for every ten customers, if we had one bad customer report, that customer would tell others. So as a small company with not many resources we try to make sure that every single customer had a good thing to say about us. I think this would apply to any business. But the point made here is that a small company won't go into an emerging market if it thinks it's going to take twenty years, or even five years, to be successful. It just won't have the investment to do that. So, smaller companies have to look to shorter term horizons to be successful.

Pervez Ghauri – Do you agree?

Arten Moussavi – Yes, I totally agree with that. I grew up with the experience of biotechnology. Very long lead times, a lot of investment in R and D, a lot of product development time, regulatory hurdles to overcome, and several rounds of venture capital to get to the point where you have something that another company either wants to acquire so you can float, or you can exit. I decided that the funding we were receiving just wasn't going to take us all the way to an exit point in that biotech business, so we diversified into the oil and gas industry. That experience is what I'm bringing now, looking for ways in which we can accelerate growth. The emerging markets, I believe, offer that opportunity. There are very dynamic businesses that have only emerged in the last fifteen years. In India, for example, there are a lot of small businesses that are now producing medicines for the NHS, vaccines for the US military. These kinds of companies have grown incredibly quickly and they are very sophisticated businesses. We're seeing that in China, we're seeing that in South Asia as well, and we want to get partners that have that ambition and that speed and those capabilities and that are investing in it.

The risks of counterfeit and intellectual property protection

Pervez Ghauri – One of the risks we come across is the danger of counterfeits, that your product can be easily copied and then you are one supplier among others selling products similar to yours. So, do you face this problem?

Arten Moussavi – Yes, we have spent the majority of our upfront costs on intellectual property protection and packaging design to make them very difficult to copy. We've had to spend more on our packaging than we would otherwise have wanted to. The nature of some of these emerging markets is such that you can't afford not to, especially if you're in the infant food market. One counterfeit episode can damage the brand across the world, so we can't afford to have that happen to us.

Pervez Ghauri – If you discover one, what do you do?

Arten Moussavi – With all the partnerships we have, we have a very strong agreement and we choose partners who will hopefully honour it. There is also a business contingency plan and it's quite a thick document. It's a bit like an emergency relief system. We will fly straight out there and try and manage media and we will try and manage product recall, because you can't afford to take the risk.

Pervez Ghauri – Carla is this a problem in your industry?

Carla Mahieu – Well if you're in, let's say, life insurance and pensions, you're offering a customer financial security over time. That is something you can't easily copy because it depends on so many other things, it's not just the product. It's also the financial stability and capability of the whole company and what the brand stands for. If you're in the electronics industry, where I worked for many years, then you would worry about intellectual property. So it depends on what sort of business you're in, on the nature of your business.

Pervez Ghauri – Paul, do you face these problems?

Paul D'Arcy – With sophisticated defence electronics equipments, we have to protect the know-how, the IP. The biggest challenge there today is probably cyber attack on the corporation, so a large part of our business is cyber security.

Ian Stevens – With Mpathy, the market that we went into was very competitive and the intellectual property space was quite crowded.

There had been a lot of activity in terms of stealing other large multinational company's intellectual property. Actually, we were reasonably well protected against that. First, because we had some good intellectual property. Secondly, because there were four or five other players in the market and our aim was to be purchased by one of them. So ripping off our intellectual property was only going to cause a problem for whoever did it. Ironically, we were sued, for patent infringement, by the company that then purchased us six months later. They did that to try to depress our value in the view of the other companies in the market. So counterfeiting by the backdoor, I guess.

Pervez Ghauri – So that worked for them?

Ian Stevens – No it didn't work, we protected ourselves very well, but it was a little bit annoying at the time.

Learning for internationalization

Pervez Ghauri – Let's talk a little bit about learning. We do a lot of research about that. Do you learn form one market when you go to the next. So, if you have been in Poland, let's say, do you think the rate of success will be higher if you got to Hungary? What do you think? So, do you really learn in this way, what do you learn, and how does it help you, every time you go to a new market?

Carla Mahieu – I think you always do learn and I think when we go in to new markets there is knowledge and there are people that we transfer to bring that knowledge across to speed up the learning in that sense. Some of our people went from more mature markets to emerging markets. I now also see the reverse happening, and recently on a company visit to India, I asked the local business development guy, 'So how long did it take you to develop that product?' and he said 'well, six to eight weeks'; and the colleagues with me from mature markets started to mumble, 'Now we really mean from the beginning to the end, how long did it take?' 'Six to eight weeks', came the answer. Again mumbling, 'No, we mean including the IT solution to bring it to the customer, so how long did it take?' He said 'Six to eight weeks'. I think it is that type of learning that is coming from the emerging markets in to the mature markets.

Pervez Ghauri – Arten, what do you think?

Arten Moussavi – We're a small business and we've got a lot to learn. We have learnt a lot about what not to do, and you learn quickly when you're a small company because information's passed around the company. We don't have lots of different locations, most of us share the same office. In terms of, 'Can we take our experiences from the Middle East and transfer them to the Far East?', No, we haven't really been able to do that. The cultural differences are so great that we're literally being led by the hand quite often in the Far East, and even within the Far East, there's a huge diversity. Cambodia is very different from Hong Kong, and different parts of China appear to have very different regulations and culture to deal with. But, business has become very international and we deal primarily in documentary letters of credit. We've learnt ways in which we can reduce cash flow, stress, and how not to disrupt trust, and things like that in markets, and we have been able to apply that learning across the World. But there are subtle, but very important, differences in every country market that we're in.

Pervez Ghauri – Paul?

Paul D'Arcy – The only thing I would add is that you can't take the same business model to each region, it's just not a transactional thing. The things we do, really as Carla said, is we think how we can get intelligence quickly, that's the name of our game, intelligence. Competitive intelligence, market intelligence, so that may mean you acquire someone, or you go in to a network, find out where the networks are, find out where the power players are. What are the written rules, what are the unwritten rules, who really makes the decisions? So you get connected using your government agencies or you acquire known companies there. I think we also learned to blend local home country leadership in these regions with local conventions so we don't take the business model but we take the same approach. It's more about how you can learn quickly on the ground and listen, and gain intelligence quickly. So that you can move fast. It's more of an approach to doing business, because every region is supremely different.

Pervez Ghauri – Ian?

Ian Stevens – I agree, you can't copy what you've done in one area to another, and even within America you can't copy in different states. Just bringing somebody into your organization who's got experience is not enough because every situation is different. The important thing is to become a learning organization, that there are processes in place which analyse what it was that you learnt from the last bit of work that you did, and that your people are aligned with that sort of culture. If you can get that going then you can go into any market and make a success of it, given a fair wind.

Ethics in international business

Pervez Ghauri – How about ethical issues. What sort of ethical dilemmas do you face when you go to new markets, and how do you handle them?

Ian Stevens – Well, in the medical market, the ethical side of it is absolutely crucial. Maybe, I would not quite go so far as to say that our competitors were unethical, but certainly there would be, if you like, a bit of a feeling against large medical companies: what they are doing; how powerful they are; and how they are influencing the treatments and products that are coming to the market, rather than surgeons. So, a small company has an opportunity to step in there and say well, we're talking to doctors, and we are responding. As far as pure ethics goes, there's absolutely no prospect of short-cutting or anything like that, and if you do you're dead, because your competitors will seize on it. In this environment, the FDA would seize on it straight away and shut you down. This is important from an ethical and medical point of view, but it is important even within the organization. People tend to talk about the way you run your organization.

Pervez Ghauri – Do you follow the same standards that you follow in USA also, let's say, if you go to India?

Ian Stevens – Yes, I think you should as an organization, you should do that.

Pervez Ghauri – Arten your industry is typical for this issue because there has been a lot of issues here: that all those claims by companies that their food is helping this or that nutritional condition are bogus.

Arten Moussavi – Well, the regulations vary quite a bit from country to country and so does what you can claim an infant formula actually does for your baby. It's a very sensitive issue. We are selling to emerging markets, sometimes to markets where the vast majority of the population doesn't have access to clean water, and it's a powder, it needs to be mixed. So we have partnered up with a company that produces specific mineral content sterile water and we sell that, at cost, into these markets alongside our products. What we found is that now it's a very rapidly growing market because, as you imagine, it's a commodity in short supply in those markets. From an ethics point of view, a big issue in China is counterfeit infant formula, and risk mitigation. It's sometimes not obvious what you can do about that but we try to select companies that have a long history, that haven't had any issues in terms of trade standards, and things like that. In terms of counterfeit, we're looking at other methods, as well as the tamper proof tins, that we produced. We have produced some quite expensive manufacturing processes to help with this. We don't follow our competitors' example. Some claim their infant milk improves the intelligence of the baby, over mother's milk. That's something we would never do. And we always retain the right to vet any publicity or marketing material that goes out before it's published. We check everything and all the claims.

Pervez Ghauri – So Carla what will you do, or your company I mean, what will you do if you realize that one of your partners is behaving unethically … in a market?

Carla Mahieu – Probably not continue with them. We would investigate first but for us ethical behaviour is the key to our business. So, if there really was unethical behaviour that would be the end of it.

Pervez Ghauri – Has it ever happened?

Carla Mahieu – In terms of saying farewell to a business partner? Not to my knowledge but then again we have joint ventures with very reputable companies in themselves. But, for instance, we do have towards our own employees a very stringent code of conduct. And we monitor their compliance. If there are cases where people do not comply, they get fired.

Pervez Ghauri – Has it happened to any company, that you realize that your subsidiary or your joint venture was busy with unethical activity? And how did you handle that?

Paul D'Arcy – In our industry there's been some well publicized recent examples of how contracts were secured, because every region has different ethical business behaviours. Not necessarily inappropriate or wrong, they're just different. In some countries, you have to work through third parties or intermediaries and when you're learning in certain regions, sometimes you end up in a situation where all is not what it seemed. It is as Carla described. A corporation of our size is all about being transparent, so when we do come across a situation that conflicts with our ethical standards, we have to be swift, we have to make declarations, we have to step right back. There are regions that we won't go into because we've learned through bitter experience that it's not for us. Transparency and the high standards of ethical behaviour are our name, our reputation. So we guard that supremely.

Ian Stevens – For a small company, it's a massive risk. There is a human side to it, you know. We had an example of a doctor who was going to be a consultant for us, but there was some background, not proven, of impropriety in the past. And we just couldn't work with him, because of the risk to the corporate name of that association, even though it seemed rather unfair at a human level. But at a corporate level, we just couldn't do it.

Pervez Ghauri – OK, thank you all very much. I think we have touched on many of the issues that we research, so now the floor is open for questions.

Questions from the floor

Floor question – All of you have mentioned data gathering, but I see difficulties, especially for small companies, since it costs a lot of money. What types of data, do you find particularly useful?

Carla Mahieu – I was saying how I've seen paralysis by analysis. You have to be quite specific about the data and at a very granular level. I've seen, not in Aegon, cases where every year we said, 'We need to expand in China', and every year it didn't happen. And the reason was, at a high level, that a lot of information that we were given was never granular enough. It should have said, this is the product line and this is the specific market and this is the region that we will be targeting and, by the way, we will get more sales people in to do it. It never got to that granular level. Once it started to become more granular, and once the company started to organize for it properly, then it also became reality. But I've seen situations in big companies where a lot of information is being gathered is too generic to to put into action.

Ian Stevens – There are two layers to it. First of all look at the market size, look at what the prices were on the market, and compare that with how much our products cost to make and say, 'OK, is there a business to be had here?' Because then you need to go into the business, into the market and find out all the other things. So, the data that was interesting to us was OK, and we're going to sell to surgeons. Where are the surgeons? how many surgeries are they doing? in which geographical locations? That's data we should buy. So first of all, is there a market? Secondly, we're now going to hire people – where do we hire them? Where do we get the data for that?

Arten Moussavi – You're right, market research, especially the primary level, is very expensive and, as a small company, we can't afford to spend too much time gathering data. We spent money and time promoting quite a highly defined set of products and we're getting market pull. Every day, we're inundated with offers to be our distributors and we spend a lot of time sifting through them and then looking at the market potential of the countries. If we have a distributor that provides us with a lot of information, we'll ask them. Quite often they'll provide their own data research for us to look at before we enter in to negotiations.

Floor question – How do you choose, and work with, your business partners, particularly in emerging markets?

Paul D'Arcy – We will collaborate with people known to us. Almost all competitors will be in parts of big consortiums. So we actually know who they are. When we form our alliances, local alliances, then we will do an ethical calibration to our standards. If we can't harmonize with ourselves ethically, then that's just not a partnership for us. Ethically you have to be synchronized, in our opinion.

Arten Moussavi – Despite being a very small company, we offer, we don't force, we offer training seminars, especially with distributors that we have selected because they have a gap in their portfolio. So they may be selling special vitamin drops for infants, and so they have a relationship established with the primary care and medical community and pharmacies, but they don't have, for example, infant nutrition. So we will go in and organize sales seminars for the sales rep's that are going to be selling that product. Other than that, there has to be a huge level of trust and we try our very best to screen out companies we don't feel we're going to have a long term relationship with.

Carla Mahieu – I would say it's never a casual sort of relationship. So, do you find out data about your prospective partners? The answer is always, 'Yes'. To the point, almost, where you do diligence on each other. So it's a mutual thing. Training depends a little bit on the nature of the relationship with your partner. There are sometimes joint ventures that are maybe the sort where the shares are divided, but not necessarily the operations, so it depends a little bit on how you operate the joint venture whether you exchange a lot of learning. But if that happens, it's usually a mutual thing, again. In terms of trust, I would say that, if you don't trust your business partner, don't do it. The whole idea is that you trust each other, and you sort of subscribe to the same way of doing business, otherwise there is no point in doing it.

Ian Stevens – I'll start by going back to the trust thing, it's very important. You're not going to do business with people you don't like and trust. With regard to training, I'd like to just adapt again to the situation I've been in. I would answer the question more in terms of core competencies. So, for example, for our company, we hired a direct sales force. So training was extremely important, for those people to be part of the culture that we had. But, the closest we had to joint ventures in terms of training other organizations was our suppliers.

And, yes, it was absolutely vital to make sure that the processes that they were following were the ones that were important for our company. We kept control of the approval of every product that went out the door, and we made sure they were trained properly to do that, so, you know, it's just vital.

Floor question – What gives you the ability to last, to survive, to go on?

Arten Moussavi – There's not a huge amount of difference between our product and other infant formula, for example, when compared with a lot of the other products on the market. We do add where we can the very best additives according to the latest regulations and the latest medical opinion, but you have to be careful in terms of the costs because we're taking products from Europe and putting them into emerging markets, and that means we are going to the top end of the market, that's our niche. There is a lot of pressure in terms of differentiation and our distributors are always looking to do that. But I feel our success, in terms of entering the market from a small company perspective, has been the ability to change rapidly and flexibly. we have that, as I say, as a very small business, and we learn from the market very quickly. One person gets a call or gets a visit and they'll tell everybody. Everyone will know a little bit more about that market quite quickly. And that gives us a huge advantage over some of the big well-established brands in Europe that are losing market share to us in, for example, the Middle East or South East Asia. We're able to meet market demands, which are fresh and incoming, there's quite a dynamic emerging market. Especially when there are some things you wouldn't necessarily factor in at the beginning of your campaign, but you want to put it in towards the end. We found that mothers, for example, in many of the Middle Eastern countries, were tasting the more advanced formulas for toddlers aged one to three years, and it was their taste preference that dictated what products they were buying, not the infants, which is interesting. So we modified, really, to satisfy the mothers and we started to see rapid growth.

Floor Question – When going into emerging markets now, how have things changed, say, compared to a few years ago?

Carla Mahieu – The change that I've seen, from a focus on production, to market, to source of innovation, is actually something I've seen across sectors over the years. And I think it will reverse some of the flows that we have seen in the past. For instance, there used to be a quite acceptable model for expatriates to be sent out to emerging countries from the more mature markets to set up a business and to basically stay there for a very long time. What you see happening, though, is that very often, with the downsizing of the original business in the home countries, there's no return ticket for any of the expatriates anymore. More importantly, the emphasis has shifted from the production to the marketing. So the skills required in many of the countries, including the emerging countries, are much more marketing focused these days than purely operational or production focused. In that sense, I've seen a skills shift. And what I now expect to see also is a reverse flow, the example I gave of the business development person in India is something that left, particularly American, colleagues with a lot of envy. And I'm sure that, very shortly, he will get an invitation to move from India to the US to actually explain what it is he's been doing, and how he's been doing it. And maybe he might even expect an assignment from, in this case, India, or it could well be China, to a market like the US. So, I think we've seen some really dramatic shifts, both in terms of skills sets that were required in emerging markets and how companies were organizing for it: in the first instance by sending people out but I think we will see a reverse flow.

Floor question – I just want to know, what is the importance and role of corporate and social responsibility as you go into emerging markets?

Arten Moussavi – We contribute to the education of the organization we're partnered with as much as we can. We provide nutritional and scientific training because we're dealing with a sensitive product. Infant milk has got a reputation. Unfortunately, in the past it has been mis-sold in many instances. What we're doing is, we know there's a medical need and that's what we're trying to address. We're not big enough to set up a charitable trust or a fund or that kind of thing. We're hoping we will be, we've only been going for months not years, but when we reach a point where we can, we certainly will.

Carla Mahieu – When we go in to emerging markets we go there to stay. And we want to act as responsible citizens, obviously. Also I think we go there with the intention of making sure that our local organization is strong, or will become strong, so we'll invest heavily in terms of training and developing people. Equally, we also spend money and time. It's not just money, it's particularly also time, more and more, I would say. I see that also as a trend with quite a few other companies as well, in terms of doing things in and with the community. That differs with countries, so there's not one recipe. It depends a little bit on what we feel is appropriate in that particular country.

Paul D'Arcy – One of our contributions is that we intend to stay, as Carla says, as well as bring in high value, professional jobs. We will, for instance, partner with universities and educational establishments. We will invest in maths and the sciences, right through the ranges. That tends to be out of investment. The big challenge we have in certain regions is retention and turnover. So, you want to stand out from the crowd in terms of who you are and what you're about, even to keep and attract the talent. So, we'll invest locally as well as in just the economy. More so in the educational arena, that's been a big thing for us. So we'll look to local education because we're going to draw the talent from there.

Floor Question – What in your experience has been the role of planning and systematic thinking versus emergent opportunity-taking.

Arten Moussavi – In the past two months we've entered two new countries and we didn't plan to do that. As I said, there is a market pull and demand. If we had enough money, we could start to go in to a lot more, more quickly, but we just don't have the monetary focus or resources to do it. So a lot of it is unplanned. But, once we have made the decision to enter in to a country market, we do have quite a systematic approach to that. It goes through partner selection, all the way through to the education I mentioned, and deals with, for example, promotion. Also, making sure the company we're partnering with knows what to do in case of a product recall event, which we haven't had, but it's a very important part of what we do.

Ian Stevens – I know it might seem, you know, that if it's a small company, it's bound to be disorganized, because why would it be organized when there's no processes in place. But one thing we haven't really talked about today is investors and, you know, investors require you to make business plans and have milestones against which you either deliver, or you go bust. So, my experience has been that we did plan to go to a certain place and do certain things but they didn't always turn out the way we planned. But, there was always a strategic plan and there was an exit plan as well. I think unless you've got that in place, you are relying on getting lucky.

Carla Mahieu – Indeed, there is always a business plan, but I think it then subsequently comes down to how do you start organizing for it. It is possible to actually tip-toe in to the market first and that could still alter the whole picture. So, there could be a business plan with every rationale to go for it. If you don't have the people, if you don't find that business partner that you probably need, then it's going to be really difficult and it could change the whole picture.

Floor Question – I'd like to ask Arten why he has not considered a massive growth market like China?

Arten Moussavi – We're in the process of entering the Chinese market and it's not something we wanted to do initially, and it was because of the right partner coming in at the right time. They did a lot to persuade us that the big risk was going to be managed, because if we have an event, and there have been many events in the past year in China that have had serious consequences, it would ruin our brand image in other parts of the world. So, we reluctantly entered into negotiations but now we're actually quite enthusiastic and looking forward to the Chinese market. Counterfeiting was one of the reasons why we were reluctant in the first place.

Pervez Ghauri – Thank you all very much. This has been a useful session. Please join me in thanking our speakers.

13
Practices of Innovation in Mobile Computing Alliances

Yong Kyu Lew and Rudolf R. Sinkovics

Introduction

Global technology alliances (GTAs) and innovation capabilities are the two main themes in this chapter. Drawing on innovation concepts and the resource-based view, this chapter explains how firms gain access to complementary resources, dispersed in the international realm, and incorporate these within their organizations through GTAs. This emergent form of international resource-seeking and network collaboration across borders can be seen as a new phenomenon in international business (IB) (Kogut and Zander, 1992; Rugman and D'Cruz, 2000; Yamin, 2011). Innovation capabilities can be attained by combining a firm's technology resources with those of overseas alliance partners, offering progress towards enhancement of competitive advantage. From a theoretical aspect, we combine the resource-based view with innovation concepts, and comprehensively examine the dynamics of resources and innovation at both a firm and a network level.

Foreignness provides firms with innovation-creating opportunities in terms of a wider range of resource availability and accessibility (Glaister and Buckley, 1996; Kafouros et al., 2008; Kotabe, Srinivasan, and Aulakh, 2002). However, due to bounded rationality and heterogeneity, firms cannot keep their entire set of resources in house and, at the same time, capture all of the market opportunities available in global high-velocity environments (Johanson and Vahlne, 2009; Ohmae, 1989). From technology and market development perspectives, GTAs permit firms to explore and exploit technological partnership opportunities in order to develop and sustain their competitive advantage (Eisenhardt and Schoonhoven, 1996; Podolny, 1994). Thus, firms utilize resources from external actors to increase their technological capabilities, thereby achieving product innovation and market competence (Danneels, 2002; Hagedoorn, 1993; Hill and Rothaermel, 2003; Narula and Hagedoorn, 1999; Osborn and Baughn, 1990; Song et al., 2005; Stuart, 2000).

There is a growing interest in the business activities of high-tech firms in upstream value chains. Yet, little international business (IB) research has looked at GTAs and innovation. Despite the fact that a large amount of value is generated through the research and development (R&D) activities of firms in the upstream value chain (Hamel and Prahalad, 1991; Mudambi, 2007), the majority of global strategic alliance studies to date have focused on downstream segments of the value chain (for example, manufacturer-distributor relationships). Empirical GTA studies in the IB literature, mostly focus on a macro-level unit of analysis, based on secondary data sources, failing to explain the firm-level innovation capabilities attributable to GTAs in specific industry contexts. This leads to the following questions: Are GTAs critical to the innovation capabilities of firms in high-tech industries? If so, how do firms create idiosyncratic innovation through GTAs? Accordingly, the aim of this chapter is to explain the innovation capabilities of GTAs. It also aims to explore the validity of the conceptual arguments, by illustrating the use of GTAs in a specific high-tech market, from the perspective of a focal firm.

The remainder of the chapter is structured as follows. In the next section, we examine GTAs and resource complementarity in high-tech industries. After this, innovation landscapes and the resource-based view are reviewed from a theoretical perspective. Integrating these elements conceptually, we discuss innovation capabilities from the aspects of new product development and market development. The subsequent sections illustrate a software firm's innovation through GTAs in the mobile computing market, and the final section provides conclusions to the chapter.

GTAs in high-tech industries

The rationale for GTAs in high-tech industries

A firm cannot internalize all of the resources available in the market so technology alliances are a good strategic option for firms seeking specific technology resources. GTAs allow a firm to access the resources it requires but which do not exist in its own local market, thus enabling it to bring the acquired complementary external resources within its own boundaries (Doz, 1988; Kotabe and Swan, 1995; Mathews, 2006). By forging non-equity-based organizational arrangements, a firm can efficiently anchor its technological position in global high-tech markets (Cantwell and Narula, 2001; Osborn and Baughn, 1990). For this reason, there are a growing number of GTAs worldwide in high-tech industries (Hagedoorn and Narula, 1996; Narula and Hagedoorn, 1999). GTAs encompass governance structures, such as joint R&D agreements, R&D contracts, co-production or co-development contracts, technology licensing, and technology sharing (Narula and Hagedoorn, 1999). Generally, market-related alliances which are accompanied by GTAs can also be included in this list (Oxley and Sampson, 2004; Swaminathan and Moorman, 2009). In this respect, GTAs are not only oriented towards technology development (for example, technology complementarities, or a reduction in the innovation time span), but also market access, market expansion, and influencing market structures (Glaister and Buckley, 1996; Hagedoorn, 1993; Jaworski, Kohli and Sahay, 2000; Varadarajan and Cunningham, 1995).

One result of internal and external R&D investment in high-tech industries is that a firm's absorptive capacity, upon which its resource allocation for innovation rests, is increased (Cohen and Levinthal, 1990; Dyer and Singh, 1998; Miozzo and Grimshaw, 2005; Rothaermel and Deeds, 2006). There is a propensity for firms in technology-intensive industries (for example, software, computers, semiconductors, and pharmaceuticals) to spend more R&D expenditure on sales (Cantwell and Fai, 1999; Kafouros et al., 2008; Kotabe, Srinivasan and Aulakh, 2002; Osborn and Baughn, 1990). As technology investment can be taken as a proxy for innovation (Ahuja and Katila, 2001; Teece, 1996), valuable technology resource acquisitions, through external linkages, guarantee a firm's innovation. Therefore, taking into account the notion that innovation equates to technological invention and market competence, it can be seen that GTAs contribute to a firm's innovation capability, which gives it a competitive advantage (Chesbrough, 2003; Cooper, 2001; Danneels, 2002; Teece, 1996).

GTAs and resource complementarity

Firms ought to identify their core technologies and strategically obtain new external technology resources in order to gain a competitive advantage in high-velocity industry environments (Porter, 2004; Prahalad and Hamel, 1990). As GTAs deal with complex relationships between different legal entities, partnering firms should identify how much resource complementarity exists prior to entering GTAs, and then develop resource exchange governance mechanisms in the GTA structures (Gulati and Singh, 1998; McCutchen, Swamidass and Teng, 2008). Proper governance of the exchange of technology resources in GTAs is critical to generating mutually beneficial outcomes (Hoetker and Mellewigt, 2009). Owing to knowledge tacitness, (Inkpen, 2000; Kogut and Zander, 1993), the more high-tech and knowledge intensive the industry, the more complex the technology knowledge transfers between the partnering firms are. A firm can benefit from valuable external resources, which can help it to overcome technological difficulties and the risks involved in complex product development in high-tech industries (Mitchell and Singh, 1996). Thus, whether potential partners are capable of complementing their own technological innovation is critically important (Shapiro and Varian, 1999).

A firm, as a repository of knowledge, has unique technological capabilities which differentiate it from other firms (Kogut and Zander, 1992). The firm can create technological opportunities and successfully implement new technologies when it appropriately adapts technology resources to environments (Leonard-Barton, 1988). As such, resource complementarity between partnering firms leads to technology dependence on partners, in that the focal firm is making an effort to appropriate complementary resources from its partners in order to attain competitive heterogeneity (Lambe, Spekman and Hunt, 2002; Richey, Daugherty and Roath, 2007). Thus, the presence of complementary resources is an important criterion for selecting partners, and technology alliances provide partnering firms with the resources they need to create value (Harrison et al., 2001; Hitt et al., 2000). From a focal firm's perspective on GTAs, how to obtain complementary resources from external actors and achieve innovation is of crucial importance. To elaborate on this, the following sections discuss the theoretical foundations of this chapter, integrating the resource-based view with innovation concepts.

Innovation and a resource-based view

Innovation landscapes

There is a large volume of innovation literature, ranging from sociology and economics to management. This chapter limits the scope of the discussion to product innovation perspectives, whilst taking into account resource acquisition through GTAs (Eisenhardt and Martin, 2000; Powell, Koput and Smith-Doerr, 1996; Srinivasan, Lilien and Rangaswamy, 2002). Teece (1996) defines innovation as a quest into the unknown that includes examining and exploring technological and market opportunities. Similarly, Chesbrough (2003) distinguishes innovation from invention, stating that innovation has market-orientation. By processing the development and application of new ideas, a firm is able to create a new product, process, or business model (Galbraith, 1982). As such, product innovation is one of the key dimensions of innovation, as technology resources encourage firms to innovate new products (Cooper, 2001; Goffin and Mitchell, 2005). Exploration and exploitation, in relation to radical and incremental innovation, are frequently recurring topics in the literature (see, for example, Eisenhardt and Martin, 2000; Hill and Rothaermel, 2003; McGrath, 2001; Rothaermel and Deeds, 2004; Zahra, Ireland and Hitt, 2000). This group of studies refers to March's work (1991, p.71):

> Exploration includes things captured by terms such as search, variation, risk taking, experimentation, play, flexibility, discovery, innovation. Exploitation includes such things as refinement, choice, production, efficiency, selection, implementation, execution.

Recent product innovation studies show that a firm's innovation capability is related to its level of radical or incremental innovation attributes (see, for example, Atuahene-Gima, 2005; Atuahene-Gima and Murray, 2007; Yalcinkaya, Calantone and Griffith, 2007). This being the case, how can firms in high-tech industries successfully acquire and coordinate technology resources for product invention, and then successful commercialize these combined resources? Technology management and innovation scholars seek an answer in the concept of open innovation (see, for example Chesbrough, 2003, 2007; Dahlander and Gann, 2010; Laursen and Salter, 2006; Lichtenthaler, 2008).

The idea of open innovation is that a firm's innovation activities can go beyond its internal R&D boundary in pursuit of open inbound (for example, acquiring or sourcing resources) and outbound innovation (for example, selling or revealing resources) (Chesbrough, 2003; Dahlander and Gann, 2010; Lichtenthaler, 2005). In other words, the use of internal and external technology resources and paths to the market help a firm to develop new ideas and accomplish innovation. Taking open strategic initiatives, a firm can create and capture new value from the contributions of outside institutions, such as communities, partners, volunteers, and its own business ecosystem, thereby achieving innovation quickly and economically (Broughton, 2010; Chesbrough, 2007; Chesbrough and Appleyard, 2007). The concept of open innovation fits well with recent new business phenomena in high-tech industries, such as open-source software and community-based web businesses. In this respect, GTAs allow greater access to complementary resources, thus offering appropriated relational rent and inbound spillover rent (Lavie, 2006).

Resource-based view

According to the resource-based view, a firm's valuable, inimitable, rare, and non-substitutable (VIRN) resources contribute to its competitive advantage (Barney, 1991; Dyer and Singh, 1998; Oliver, 1997). From a focal firm's perspective on GTAs, the resource-based view complements the concept of innovation, in that it fundamentally assumes resource ownership and the heterogeneity of the firm. A commonality in the literature about the resource-based view is that salient resources enable a firm to sustain a competitive advantage through its intentional firm-specific investments and its use of resources (Barney, 1991; Barney and Clark, 2007; Cockburn, Henderson and Stern, 2000; Ethiraj et al., 2005). Accordingly, a firm attains competitive heterogeneity by exchanging complementary technology knowledge with external firms (Cantwell and Narula, 2001; Choi and Lee, 1997). Resources acquired through exchange relationships, that is, GTAs, ought to contribute inwardly to a firm's capability to gain successful relationship outcomes and create a competitive advantage (Hitt et al., 2000; Oliver, 1997; Powell, Koput and Smith-Doerr, 1996; Rothaermel and Deeds, 2006). As such, explicit and tacit technological knowledge is embedded in resource exchange relationships (Grant and Baden-Fuller, 2004; Kogut and Zander, 1996; Nonaka and Takeuchi, 1995).

Tacit knowledge exists in firms in the form of rare and imperfectly-imitable resources embedded in the organizational routines (Makhija, 2003; Verbeke, 2003). In this regard, a firm seeks to obtain requisite complementary resources by forming relationships with external firms (Hitt et al., 2000; Lorange and Roos, 1993). From the resource-based view, it is critical for a firm to identify the resources it needs in order to build up its innovation capabilities. Thus, the resource-based view can be effective in explaining GTAs, as it regards a firm as a bundle of resources, made up of both skills and knowledge (Eisenhardt and Schoonhoven, 1996; Madhok, 2002).

Integrating the resource-based view with the concept of innovation

Following the innovation concept of technological invention leading to market commercialization, a two-by-two matrix has been developed and is presented in Table 13.1. The matrix shows that the resource-based view can be encapsulated using innovation concepts. The horizontal line shows two different sources of technology resources that can be used for technology development: internal and external; the vertical axis represents levels of value-capturing actors involved in the commercialization of technological developments, given the two groups of resources. The resource-based view explains cells A and B at the bottom of the matrix, since this view looks upon a firm as the owner of VIRN resources, which give it heterogeneity and a competitive advantage. These cells allow for technology development through the use of internal and external resources and also for their value-capturing commercialization by an economic actor at the firm level. By following this logic, firms in cell A (closed innovation), first, create and capture innovation, based on internal R&D. In the Chandlerian innovation system, the traditional hierarchy (a firm) would be an example (Hedlund and Rolander, 1990; Kristensen, 2010; Williamson, 1971, 1979).

Table 13.1 Integrative innovation matrix from resource and openness perspectives

Commercialization

Network level	C. *Inside-out innovation* (e.g. Open platform – Google Android operating system)	D. *Open network innovation* (e.g. Open community – Linux open source software)	Resource Externalization
Firm level	A. *Closed innovation* (e.g. Internal R&D – hierarchy in Chandlerian innovation system)	B. *Inbound innovation* (e.g. Quasi-hierarchies – strategic technology alliances)	Resource Internalization
	Firm's internal resources	Resources external to the firm	
	Source of technology development		

Secondly, external resources contribute to a firm's technology development and commercial success through resource exchange governance mechanisms between economic actors (Gulati and Singh, 1998; Sinkovics et al., 2011). With respect to this, an organizational form of quasi-hierarchy or quasi-market (for example, a joint venture, or non-equity based technology alliance) exemplifies cell B, inbound innovation. Thus, the bottom cells (A and B) illustrate resource internalization at the firm level.

By employing the open innovation concept, the level at which value is gained can be further extended from the firm to the network (Chesbrough, 2007; Henkel, 2006; Johanson and Mattsson, 1987). Herein, network is taken to mean a group of value-capturing economic actors outside a resource-contributing firm. For instance, a network could be a focal firm's partners or ecosystem, an unspecified constellation of firms, or a community.

Cell C is termed 'inside-out innovation' not only to highlight resource externalization, but also to distinguish the term from pecuniary outbound innovation in the literature (e.g. selling internal resources, or outsourcing). Good examples of inside-out innovation, are OpenJDK (free Java software), developed by Sun Microsystems, and Google's Android operating system. OpenJDK is freely available as a part of Linux operating systems, such as Debian and Ubuntu. Even multinational enterprises (e.g. Motorola, Samsung, LG, Motorola, Huawei, and HTC) have recently begun to adopt Google's free Android platform as their operating system, thereby producing commercially successful Smartphones. These firms have saved on resource-acquisition costs, as well as internal technology development time, by using free Open Source software (Stallman, 1999). Google, on the other hand, as a resource contributor, gains value by directing the numerous customers of such devices, through the Android platform, to its internet site.

Finally, cell D is termed 'open network innovation' because networks of actors can benefit from the technology developments contributed by networks of actors (for example, volunteer communities or a business ecosystem). The well-known case of the Linux open source kernel, initiated and released by open communities, belongs to cell D. Interestingly, resource contributors to cell C, such as Sun Microsystems and Google, are also beneficiaries of open network innovation, as they use open resources in their products. Thus, the upper cells (C and D) indicate that value can be created through externalizing resources, capturing and commercializing them at the network level. This implies that high-tech firms adopt their innovation strategies selectively with regard to the level of openness they apply to the innovation process. As this chapter deals with firm-level GTAs and innovation capabilities, we highlight phenomena that illustrate cell B in the case study sections.

GTAs and product innovation

In the resource-based view, a firm can infuse new technology resources accessed through GTAs, into its organizational structure through internal bonding mechanisms, in order to generate capabilities (Amit and Schoemaker, 1993). Product innovation and strategic alliances are entwined with firms' capabilities in high-tech industries, in that external linkages such as GTAs feed situation-specific new knowledge into the firm's technological innovation (Eisenhardt and Martin, 2000; Teece, 1996). Thus, the more innovation-oriented firm is likely to cooperate with external actors regarding technology (Chesbrough, 2003; Eisenhardt and Schoonhoven, 1996). Reflecting cell B in Figure 13.1, a firm's technological capability is determined by how it leverages internally-existing and externally-fuelled resources (Chesbrough, 2003; Luo, 2000; Metcalfe and Boden, 1992; Teece, Pisano and Shuen, 1997). A corollary of its improved technological capability is the ability to improve and refine existing products and explore unique new product developments (Atuahene-Gima, 2005; Grant and Baden-Fuller, 2004; March, 1991). Nevertheless, technologically advanced and innovative products will be unable to permeate the market unless the firm is capable of commercializing its ideas and technologies (Chesbrough, 2004; Day, 1994; Gittelman and Kogut, 2003; Lichtenthaler, 2008). When it comes to product innovation, therefore, the firm must have market development capabilities to complement its new product development capabilities.

An illustration: a software company's GTAs and innovation capability

Based on the theoretical discussions above, the following sections explore how firms exchange complementary technology resources through GTAs and use these to augment their innovation capabilities, in the context of the mobile computing market. Based on interviews with senior managers and secondary sources of information, we will illustrate a GTA between a personal computer (PC) software firm in South Korea and its global hardware and software technology partners. Ranked second in the local software industry, the focal firm used to develop PC software applications and server operating systems in the local market. This single case study will show how the focal firm gains access to overseas complementary resources through GTAs, internalizes the resources, develops technologically new products, and commercializes them in the new mobile computing market.

GTAs in the mobile computing market

Wireless technologies (for example, 3G, Wi-Fi, Bluetooth) have triggered the formation and expansion of the mobile computing market (ABI Research,

2008; Ansari and Garud, 2009). Market growth has recently accelerated, due to advancements in central processing unit (CPU) technologies (low battery power consumption, high CPU performance) (ARM, 2009; Intel, 2009). The upstream value chain of the market consists of software and hardware firms, numerous component suppliers, and device manufacturers. Cross-industry cooperation between IT firms has contributed to some highly innovative and rapid product development (for example, high-end smartphones, portable net-books, and touchbooks).

The latest products support mobile communication functionality, a high level of computing power, and internet-supported multimedia data streaming (ARM, 2009; Intel, 2009; Sharon and Eric, 2009). Third-party applications are also embraced. There are growing numbers of GTAs between software (for example, operating systems, application platforms, and application software) and hardware (for example, chip design, microcontrollers, system-on-chips, and graphics/video) firms at the end of the upstream value chain, an example of which is shown in Figure 13.1 (Waters, 2011). A firm's strategic decisions as to how it cooperates with other firms determine its success or failure in turbulent markets (Kale, Singh and Perlumutter, 2000; Shapiro and Varian, 1999). External linkages allow firms in the upstream value chain to secure complementary technology resources and develop innovative products (Harrison et al., 2001; Jaworski, Kohli and Sahay, 2000; Kotabe and Swan, 1995; Teece, 1996). As such, technology alliances are an indispensible part of the strategies of software and hardware firms in the mobile computing market.

It is unlikely, and certainly not current practice, that IT firms would internalize all the technology resources available. As such, a brief case study in the following section illustrates how a software firm based in South Korea has generated innovation capabilities through its GTAs with heterogeneous foreign firms. For readers' better understanding of the context of this case, Figure 13.1 shows the geographical locations and value chain positions of the case firms. It also shows a simple architecture of the mobile computing device, split logically into its components. Firm A is the focal firm and B, C, and D are its GTA partners in the case study.

Building a relationship through a GTA

Originally, most of firm A revenues were generated by PC package software distribution and licensing to companies, the government, and educational institutions. As the PC software market matured and became saturated, the focal firm A invested in mobile software technology development and explored the market opportunities. It was commercially unsuccessful until entering into a GTA with a hardware firm in the US. Firm C is a leading 'fabless' semiconductor and telecommunication technology developer, which specializes in the design and sale of hardware devices and semiconductor chips while outsourcing the

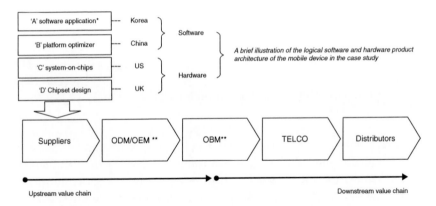

Figure 13.1 Firms in the case study – product architecture and value chain

Notes: *A focal firm in the case study.
**ODM (Original Design Manufacturer), OEM (Original Equipment Manufacturer), OBM (Original Brand Manufacturer).

fabrication or 'fab' of the devices to a specialized manufacturer, called a semi-conductor foundry. Both firms A and C required resources from each other in order to develop new products and penetrate the growing mobile computing device market, worldwide. After a negotiation stage, contracts were drawn up and signed, laying down co-development and co-marketing agreements, whose scope covered worldwide territories. The vice president of product management in firm C commented on this way of forming and managing strategic partnerships:

> We see ourselves as system architects...we identify the building blocks of the architecture. Then we identify partners that we want to work with on a building block. By building blocks and then we exchange appropriate information with these partners. We constantly re-define new technologies and new products and bring them successfully to market and they need commit the requirements of customers of the industries all the time, which means all the time we have to assess what are the partners really to work with; and what are the projects that we build with those partners.

Firm C required key software applications (for example, communication, productivity, multimedia, entertainment) to develop feasible hardware architecture in order to commercialize its hardware product, chipsets. The director of product management in the software firm A reflected on the GTA as follows:

> At that time, my company didn't monetize our technologies on the mobile platform [by partnering with C], our company management turned to pay

attention to this area and allocated more engineering resources...our partner had been prepared for GHz CPU powered chipset for a long time and
software partners was very important for them because they needed to show
directly working software applications on their new high performance CPU
to the market. They wanted to make a partnership with us to effectively
develop software stacks on the top of their hardware platform.

The new mobile software product development environment was different
from that of PC hardware, in which software firm A was used to working. Also,
it was unable to obtain this new type of technology resources from its previous hardware partner in the local market. Thus, the GTA with hardware firm
C allowed it to complement its own software technology resources with the
new hardware resource, and integrate this new resource into its existing operations in order to develop new mobile software products. The vice president of
the hardware firm pinpointed partnerships as one of the most critical factors
behind successful new product developments:

> First, a very good understanding of the status of the industry. Second, it is
> a very creative and innovative workforce with attitude toward driving new
> technologies, new products and new ideas that meet the needs of custom-
> ers. And, third, an ability to build the relationships within the new indus-
> tries in order to build a market. Without partnerships, we cannot build the
> market.

Through the GTA, firm A was provided with the proprietary hardware platform
resources and knowledge it needed for its software development by hardware
firm C. The Chief Technology Officer of firm A made the following comment
about the resource exchange governance in the GTA:

> At the beginning, we shared development tasks through sorts of workshops
> and reviewed problems and tasks and discussed development milestones.
> They [firm C] continuously provided us with testable environments and
> engineering units. So, we easily managed project tasks.

Complementary resources for new product development

Firm A confronted technological difficulties in integrating its software prototype with the hardware platform from firm C during the new product development stage. In order to resolve this, firm A needed technology resources
in the form of low-level (kernel) system knowledge and the optimization of
software with hardware. Thus, it entered into additional GTAs with firms B
and D to tackle the technological problems it was encountering in its new
product development with firm C. B is an operating system development firm
in China and D a chipset design firm in the UK. Since both firms already had

close relationships with firm C, the focal software firm was able to extend its technology development relationships to include them quite smoothly. The director of firm A discussed the difficulties of new product development, as shown below:

> Developing a new product is not a simple technical task. Many issues are interlinked so that the important point is to know what a problem is and how to solve the problem...There were problems originated from the code optimization of the hardware system and there were problems with hardware-runtime from operating system issues. During the product development process, we identified further development tasks and issues to resolve. Although the project was initiated by the chipset company [firm C] and software application provider [firm A], other cooperative firms were also involved in the product and we resolved problems together. Without the other partners, we couldn't reach the project goals.

By sharing technology knowledge about kernel-level operating systems with firm B, firm A was able to optimize its development of mobile application software using firm B's different types of kernel-level systems, including Android, on top of firm C's hardware architecture (see Figure 13.1). Subsequently, firm A forged a partnership with firm D by joining that firm's global software ecosystem, after being introduced by its initial hardware partner, C. Firm D was the original intellectual property (IP) designer of the core technologies used in the chipset of firm C. The GTA with firm D provided firm A with greater access to mobile hardware and software technologies (for example, application platforms, power-saving, audio and graphic technologies). The GTA also enabled the focal firm to gain a better understanding of the whole technology architecture and dynamic market trends. Table 13.2 summarizes the series of GTAs from the aspect of the focal software firm.

Market development

Besides the co-development that went on between firms A and C, they also actively exchanged market development strategies and key market information and engaged in joint pre-marketing by demonstrating their prototype at key IT exhibitions worldwide. Furthermore, the business development teams of both firms carried out co-market development activities geared towards potential customers (for example, ODM, OBM, and telecommunication firms), in order to introduce their new software and hardware quickly. One of our interviewees commented on the criticality of commercializing new innovative products, as follows:

> The successful factor of a project is to develop a product that we can sell to the market...To develop a product that did not exist in the market, we had

Table 13.2   Summary of GTAs between the focal firm and its network

Perspectives	GTA partner 'C' (Fabless semiconductor)	GTA partner 'B' (Operating system developer)	GTA partner 'D' (Chipset IP designer)
Key business	– Licensing system-on-chips to OxM* customers	– Engineering service and license solutions to OxM	– Licensing designed blueprints to semicon-ductor/ OxM
Sequence, relationships	●————————————————————►●————————————————————►●·················►		
	(2007)	*(2008)*	*(2008)*
Motivation from partners' aspects	– Develop new product – Build a feasible product architecture	– Develop a software solution – Build new business model	– Build mobile software ecosystem – Expand its architecture base
Benefit to firm 'A'			
Resource	– Hardware development resources and technicalsupport	– Different types of optimized operating systems	– Prototype development platform
New product development capability	– Knowledge about mobile development environments – Hardware integration skills	– Operating system integration skills – Kernel-level knowledge	– Identify technology development roadmap – Hardware knowledge
Market development capability	– Market sensing – International marketing – New market development	– Customer development – Understand Chinese market	– Industry-wide market trend and dynamics – Customer creating and linking opportunities
Performance	– Increased product launch – Create new business models both B2B and B2C – Relational rent (access to network resources of firm 'B' and 'C') – Increased global reputation	– Include new products in ready-to-use solution of firm'B' – Increased customer base	– Access to new software and hardware resources – Form new partnerships in the joined ecosystem – Increased global reputation

Note: *OxM: OEM, ODM, OBM.

to develop a prototype and promote and expose this worldwide. For this, we invested a lot on engineering resources to develop marketable products.

As a result of the market development activities, the focal software firm was able to launch three new mobile software products in 2009 successfully, which were new to the market. The firm's new products were operationalized on top of firm C's hardware platform which used firm D's core technology. Also, the software firm created additional B2B and B2C business models, providing mobile software licences to OxMs and App store distribution to end users. In addition, firm A was able to build relationships with other foreign software and hardware firms within the ecosystem of firm D, thus increasing its product functionality and quality. The management of the software firm expected the new mobile products to account for ten per cent of annual revenues in 2010. This Figure 13.2 encapsulates the illustrated case from the focal software firm's perspective. Its initial need for mobile hardware technology resources led to sequential GTAs with semiconductor, operating system, and chipset design firms. External resources gained through these relationships invigorated its technological and market development capabilities, giving it a competitive advantage.

Conclusion

In this chapter, we have investigated the interrelationships between complementary resources, GTAs, and innovation capabilities in the context of the high-tech market. To do this, we have attempted to develop an integrative matrix, encompassing the resource-based view and innovation concepts, thus typologizing closed, inbound, inside-out and open network innovation. This approach allows external actors to contribute resources to the technological value of a firm and allows the firm to gain commercial value-capturing rent from the resource-based view and innovation aspects (Chesbrough and Appleyard, 2007; Lavie, 2006). Particularly, we have focused on the inbound innovation, cell B in Table 13.1, in order to explain the contribution of external resources from international partners on a firm-level product innovation. As such, we have further explored the conceptual discussion by illustrating how an idiosyncratic firm created innovation capabilities through GTAs in the mobile computing market. This allowed us to identify a sequence of relationships between three dimensions: resources, relationships, and capabilities. Firstly, the resource complementarity of firms inspires them to forge GTAs in high-tech industries; secondly, these GTAs help to increase firms' innovation capabilities.

This work contributes to the IB field on both a theoretical and an empirical level. Firstly, a theoretically-integrated matrix, in terms of the resource-based view and innovation, allows for a dynamic perspective, capturing resource internalization and externalization and encompassing the notion of open innovation. This also explains how GTAs contribute to firm-level product innovation and commercialization. Secondly, this chapter extends the extant

Figure 13.2   Relationships between resources, GTAs and innovation capabilities in the case study

IB literature that has primarily focused on interfirm relationships in the downstream value chain, from a marketing perspective, to the upstream value chain, looking at the context of technology. Thirdly, the illustrated case shows how GTAs allow a firm to acquire value-creating complementary resources which are not available and accessible in the local market, thereby creating new business models and penetrating a new market. Thus, company managers engaged in international business activities should be aware that internationalization of a firm in the innovation process can play a critical role in strengthening and reinforcing innovation capabilities in high-tech industries. Also, managers in R&D or product management functions should understand the criticality of value-capturing market development capability as well as technological product development capability in product innovation.

Finally, the conceptual matrix and explorative case study in this chapter provide a basis for empirical research. An empirically-tested model would be able to explain to what extent complementary resources, obtained through resource bonding mechanisms in GTAs, contribute to the capability to create a competitive advantage through innovation. Although we have endeavoured to provide a rich description of the relationships between the focal firm and its GTA partners, it is difficult to generalize our findings based on this single case. It may be applicable and limited to explaining phenomena in the mobile computing market. In this respect, a large-scale primary survey would be a useful area of future research. We would recommend including the openness construct, and using the context of high-tech industries, which have rarely been investigated in the IB literature. This would enrich the limited discussions provided in this chapter and allow for the capture of dynamic *bona fide* GTA and innovation phenomena.

References

ABI Research (2008) *Mobile Internet Devices* (Oyster Bay: ABI Research).

Ahuja, G. and Katila, R. (2001) 'Technological Acquisitions and the Innovation Performance of Acquiring Firms: A Longitudinal Study', *Strategic Management Journal*, 22(3), 197–220.

Amit, R. and Schoemaker, Paul J. H. (1993) 'Strategic Assets and Organizational Rent', *Strategic Management Journal*, 14(1), 33–46.

Ansari, S. and Garud, R. (2009) 'Inter-Generational Transitions in Socio-Technical Systems: The Case of Mobile Communications', *Research Policy*, 38(2), 382–92.

ARM (2009) *Enabling Innovation Creating Value: Annual Review 2008* (Cambridge: ARM).

Atuahene-Gima, K. (2005) 'Resolving the Capability – Rigidity Paradox in New Product Innovation', *Journal of Marketing*, 69(4), 61–83.

Atuahene-Gima, K. and Murray, Janet Y. (2007) 'Exploratory and Exploitative Learning in New Product Development: A Social Capital Perspective on New Technology Ventures in China', *Journal of International Marketing*, 15(2), 1–29.

Barney, Jay B. (1991) 'Firm Resources and Sustained Competitive Advantage', *Journal of Management*, 17(1), 99–120.

Barney, Jay B. and Clark, Delwyne N. (2007) *Resource-Based Theory* (1st edn, Oxford: Oxford University Press).

Broughton, P. D. (2010) 'Another Way to Develop Ideas', *Financial Times*, London, 18 November 2010, p.16.

Cantwell, J. and Fai, F. (1999) 'Firms as the Source of Innovation and Growth: The Evolution of Technological Competence', *Journal of Evolutionary Economics*, 9(3), 331–66.

Cantwell, J. and Narula, R. (2001) 'The Eclectic Paradigm in the Global Economy', *International Journal of Economics of Business*, 8(2), 155–72.

Chesbrough, Henry W. (2003) *Open Innovation* (1st edn, Boston: Harvard Business School Press).

Chesbrough, Henry W. (2004) 'Managing Open Innovation', *Research Technology Management*, 47(1), 23–6.

Chesbrough, Henry W. (2007) 'Why Companies Should Have Open Business Models', *MIT Sloan Management Review*, 48(2), 22–8.

Chesbrough, Henry W. and Appleyard, Melissa M. (2007) 'Open Innovation and Strategy', *California Management Review*, 50(1), 57–76.

Choi, C. J. and Lee, S. H. (1997) 'A Knowledge-Based View of Cooperative Relationships' in Beamish, Paul W. and Killing, J. Peter (eds), *Cooperative Strategies* (San Francisco: The New Lexington Press), 33–54.

Cockburn, Iain M., Henderson, Rebecca M. and Stern, S. (2000) 'Untangling the Origins of Competitive Advantage', *Strategic Management Journal*, 21(10–11), 1123–45.

Cohen, Weseley M. and Levinthal, Daniel A. (1990) 'Absorptive Capacity: A New Perspective on Learning and Innovation', *Administrative Science Quarterly*, 35(1), 125–52.

Cooper, Robert G. (2001) *Winning at New Products* (3rd edn, New York: Basic Books).

Dahlander, L. and Gann, David M. (2010) 'How Open Is Innovation?', *Research Policy*, 39(6), 699–709.

Danneels, E. (2002) 'The Dynamics of Product Innovation and Firm Competences', *Strategic Management Journal*, 23(12), 1095–121.

Day, George S. (1994) 'The Capabilities of Market-Driven Organizations', *Journal of Marketing*, 58(4), 37.

Doz, Yves L. (1988) 'Technology Partnerships between Larger and Smaller Firms: Some Critical Issues' in Contractor, Farok J. and Lorange, P. (eds), *Cooperative Strategies in International Business* (Lexington: Lexington Books), 317–38.

Dyer, Jeffrey H. and Singh, H. (1998) 'The Relation View: Cooperative Strategy and Sources of International Competitive Advantage', *Academy of Management Review*, 23(4), 660–79.

Eisenhardt, Kathleen M. and Martin, Jeffrey A. (2000) 'Dynamic Capabilities: What Are They?', *Strategic Management Journal*, 21(10/11), 1105–21.

Eisenhardt, Kathleen M. and Schoonhoven, C. B. (1996) 'Resource-Based View of Strategic Alliance Formation: Strategic and Social Effects inEntrepreneurial Firms', *Organization Science*, 7(2), 136–50.

Ethiraj, Sendil K., Kale, P., Krishnan, M. S., and Singh, Jitendra V. (2005) 'Where Do Capabilities Come from and How Do They Matter? A Study in the Software Services Industry', *Strategic Management Journal*, 26(1), 25–45.

Galbraith, Jay R. (1982) 'Designing the Innovating Organization', *Organizational Dynamics*, 10(3), 4–25.

Gittelman, M. and Kogut, B. (2003) 'Does Good Science Lead to Valuable Knowledge? Biotechnology Firms and the Evolutionary Logic of Citation Patterns', *Management Science*, 49(4), 366–82.

Glaister, Keith W. and Buckley, Peter J. (1996) 'Strategic Motives for International Alliance Formation', *Journal of Management Studies*, 33(3), 301–32.

Goffin, K. and Mitchell, R. (2005) *Innovation Management* (1st edn, New York: Palgrave Macmillan).

Grant, Robert M. and Baden-Fuller, C. (2004) 'A Knowledge Accessing Theory of Strategic Alliances', *Journal of Management Studies*, 41(1), 61–84.

Gulati, R. and Singh, H. (1998) 'The Architecture of Cooperation: Managing Coordination Costs and Appropriation Concerns in Strategic Alliances', *Administrative Science Quarterly*, 43, 781–814.

Hagedoorn, J. (1993) 'Understanding the Rationale of Strategic Technology Partnering: International Mode of Cooperation and Sectoral Differences', *Strategic Management Journal*, 14(5), 371–85.

Hagedoorn, J. and Narula, R. (1996) 'Choosing Organizational Modes of Strategic Technology Partnering: International and Sectoral Differences', *Journal of International Business Studies*, 27(2), 265–84.

Hamel, G. and Prahalad, C. K. (1991) 'Corporate Imagination and Expeditionary Marketing', *Harvard Business Review*, 69(4), 81–92.

Harrison, Jeffrey S., Hitt, Michael A., Hoskisson, Robert E. and Ireland, R. Duane (2001) 'Resource Complementarity in Business Combinations: Extending the Logic to Organizational Alliances', *Journal of Management*, 27, 679–90.

Hedlund, G. and Rolander, D. (1990) 'Actions in Heterarchies: New Approaches to Managing MNC' in Bartlett, Christopher A., Doz, Yves and Hedlund, Gunnar (eds), *Managing the Global Firm* (1st edn, New York: Routledge), 15–46.

Henkel, J. (2006) 'Selective Revealing in Open Innovation Processes: The Case of Embedded Linux', *Research Policy*, 35(7), 953–69.

Hill, Charles W. L. and Rothaermel, Frank T. (2003) 'The Performance of Incumbent Firms in the Face of Radical Technological Innovation', *Academy of Management Review*, 28(2), 257–74.

Hitt, Michael A., Dacin, M. Tina, Levitas, E., Arregle, J. L. and Borza, A. (2000) 'Partner Selection in Emerging and Developed Market Contexts: Resource-Based and Organizational Learning Perspectives', *Academy of Management Journal*, 43(3), 449–67.

Hoetker, G. and Mellewigt, T. (2009) 'Choice and Performance of Governance Mechanisms: Matching Alliance Governance to Asset Type', *Strategic Management Journal*, 30(10), 1025–44.

Inkpen, Andrew C. (2000) 'Learning through Joint Ventures: A Framework of Knowledge Acquisition', *Journal of Management Studies*, 37(7), 1019–43.

Intel (2009) *Mobility's Next Wave of Growth* (Sunnyvale: Intel Corp).

Jaworski, B., Kohli, Ajay K. and Sahay, A. (2000) 'Market-Driven Versus Driving Markets', *Journal of the Academy of Marketing Science*, 28(1), 45–54.

Johanson, J. and Mattsson, L.-G. (1987) 'Interorganizational Relations in Industrial Systems: A Network Approach Compared with the Transaction-Cost Approach', *International Studies of Management & Organization*, 17(1), 34–48.

Johanson, J. and Vahlne, J. E. (2009) 'The Uppsala Internationalization Process Model Revisited: From Liability of Foreignness to Liability of Outsidership', *Journal of International Business Studies*, 40(9), 1411–31.

Kafouros, Mario I., Buckley, Peter J., Sharp, John A. and Wang, C. (2008) 'The Role of Internationalization in Explaining Innovation Performance', *Technovation*, 28(1–2), 63–74.

Kale, P., Singh, H., and Perlumutter, H. (2000) 'Learning and Protection of Proprietary Assets in Strategic Alliances: Building Relational Capital', *Strategic Management Journal*, 21(3), 217–37.

Kogut, B. and Zander, U. (1992) 'Knowledge of the Firm, Combinative Capabilities, and the Replication of Technology', *Organization Science*, 3(3), 383–97.

Kogut, B. and Zander, U. (1993) 'Knowledge of the Firm and the Evolutionary Theory of the Multinational Corporation', *Journal of International Business Studies*, 24(4), 625–45.

Kogut, B. and Zander, U. (1996) 'What Firms Do? Coordination, Identity, and Learning', *Organization Science*, 7(5), 502–18.

Kotabe, M., Srinivasan, Srini S. and Aulakh, Preet S. (2002) 'Multinationality and Firm Performance: The Moderating Role of R&D and Marketing Capabilities', *Journal of International Business Studies*, 33(1), 79–97.

Kotabe, M. and Swan, K. Scott (1995), 'The Role of Strategic Alliances in High-Technology New Product Development,' *Strategic Management Journal*, 16(8), 621–36.

Kristensen, Hull Peer (2010) 'Transformative Dynamics of Innovation and Industry: New Roles for Employees?', *Transfer: European Review of Labour and Research*, 16(2), 171–83.

Lambe, C. Jay, Spekman, Robert E. and Hunt, Shelby D. (2002) 'Alliance Competence, Resources, and Alliance Success: Conceptualization, Measurement, and Initial Test', *Journal of the Academy of Marketing Science*, 30(2), 141–58.

Laursen, K. and Salter, A. (2006) 'Open for Innovation: The Role of Openness in Explaining Innovation Performance among U.K. Manufacturing Firms', *Strategic Management Journal*, 27(2), 131–50.

Lavie, D. (2006) 'The Competitive Advantage of Interconnected Firms: An Extension of the Resource-Based View', *Academy of Management Review*, 31(3), 638–58.

Leonard-Barton, D. (1988) 'Implementation as Mutual Adaptation of Technology and Organization', *Research Policy*, 17(5), 251–67.

Lichtenthaler, E. (2005) 'Corporate Diversification: Identifying New Businesses Systematically in the Diversified Firm', *Technovation*, 25(7), 697–709.

Lichtenthaler, U. (2008) 'Integrated Roadmaps for Open Innovation', *Research Technology Management*, 51(3), 45–9.

Lorange, P. and Roos, J. (1993), *Strategic Alliances* (1st edn, Cambridge: Blackwell).

Luo, Yadong (2000) 'Dynamic Capabilities in International Expansion', *Journal of World Business*, 35(4), 355–78.

Madhok, A. (2002) 'Reassessing the Fundamentals and Beyond: Ronald Coase, the Transaction Cost and Resource-Based Theories of the Firm and the Institutional Structure of Production', *Strategic Management Journal*, 23, 535–50.

Makhija, M.(2003) 'Comparing the Resource-Based and Market-Based Views of the Firm: Empirical Evidence from Czech Privitation', *Strategic Management Journal*, 24, 433–51.

March, James G. (1991) 'Exploration and Exploitation in Organizational Learning', *Organization Science*, 2(1), 71–87.

Mathews, J. (2006) 'Dragon Multinationals: New Players in 21st Century Globalization', *Asia Pacific Journal of Management*, 23(1), 5–27.

McCutchen Jr, William W., Swamidass, Paul M. and Teng, B. (2008) 'Strategic Alliance Termination and Performance: The Role of Task Complexity, Nationality, and Experience', *The Journal of High Technology Management Research*, 18(2), 191–202.

McGrath, R. G. (2001) 'Exploratory Learning, Innovative Capacity, and Managerial Oversight', *Academy of Management Journal*, 44(1), 118–31.

Metcalfe, S. and Boden, M. (1992) 'Evolutionary Epistemology and the Nature of Technology Strategy' in Coombs, Joseph, Saviotti, Paolo and Walsh, Vivien (eds), *Technological Change and Company Strategies* (London: Academic Press), 49–71.

Miozzo, M. and Grimshaw, D. (2005) 'Modularity and Innovation in Knowledge-Intensive Business Services: IT Outsourcing in Germany and the UK', *Research Policy*, 34(9), 1419–39.

Mitchell, W. and Singh, K. (1996) 'Survival of Businesses Using Collaborative Relationships to Commercialize Complex Goods', *Strategic Management Journal*, 17(3), 169–95.

Mudambi, R. (2007) 'Offshoring: Economic Geography and the Multinational Firm', *Journal of International Business Studies*, 38(1), 206.

Narula, R. and Hagedoorn, J. (1999) 'Innovating through Strategic Alliances: Moving towards International Partnerships and Contractual Agreements', *Technovation*, 19(5), 283–94.

Nonaka, I. and Takeuchi, H. (1995) *The Knowledge-Creating Company* (1st edn, New York: Oxford University Press).

Ohmae, K. (1989) 'The Global Logic of Strategic Alliances', *Harvard Business Review*, 67(2), 143–54.

Oliver, C. (1997) 'Sustainable Competitive Advantage: Combining Institutional and Resource-Based Views', *Strategic Management Journal*, 18(9), 697–713.

Osborn, Richard N. and Baughn, C. Christopher (1990) 'Forms of Interorganizational Governance for Multinational Alliances', *Academy of Management Journal*, 33(3), 503–19.

Oxley, Joanne E. and Sampson, Rachelle C. (2004) 'The Scope and Governance of International R&D Alliances', *Strategic Management Journal*, 25(8/9), 723–49.

Podolny, Joel M. (1994) 'Market Uncertainty and the Social Character of Economic Exchange', *Administrative Science Quarterly*, 39(3), 458–83.

Porter, Michael E. (2004) *Competitive Advantage* (New York: Free Press).

Powell, Walter W., Koput, Kenneth W. and Smith-Doerr, L. (1996) 'Interorganizational Collaboration and the Locus of Innovation: Networks of Learning in Biotechnology', *Administrative Science Quarterly*, 41(1), 116–45.

Prahalad, C. K. and Hamel, G. (1990) 'The Core Competence of the Corporation', *Harvard Business Review*, 68(3), 79–91.

Richey, R. Glenn, Daugherty, Patricia J. and Roath, Anthony S. (2007) 'Firm Technological Readiness and Complementarity: Capabilities Impacting Logistics Service Competency and Performance', *Journal of Business Logistics*, 28(1), 195–228.

Rothaermel, Frank T. and Deeds, David L. (2004) 'Exploration and Exploitation Alliances in Biotechnology: A System of New Product Development', *Strategic Management Journal*, 25(3), 201–21.

Rothaermel, Frank T. and Deeds, David L. (2006) 'Alliance Type, Alliance Experience and Alliance Management Capability in High-Technology Ventures', *Journal of Business Venturing*, 21(4), 429–60.

Rugman, Alan M. and D'Cruz, Joseph R. (2000) *Multinationals as Flagship Firms: Regional Business Networks* (Oxford: Oxford University Press).

Shapiro, C. and Varian, Hal R. (1999) *Information Rule* (Boston: Harvard Business School Press).

Sharon, P. Hall and Anderson, E. (2009) 'Operating Systems for Mobile Computing', *Journal of Computing Sciences in Colleges*, 25(2), 64–71.

Sinkovics, Rudolf R., Jean, R.-J., Roath, Anthony S., and Cavusgil, S. Tamer (2011) 'Does IT Integration Really Enhance Supplier Responsiveness in Global Supply Chains?', *Management International Review*, 51(2), 193–212.

Song, M., Droge, C., Hanvanich, S. and Calantone, R. (2005) 'Marketing and Technology Resource Complementarity: An Analysis of Their Interaction Effect in Two Environmental Contexts', *Strategic Management Journal*, 26(3), 259–76.

Srinivasan, R., Lilien, Gary L. and Rangaswamy, A. (2002) 'Technological Opportunism and Radical Technology Adoption: An Application to E-Business', *Journal of Marketing*, 66(3), 47–60.

Stallman, Richard M. (1999) 'The Gnu Operating System and the Free Software Movement' in DiBona, C., Ockman, S. and Stone, M. (eds), *Open Sources: Voices from the Open Source Revolution* (Sebastopol, CA: O'Reilly), 53–70.

Stuart, Toby E. (2000) 'Internationalization Alliance and the Performance of Firms: A Study of Growth and Innovation Rates in a High-Technology Industry', *Strategic Management Journal*, 21(8), 791–811.

Swaminathan, V. and Moorman, C. (2009) 'Marketing Alliance, Firm Networks, and Firm Value Creation', *Journal of Marketing*, 73(5), 52–69.

Teece, David J. (1996) 'Firm Organization, Industrial Structure, and Technological Innovation', *Journal of Economic Behavior & Organization*, 31(6), 193–224.

Teece, David J., Pisano, Gary P. and Shuen, A. (1997) 'Dynamic Capability and Strategic Management', *Strategic Management Journal*, 18(7), 509–33.

Varadarajan, Rajan, P. and Cunningham, Margaret H. (1995) 'Strategic Alliances: A Synthesis of Conceptual Foundations', *Journal of the Academy of Marketing Science*, 23(4), 282–96.

Verbeke, A. (2003) 'The Evolution View of the MNE and the Future of Internationalization Theory', *Journal of International Business Studies*, 36(6), 498–504.

Waters, R. (6 January 2011) 'Microsoft Needs to Rethink Tablets', *Financial Times*, London, available at http://www.ft.com/cms/s/2/2c9b4058-19cc-11e0-b921-00144 feab49a.html#axzz1kO8JIeAU.

Williamson, Oliver E. (1971) 'The Vertical Integration of Production: Market Failure Considerations', *The American Economic Review*, 61(2), 112–23.

Williamson, Oliver E. (1979) 'Transaction-Cost Economics: The Governance of Contractual Relations', *Journal of Law and Economics*, 22(2), 233–61.

Yalcinkaya, G., Calantone, Roger J. and Griffith, David A. (2007) 'An Examination of Exploration and Exploitation Capabilities: Implications for Product Innovation and Market Performance', *Journal of International Marketing*, 15(4), 63–93.

Yamin, M. (2011) 'A Commentary on Peter Buckley's Writings on the Global Factory', *Management International Review*, 51(2), 285–93.

Zahra, Shaker A., Ireland, R. Duane and Hitt, Michael A. (2000) 'International Expansion by New Venture Firms: International Diversity, Mode of Market Entry, Technological Learning, and Performance', *Academy of Management Journal*, 43(5), 925–50.

Index